Danube Bi

**Hungary, Croatia, Serbia, Romania
From Budapest to the Black Sea**

An original *bikeline* guide

Esterbauer

bikeline® Danube Bike Trail 4
From Budapest to the Black Sea
© 2008, **Verlag Esterbauer GmbH**
A-3751 Rodingersdorf, Hauptstr. 31
Tel.: ++43/2983/28982-0, Fax: -500
E-Mail: cycline@esterbauer.com
www.esterbauer.com
1st edition 2008

ISBN: 978-3-85000-250-9

Please quote edition and ISBN number in all correspondence.

We are especially grateful to Ms. Kathy Kist of Cincinnati, whose generous support made the translation of this book possible.
We wish to thank all the people who contributed to the production of this book.

The *bikeline*-Team: Birgit Albrecht, Heidi Authried, Beatrix Bauer, Michael Bernhard, Michael Binder, Veronika Bock, Karin Brunner, Nadine Dittmann, Sandra Eisner, Roland Esterbauer, Angela Frischauf, Jutta Gröschel, Dagmar Güldenpfennig, Carmen Hager, Karl Heinzel, Heidi Huber, Peter Knaus, Martina Kreindl, Sonja Landauer, Niki Nowak, Adele Pichl, Petra Riss, Gaby Sipöcz, Matthias Thal, Wolfgang Zangerl. Translated from German by Otto Mayr.
Photo credits: Cover: Birgit Albrecht; Roland Esterbauer: 21, 22, 24; Gaby Sipöcz: all other.

bikeline® is a registered trademark. The cover design is legally protected. While the greatest of care has been taken in researching the contents of this book, it is presented without guarantee. Data and information may change without notification. All rights reserved. No part of this book may be reproduced or electronically altered, reproduced or processed in any form without the publisher's written permission.

What is bikeline?

We're a young team of active cyclists who started making cycling maps and books in 1987. Today we're a highly successful publisher and have published bikeline® books in five languages in many European countries.

We need your help to keep our books up-to-date. Please write to us if you find errors or changes. We would also be grateful for experiences and impressions from your own cycling tours.
We look forward to your letters.

Your bikeline team

Preface

If you love bicycle touring and a special challenge, this book may be what you are looking for. It describes an exciting 1,600-kilometer ride from Budapest to the Black Sea. As you follow the Danube through the changing scenery of the Balkans, the great river's name also changes, from Duna in Hungary, to Dunea in Croatia and Serbia, to Dunrea in Romania. These are all derived from the Latin Danubius, the name of a Roman river god. The route crosses landscapes marked by thousands of years of European history and breath-taking natural spectacles. Arriving on the Black Sea at the Romanian city of Constanṭa, you have the option of ending your tour or continuing through the Danube delta to Tulcea, where you can board a ferry to complete the final kilometers to Sulina where the Queen of Rivers enters the Black Sea.

This bicycle touring guide includes detailed maps of the countryside and of many cities and towns along the route, precise route descriptions, information about historic and cultural sites, as well as background information and a comprehensive list of overnight accommodations. The one thing this guide cannot provide is fine cycling weather, but we hope you encounter nothing but sunshine and gentle tailwinds.

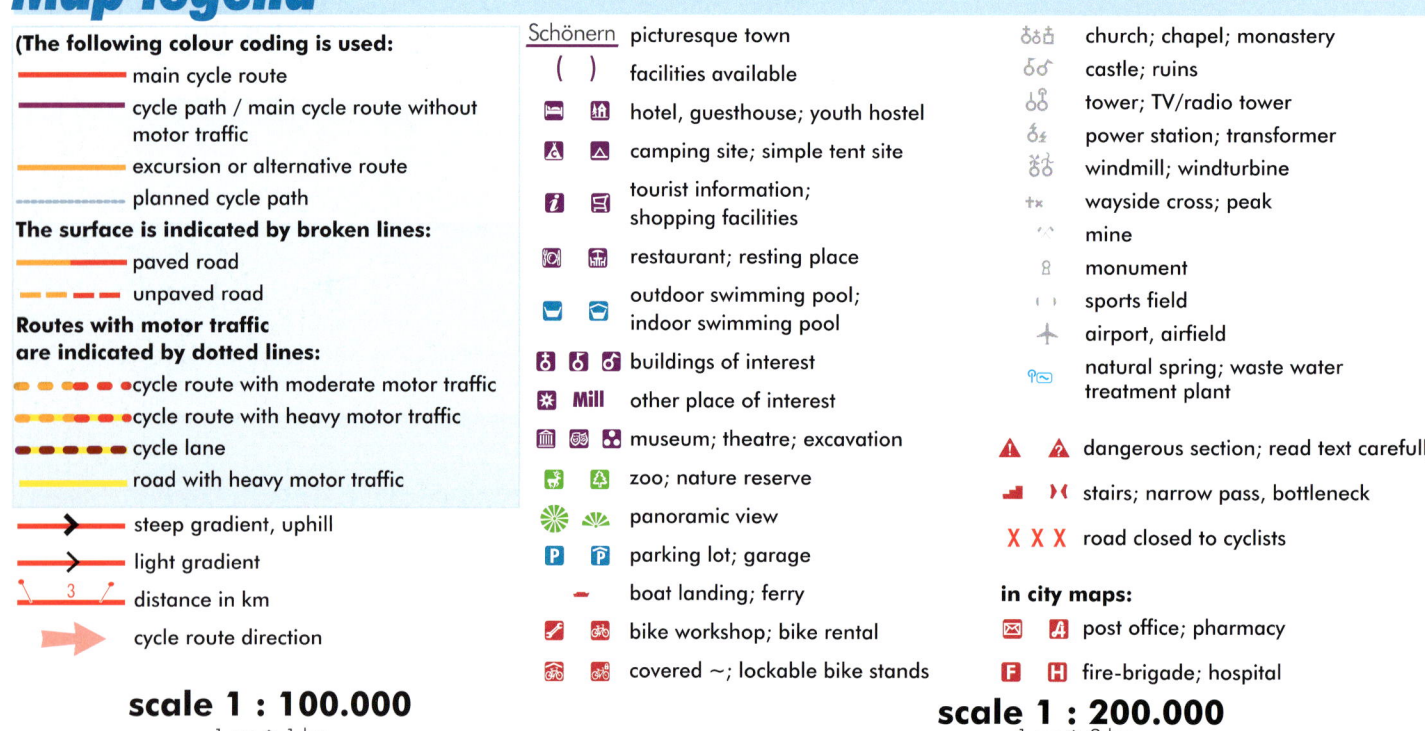

- international border
- border checkpoint
- country border
- forest
- rock, cliff
- marshy ground
- vineyard
- cemetary
- shallows
- dunes
- meadows
- embankment, dyke
- dam, groyne, breakwater
- motorway
- main road
- minor road
- carriageway
- footpath
- road under construction
- railway with station
- narrow gage railway
- tunnel; bridge

Contents

3	Preface	
4	Map legend	
6	Danube Bicycle Route from Budapest to the Black Sea	
18	About this Book	
20	**Hungary**	**201.5 km**
32	Side-trip to Lake Velence	32 km
41	Side-trip to Hajós	26 km
44	Alternate Route through the Danube-Drava National Park	74 km
59	**Croatia**	**141.5 km**
74	**Serbia**	**241.5 km/382 km**
85	Side-trip to Stari Slankomen	
86	Alternative Route via Batajnica	
115	**Romania**	**1,050.5 km/874 km**
166	Side-trip to Babadag	9 km
173	Accommodations	
179	Index of Place names	

Danube Bicycle Route from Budapest to the Black Sea

„On the Beautiful Blue Danube"
Danube so blue, so bright and blue,
through vale and field you flow so calm,
our Vienna greets you, you silver stream
through all the lands you merry heart
with your beautiful shores.

Far from the Black Forest you hurry to the sea...
From the waltz by Johann Strauss the Younger (1825-99)

The fourth part of our Danube Cycle Route series begins in Budapest and ends in Romania on the Black Sea.
With a total length of 2,845 kilometers, the Danube is Europe's second longest river (after the Volga with 3,534 kilometers), and the only one on which kilometers are counted in reverse direction, starting with kilometer zero at the mouth and ending upstream at the source.

The Danube and its significance

Greek sailors pushed upriver on the Danube from the Black Sea at Tomis, today's Constanţa, as early as the 7th century before Christ. Their exploration came to an abrupt end, however, at the Iron Gates where waterfalls, rapids and wild currents made it impossible for those early river men to navigate the river further upstream.
Hundreds of years later the Romans saw the Danube, for almost its entire length, as the barrier that separated their empire from the heathen tribes north of the river. The river also served as an important transportation link for sending supplies and troops to downstream provinces. It was not until the second century after Christ that the Romans succeeded in building a bridge over the river at Drobeta Turnu-Severin and began extending the empire into Dacia. They were able to hold that territory for only a relatively short time, until the end of the third century.

In the ninth century the Magyars, an Asian herding people, migrated into what is now Hungary and joined with Slavic peoples already there to form the Hungarian nation.
In the 11th century, the armies of the first crusades used the Danube to travel from Regensburg in Germany as far as Belgrade. More than 300 years later the Danube again provided supplies and transportation for troops as Turkish forces followed the river's course upstream during their invasions into eastern Europe.
The Danube enabled the Turks to advance quickly, and soon the first battles were being waged near Belgrade. In 1521 the Ottoman forces conquered the city and five years later, in 1526, they destroyed the Hungarian kingdom in the Battle of Mohács. The death of the Hungarian King Louis II in the battle marked the beginning of the Habsburg's control over Austria and Hungary.
The Turkish armies marched on upstream and

made it as far as the gates of Vienna three years later, where they were finally defeated. In the following centuries the Ottomans were gradually pushed out of Austria-Hungary but remained a potent political force in the Balkans until losing more territories first in the Russo-Turkish War (1768-74) and the Balkan Wars (1912-13).

The Danube provided the stage for many of these campaigns, and functioned as an essential economic and military asset. It also served as political, cultural and religious border between the orient and the occident. Today the Danube delivers drinking water for millions of people, mainly in Germany and Romania. The other bordering countries do not use the river's water because it is heavily polluted.

For Germany, Austria, Slovakia, Serbia and Romania the Danube is an important economic asset because it is used to generate electricity. The construction of generating stations, however, represent a major interference with the natural life of the river. These dams change the river's path and its speed, and prevent natural flooding of important flood plains. These changes to the river also stop fish from migrating up and down the river.

People have always used the Danube to transport themselves and goods, making the Danube one of the oldest and most important European trading routes. For millennia, the only way to move ships upstream was to tow them against the current. This resulted in tow paths that gangs of people, horses and later locomotives used to pull ships upriver. It wasn't until 1812 that the first steam ships appeared and began to put an end to the practice of towing.

During the 19th century, another method was employed to pull ships up stream. These were chain-ships that used a steam-engine on board to turn a drum that hooked onto chains laid along the bottom of the river.

Today the Danube can be navigated by larger ships from Kelheim in Germany all the way to the Black Sea at Sulina. The Main-Danube canal connects the river with the Main River that feeds the Rhine and enables ships from the Black Sea to reach the North Sea. The principle that ships of all nationalities are allowed to use the Danube was reestablished at the Conference of Belgrade in 1948.

The Danube also passes through a number of significant wine-growing regions, especially the Wachau in Austria and in Hungary. The river's importance as a fishery has declined, except in the delta where many people still live from fishing.

In recent years the Danube has become an important tourism destination. Attractions range from nature preserves and protected flood plains to great European cities, including four national capitals (Vienna, Bratislava, Budapest and Belgrade) and numerous other historic cities and towns, castles, monasteries, churches and historic sites. One way to visit many of these is with a river cruise ship. The most popular stretch for cruises is between Vienna and Budapest, but it is also possible to take a cruise from Passau all the way to the Danube delta.

Thousands of years of human activity along the Danube have given rise not just to countless legends, sagas and fairy-tales, but have inspired poets, writers and musicians. Perhaps the best-known single work about the Danube is the waltz, "On the Beautiful Blue Danube," written by Johann Strauss the Younger in 1867.

About this Bicycle Tour

The adventure presented in this book takes you first through the Transdanubia region of Hungary, past the palace of Prince Eugene of Savoy in Ráckeve and then to Hungary's paprika capital, Kalocsa. The region is famous around the world not just for its red peppers but also for its excellent wines. Test them for yourself during a visit to Europe's largest wine-cellar village, where the wines are stored in barrels that are hundreds of years old and vintners are themselves guests and delighted to serve amazed visitors. Next the route passes through the city of Baja with its glorious central Holy Trinity Square on the Danube, and to Mohács. Mohács was the site of the famous battle in 1526, where Hungarian forces were defeated by the Ottoman Empire led by Suleiman the Magnificent. There is a memorial for the battle south of the town.

The route then enters Slavonia, the breadbasket of Croatia. You ride through Osijek on the River Drava, followed by Vukovar and Ilok. The broad countryside of fields and grassy meadows conveys a sense of tranquility that belies the region's turbulent history. Much evidence remains of the most recent upheavals, the civil war of the 1990s. The route passes many ruins of bombed out houses and signs warning of landmines in the unkempt fields. Although the people in these parts of Croatia have been working hard to rebuild their shattered country, progress is slower than in Istria and Dalmatia along the coast, where tourism is stronger. Despite the suffering and hardships, the Croatian people welcome visitors to their country with hospitality and friendliness.

In Serbia the route goes through Novi Sad with its great fortress Petrovaradin, and then proceeds to the capital Belgrade and the Kalemegdan. This is followed by the high-point of the tour, the long gorge and the Iron Gates where the Danube rushes between towering cliffs as it breaks through the Southern Carpathian Mountains and enters the fertile farmlands of Romania and Bulgaria. At Sip the river is blocked by a huge dam that has transformed the Danube into a 140-kilometers long artificial lake and submerged numerous villages, towns and historic ruins. The dam generates electricity for Romania and Serbia, and includes huge locks that lift or lower ships past the dam on their way to or from the Black Sea.

After the thrilling scenery of the Danube Gorge the route enters a more pastoral kind of landscape, the vast and beautiful farmland of Romania, where the bicycle tourist shares quiet country roads with horse-drawn wagons and herds of livestock. You will pass through dozens of small villages and towns, see groups of Romani traveling as they have for centuries in their covered wagons or camped along rivers or on the edges of towns. After many kilometers the route finally delivers you to Constanța, Romania's third-largest city and main seaport. It is also a popular beach resort with a Mediterranean flair that makes it almost impossible to resist taking a break on the beach and a refreshing dip in the sea.

The final leg of the tour takes you north towards the Danube delta. Riding between the Black Sea to the east and the Danube to the west, you ride past many ancient ruins and former harbor towns that have been abandoned as the sea silted up and the coastline retreated. The final kilometers before the harbor town of Tulcea take you into one of Europe's largest and most important nature preserves.

Having made it to Tulcea, one should find an extra day or two to take a boat to Sulina and the "zero" kilometer marker that indicates the "beginning" of this great European river. Nor should one miss an excursion into the delta, where one can see a wonderful variety of wildlife, including the area's famous pelicans.

At this point we should note that this route can be recommended only for riders who are in good physical condition and prepared to deal with some strenuous conditions. The trip is long. In the cities you will be confronted with heavy traffic. There are some tough climbs and long stretches through sparsely populated countryside with few amenities. In the major cities we have given priority to describing routes that are easy to follow instead of routes that avoid the heaviest traffic. In Novi Sad and Belgrade you will be able to ride some short stretches on promenades or parks directly next to the river.

You should also be prepared to spend occasional nights in a tent. In Romania there is one stretch of more than 200 kilometers where, at the time the route was researched, there were no hotels or other tourist accommodations. You do, however, have the option of getting on a train for this section.

About the Route

Length

The total length of Part 4 of the Danube Bicycle Route is about 1,600 kilometers.

This does not include various side trips and alternative route possibilities.

Road quality and traffic

Most of the Danube bicycle route follows well-paved main roads and secondary roads. Only in Hungary do you have the option of riding on improved minor roads on top of the dikes that contain the river. The rest of the route through Croatia, Serbia and Romania takes public roads which the bicyclist must share with varying numbers of other vehicles. Especially the major cities – Budapest, Novi Sad, and Belgrade – have extremely heavy traffic. But between these urban centers you will encounter many long stretches on minor country roads with only little traffic.

Major climbs along the route include several in Croatia between Vukovar and Ilok, along the entire gorge where the Danube breaks through the mountains of eastern Serbia, and between Călăraşi and Constanţa in Romania.

Signage
With the exception of the section in Croatia, this route is not posted with signs. In Croatia, just after crossing the border from Hungary, you will see the first "Ruta Dunav" bicycle route signs. These can be followed all the way to the Serbian border.

Planning your trip

Essential telephone numbers:
The international dialing codes:
Hungary   0036
Croatia   00385
Serbia   00381
Romania   0040

Other important telephone numbers:
Hungary:
Fire: ☏ 104
Police: ☏ 105
Rescue: ☏ 106
Magyr Autklub ☏ 0036/(0)1/3451800
International emergency center: 0036/1/317-1173

Croatia:
Fire: ☏ 93
Police: ☏ 92
Rescue: ☏ 94
Croat Autoclub HAK ☏ 987
Emergency numbers for ADAC (German Automobile Club) and ÖAMTC (Austrian Auto Club): 00385/1/3440666

Serbia:
Fire: ☏ 93
Police: ☏ 92
Rescue: ☏ 94
Automobile breakdown service ☏ 987

Romania:
Fire: ☏ 981
Police: ☏ 955
Rescue: ☏ 961
Automobile breakdown service of the ACR-Automobil Clubul Roman ☏ 0040/2221553
General information about getting to Budapest can be found at www.fahrplan-online.de with additional links to arriving by rail, bus, automobile, ship and airplane.

Diplomatic missions

Hungary:
Embassy of the United States of America
Szabadság tér 12, H-1054 Budapest
☏ (36-1) 475-4400, After-hours emergency calls (36-1) 475-4703/4924
E-mail: acs.budapest@state.gov
http://hungary.usembassy.gov/

Embassy of Canada
1027 Budapest, Ganz u. 12-14.
☏ +36 1 392-3360
http://geo.international.gc.ca/canada-europa/hungary

British Embassy
1051 Budapest, Harmincad utca 6.
☏ +36 1 266 2888, Fax: +36 1 266 0907
www.britishembassy.gov.uk/hungary

Australian Embassy
Kiralyhago ter 8-9, Budapest 1126
☏ +36-1 457 9777, Fax +36-1 201 9792
www.dfat.gov.au/missions/countries/hu.html

Croatia:
Embassy of the United States of America
2 Thomas Jefferson Street
10010 Zagreb, Croatia

☏ 385-1-661-2200, www.usembassy.hr
Canadian Embassy
Prilaz Gjure Dezelica 4
10000 Zagreb, Croatia,
☏ (385) 1 488 1200,Fax (385) 1 488 1230
E-Mail_ zagrb@international.gc.ca
http://geo.international.gc.ca/canada-europa/croatia/
British Embassy
Ivana Lucica 4, 10000 Zagreb
☏ +385 (0)1 600 9100
Fax: +385 (0)1 600 9111
british.embassyzagreb@fco.gov.uk
www.britishembassy.gov.uk/croatia
Australian Embassy Zagreb
Centar Kaptol, 3rd floor
Nova Ves 11, 10 000 Zagreb, Croatia
☏ (385 1) 4891 200, Fax: (385 1) 4891 216
Email: australian.embassy@zg.t-com.hr
www.croatia.embassy.gov.au
Serbia:
Embassy of the United States of America
Kneza Miloša 50, 11000 Belgrade
☏ Embassy Switchboard: +381 11 361 9344
http://belgrade.usembassy.gov

E-mail: BelgradeACS@state.gov
Embassy of Canada
Kneza Milosa 75, 11000 Belgrade, Serbia
☏ 381 11 306 3039, Fax: 381 11 306 3040
Email: belgrade-im-enquiry@international.gc.ca
www.dfait-maeci.gc.ca/canada-europa/serbia/
British Embassy
Resavska 46, 11000 Belgrade
☏ (381) (11) 2645 055, Fax:(381) (11) 2659 651www.britishembassy.gov.uk/serbia
Australian Embassy
13 Cika Ljubina, Belgrade
☏ 330 3400 - Fax: 330 3409
http://www.serbia.embassy.gov.au
Romania:
The United States Embassy
7-9, Tudor Arghezi, Bucharest
☏ (40-21) 200-3300
E-mail: acsbucharest@state.gov
http://bucharest.usembassy.gov
Canadian Embassy
1-3, Tuberozelor St.
011411, Bucharest, sector 1
☏ 40 (21) 307-5000
E-mail: bucst@international.gc.ca

http://geo.international.gc.ca/canada-europa/romania
British Embassy
24 Jules Michelet, Sector 1
010463 Bucharest
☏ switchboard: (40) (21) 2017200
www.britishembassy.gov.uk/romania
Australian Consulate-General
World Trade Center,
Entrance F, Regus Centre 10
Montreal Square, Bucharest 011469
☏ +40 21 316 7558, Fax+40 21 316 7562
www.dfat.gov.au/missions/countries/ro.html

Central Tourism Offices

Hungarian center for tourism – Tourinform, 1052 Budapest, Deák Tér/Sütö utca 2, ✆ 3179800, Hotline from outside Hungary ✆ 0036/60550044.
www.hungary.com
www.gotohungary.com

The Croatian National Tourism Board website is www.croatia.hr
www.croatiatouristcenter.com

National Tourism office Serbia (NTOS), Deansak 8, 11000 Belgrad, ✆ 3342521, www.serbia-tourismus.org

National tourism office Romania, Str Apolodor 17, Bucharest, ✆ 21/4101262, www.turism.ro
www.romaniatourism.com

Exchange rates
1 € = 250 HUF (Hungarian Forint)
1 HUF = 0.004 €
1 € = 7.2 HRK (Croatian Kuna)
1 HRK = 0.14 €
1 € = 80 CSD (Serbian Dinar)
1 CSD = 0.012 €
1 € = 3.5 ROL (Romanian Lei)
1 ROL = 0.29 €

In all four countries you should carry the local currency as well Euros because not all stores will accept the Euro in payment. Spend or exchange any unneeded Romanian Lei before you leave the country. Exchanging the Lei outside of Romania is usually impossible or possible only at very disadvantageous exchange rates. Because keeping track of the value of four different currencies may prove difficult, it is a good idea to keep a small calculator handy to figure out what things cost in Euros. It can save you from paying too much. It is also a good idea to ask for small denomination bills when changing money. If you are seen paying with large bills, some merchants may assume you have much money and suddenly raise their prices. If possible, ask for a receipt.

Time
Hungary, Croatia, Serbia   CET = GMT+1
Romania   EET = GMT+2
(GMT= Greenwich Mean Time)

Getting there and getting back by rail

Traveling to the starting point of the trip, Budapest, by rail from Germany, Switzerland or Austria is not a problem. For information about prices, applicable discounts and schedules: in Germany contact ✆ 01805/996633 or www.bahn.de, www.reiseauskunft.bahn.de (international travel information); in Austria ✆ 0043/1/930007755 or www.oebb.at; in Switzerland ✆ 0041/0/512201111 or www.sbb.ch; in Hungary ✆ 0036/1/4165500, www.mav.hu or www.elvira.hu. Inquire carefully to make sure you get all the information you need and learn about any possible discounts.

The return trip from Tulcea is also possible by rail. First you take a train back to Constanţa where you change to a train bound for the main station in Bucharest, the Gar Nord (✆ 2232060). From Bucharest there are several trains per day to Budapest.

Tickets and seat reservations can be purchased at the Agentie de Voiaj CFR Office, ✆ 3132643, www.cfr.ro. Conditions on Romanian regional trains are, by western European standards, very poor. The trains are often overcrowded and slow.

The toilets are usually filthy. Train windows are usually also dirty and often cannot be opened. The return trip from Bucharest will take more than a day.

Travel times to a few destinations: Bucharest – Berlin 26-29 hours; Bucharest – Munich 24 hours; Bucharest – Vienna 17-18 hours; Bucharest – Zürich 26-29 hours. All connections involve several train changes.

Getting there and back by automobile

If you wish to drive an automobile to Budapest, the best routes are as follows: From Berlin the A13/E55 to Prague, then the D1/E65 to Brünn, the D2/E65 to Bratislava on the M1/E75 via Györ to Budapest (total circa 11 hours); From Munich on the A8/E52, then the A1/E60 to Vienna, then the A4/E60 to Györ and the M1/E75 to Budapest (total circa 7 hours); Vienna on the A4/E60 to Györ and the M1/E75 to Budapest (total circa 2.5 hours); Zürich take the A1/E60 and A7 to Munich, then the A8/E52 and A1/E60 to Vienna, then the A4/E60 to Györ and the M1/E75 to Budapest (total circa 10 hours). Remember to organize a secure place to park your automobile for the duration of the bicycle tour. Also remember to purchase the Autobahn usage sticker required in some countries. Using the motorways in these countries without the sticker results in expensive fines.

Getting there and back by airplane

Most major European airlines fly to Budapest. The Hungarian national airline Malev offers direct flights to the Hungarian capital from many European cities. Most airlines allow bicycles as luggage for an additional fee. Bicycles must be packed. Check with the airline for special restrictions and contact the airports about the availability of packaging for the bicycle.

For the return flight you must first take the train from Tulcea to Constanța or Bucharest. There are daily flights from Otopeni international airport in Bucharest (☏ 2014050, 2041423, www.otp-airport.ro) to Warsaw, Zürich and Vienna and other European cities.

Getting there and back by bus

Long distance buses also serve routes between various cities in Germany, Austria and Switzerland and Budapest and Bucharest. For schedules and information about transporting bicycles as luggage contact 01/7982900 or www.eurolines.at. Eurolines offices in Germany: www.deutsche-touring.com; Austria: www.eurolines.blaguss.at; Switzerland: www.eurolines-schweiz.ch; Hungary: www.volan.hu. For example, departures from Vienna Airport several times a day (circa 3 hours).

Getting there and back by ship

Hydrofoil boat service between Vienna and Budapest offers another travel option. These fast boats will take bicycles for an extra fee, if the bicycle space is reserved in advance. Check-in one hour before departure. Prices and information available at www.ddsg-blue-danube.at or wien-tragfluegel-boot.budapestreisen.com.

Another option is hovercraft service between Vienna, Bratislava and Budapest. Available April-Oct, Mon-Sat (total circa 5.5 hours). For more information contact Machart in Budapest 01/4844013, www.machartpassnave.hu or in Vienna at 01/7292161.

Bike and Rail

It is always possible to bypass sections of the route by taking a train. For instance, in Belgrade you can board trains to avoid most of the traffic, or you can use trains to skip the segment between Calafat and Corabia or Turnu Magurele. Information about schedules and prices can be had at the main train station in Belgrade, Sawski trg 2, ✆ 011/629-400, 645-822 (0-24 o'clock), ✆ 636-493, 641-488 (6-22 o'clock) or at www.yurail.co.yu. In Romania go to www.cfr.ro.

Bike and Boat

In the fall of 2005 the destroyed bridge at Novi Sad was replaced and the temporary pontoon bridge was removed, making the Danube navigable once again for the entire length from the Black Sea to Kelheim in Germany. Even so, it is not possible to board ships for short distances along the river because these types of ferries do not exist. The passenger ships that do ply the Danube are mostly cruise ships. One could, for instance, book a cabin on such a river cruise ship for the return trip from the Black Sea. However, these cruises take relatively long, are expensive, and there are only a limited number of cabins and dates available. For more information contact www.danube-river.org, www.donauschifffahrt.com or www.donaustationen.at.

Visa requirements

Obtain up-to-date immigration and visa information before beginning your trip. In Germany contact www.zoll.de or Zoll-Infocenter ✆ 069/46997600. In Austria www.bmf.gv.at or Zollamt Villach ✆ 04242/33233. In Switzerland www.zoll.admin.ch or Zollkreisdirektion in Basel ✆ 061/2871111.

Hungary: EU citizens do not need a visa to enter Hungary, even for stays longer than 90 days. Just show a passport or EU identification at the border. Currency worth about 4,000 Euros may be brought into or out of the country without any special requirements. To enter the country with an automobile, you must purchase a motorway "vignette" or sticker valid for 4, 10, 31 days or a year. It can be purchase directly at the border. Drivers must also show drivers license, automobile registration and the green proof of insurance card. Seat belts must be worn at all times. Headlights must be on low-beam during day light hours, and drivers may not have any alcohol in their blood (0.0 promille).
Vaccinations are not required.

Croatia: Citizens of Germany need a valid identification card or passport to enter Croatia for up to three months. Travelers from Switzerland or Austria must have a passport. There are no limits on the amounts of foreign currency that may be brought into or out of Croatia, but it is not legal to transport more than about 280 Euros worth of Kuna out of the country. Expensive equipment or devices must be declared (with the exception of a personal camera).
Vaccinations are not required.

Serbia: To enter Serbia you need a passport that will still be valid when you leave the country. A visa must be obtained to stay longer than 90 days. Foreign currency up to 2,000 Euros may be brought into or out of the country without special requirements. Higher amounts must be declared. When leaving the country, the amount of currency being transported may not exceed what was declared when entering the country.
Vaccinations are not required.

Romania: To enter Romania you must have a passport or EU identification valid for at least 6 more months. No visa is required to stay for up to a total of 90 days within a half-year period starting on the day of first entry. Foreign or Romanian currency in value up to about 7,900 Euros is permitted. Amounts exceeding 790 Euros must be declared. The amount of currency you carry out of the country may not exceed the declared amount you entered with. Meat or dairy products may not be imported into the country. Vaccinations are not required.

Security

Hungary: Do not carry large amounts of cash with you in large cities and in areas frequented by tourists. Pickpockets are not uncommon, especially after dark.

Croatia: Crime is not generally a problem in most of Croatia. The only exception is the Adriatic coast, where pickpockets can be common. The country has become much safer since the end of the civil war in the 1990s. Travelers should, however, take seriously the warning signs about land-mines. Note also the warnings in the Croatia section of this book.

Serbia: Serbia can also be considered a safe place to travel. In Belgrade and other larger cities you can move about safely day and night. The streets feel peaceful and civilized. Special care should be taken only in the vicinity of political demonstrations and in the few areas where ethnic tensions persist.

Romania: Follow the same precautions as in Hungary. Avoid panhandling children in cities as well as in rural areas. Roaming stray dogs in Bucharest also pose a danger. Do not travel overland at night. The roads are dark and in poor condition and you may encounter unlit horse-drawn wagons or herds of animals. Guard personal possessions closely on trains at night.

Some important general rules:

Photography of military or other strategically important assets is strictly prohibited.

Police checkpoints are frequent in Romania and in Serbia.

Change money only at banks or official exchange offices. Do not change money with unofficial traders in the streets.

Do not carry large amounts of cash with you, especially in cities.

Keep valuable documents and items in a pouch belted to your body or hanging from your neck under your shirt.

Keep photocopies of travel documents in a separate location in your baggage. Such copies can save a great deal of inconvenience if the originals are lost or stolen. (Refer also to the chapter on "In an Emergency")

When staying in hotels or inns, ask for a locked room or space to store your bicycle safely. If no such space is available, bring your bicycle into your room.

If you have an encounter with the police, do not attempt a bribe.

In an emergency

The most important thing in an emergency is: do not panic! If your travel documents are lost or stolen, go to the nearest police station and declare the loss. Then contact your embassy or consulate. In such a case it is useful to have photocopies of the documents quickly available. Also contact the local police and your embassy or consulate if your money is lost or stolen. Then contact your bank about how money can be transferred to your location. In some cases your embassy may provide a loan to help you return home.

If credit cards or travelers checks are lost, contact the issuing bank immediately and have the cards or checks cancelled. Keep handy all necessary phone numbers and data for this purpose.

In other kinds or emergencies or accidents, contact the emergency numbers shown above.

First aid supplies

Ask your personal doctor to recommend medications you may need on the trip. Be sure you include something for diarrhea. You may also wish to bring water purification tablets in case you are unable to purchase bottled water. Sun block and insect repellent are also important.

Meals and provisions

Getting sufficient food and supplies is not a problem in any of the countries this tour passes through. Almost every village has a store with food and beverages, so there is no need to carry large supplies of food. In Romania you may also encounter rolling stores that sell baked goods, beverages or other supplies from the back of a truck.

Overnight accommodations

Finding a place to stay, on the other hand, can be more difficult. In Hungary, Croatia and Serbia the problem is not as critical as in Romania. In the first three countries you can be sure to find a hotel or inn in every larger town or city. Larger hotels will be found only in main cities. Smaller motels and inns are generally well marked or advertised. In Romania, however, most people still live from farming. There is little if any tourism infrastructure. That means smaller towns and villages rarely have inns or even private homes that offer accommodations. Hotels in larger cities sometimes charge excessive prices with foreign guests even when the level of comfort is not high. Often hotels do not offer breakfast, so you will be obliged to find food and beverages on your own. In parts of Romania, the distance between hotels or inns may be much more than you wish to ride in a single day. In this case, we recommend boarding a train (for instance, from Calafat to Turnu Magurele. For additional details refer to the route description of this segment. If you do not wish to take a train, be sure you have a tent and camping gear. Camping in the rough is allowed in most parts of Romania, with the main exceptions being along the Black Sea coast and in the Danube delta.

Camping rough is prohibited in Hungary and Croatia. In Croatia it may also be life-threateningly dangerous due to the possibility of landmines. Always respect warning signs about landmines and do not wander through meadows or woods. Camping rough is not banned in Serbia, though we recommend doing so only at some distance from the road or asking local farmers whether you may spend a night on their property. As a general rule, if during your trip you come into contact with local people and they will invite you to eat or sleep in their home, do not say no! Although most people do not have much wealth, they tend to be extremely friendly and hospitable.

The right bicycle

This demanding tour demands a tough and comfortable high-quality touring bicycle that can safely carry a large amount of baggage. Avoid bicycles with complicated or unusual technical features like hydraulic or disk brakes. If something breaks, it will be difficult or impossible to find replacement parts. Many experienced bicycle tourists recommend bicycles with 26-inch wheel (the standard size for mountain bikes) because tires and other spare parts for these sizes are generally easier to find.

Because even the best bicycle can break down, bring a basic supply of spare parts including brake and shifting cables, spare inner tubes, spokes, duct tape and appropriate tools.

Traveling with children

The Danube bicycle route from Budapest to the Black Sea is not appropriate for small children. The distances are big. The major cities (Budapest, Novi Sad, Belgrade) have heavy and difficult traffic and very little bicycle infrastructure. There are some long and difficult climbs.

Clothing

The right clothing also plays an important role if you are to enjoy the tour and stay comfortable during long days in varying kinds of weather.

The guiding principle should be "dress like an onion." Numerous layers of apparel can fulfill various functions and can be combined in a variety of ways according to conditions.

Underwear should be of a material that quickly transports moisture away from the skin. Padded bicycling pants will significantly enhance your comfort when sitting on the small bicycle seat for long periods of time!

Depending on the temperature, the second layer should generally be a light and compact fleece pullover or jacket that retains warmth but not moisture.

The outer layer should keep wind and rain out but at the same time breathe to allow sweat to evaporate away from your body. The result is always a compromise between how rain proof and how "breathable" your clothing is.

Sweaters and even light underwear made of high quality sheep's wool take longer to dry but offer the advantage of retaining warmth even when wet and do not quickly begin to smell of body odors. This is not, however, true of cotton clothing, which is less suitable for sportswear. Especially with underwear, a close snug fit is important to provide the desired function. The same applies to jackets and pants, on which elastic components like sleeve loops and variable zippers help reduce annoying wind flap.

Good rain gear is also essential. If it starts to rain while you are on some long and lonely stretch of country road far from shelter, you will be glad to have invested in the right equipment.

Best touring season

All four countries have mostly continental weather: relatively hot summers, cold winters and little precipitation.

The best times of year for this tour are between the middle of May to the end of June and from early September until well into October.

The hottest months, July and August, are less ideally suited because you will spend many hours in the heat of the summer sun with little chance of finding shady spots for breaks. Even a breeze in this time of year is mostly hot and does little to cool the body.

Other things to consider

- Do not travel alone. There is always the possibility of a serious breakdown or an accident.
- Call friends or relatives regularly to keep someone informed of your progress.
- Make sure you have a supply of basic medications and adequate tools to maintain your equipment.
- A flash-light and folding pocket knife frequently come in handy.
- Keep photocopies of important documents in a separate place
- Do not forget important addresses and telephone numbers.
- When planning your trip, schedule the occasional day off for tourism, rest or repairs, or just to skip a rainy day.
- Do not camp directly near a road where traffic can easily see you. The risk of accident or robbery is too great.
- Avoid groups of begging children. Some of them may be pickpockets.
- Always make sure you have sufficient drinking water
- Last but not least: Never forget that you are a guest in the country you are visiting. Behave accordingly.

About this book

This cycling guide contains basic information you need for a cycling vacation along the Danube River: Precise maps, a detailed description of the route, a comprehensive list of overnight accommodations, numerous detail maps of cities and towns, and information about tourist attractions and sights.

And all of that comes with our *bikeline* pledge: Every meter of the route described in this book has been tested and evaluated in person by one of our editors. To assure that our books stay as up to date as possible, we gladly accept any corrections or changes that users of these books or local authorities send us. We cannot, however, always verify such corrections before our editorial deadline.

The maps

The inside of the guide's front cover shows an overview of the geographic location area covered by this guide. It also depicts the area covered by each of the detail maps inside the guide, and the detail map's number. Maps for

Hungary, Croatia and Serbia are produced in a scale of 1 : 100,000. That means 1 cm on the map represents 1000 meters on the ground. Maps of Romania are produced in a scale of 1 : 200,000 (1 cm on the map = 2 kilometers on the ground). In addition to exactly showing the route, these maps also provide information about roadway quality (paved or unpaved), gradients (gentle or steep), distances, as well as cultural and gastronomic highlights. Because distances are rounded up or down to the nearest half-kilometer, you may discover small differences in the number of kilometers you actually ride.

Even with the most precise map, it may be necessary at times to consult the written descriptions of the route. Locations where the route is difficult to follow are shown by this symbol ⚠. The same symbol can then be found in the written description where the route is explained in detail. Please note that the recommended main route is always shown in red or purple; alternative and excursion routes in orange. The individual symbols used in the maps are explained in the legend on pages 4 and 5.

The text

The maps are supplemented by a written text that describes the recommended main route. Individual or key instructions about the route are separated by the ～ symbol to make them easier to find and follow.

The description of the main route is also interrupted by passages describing alternative and excursion routes. These are printed in orange type.

Furthermore, the names of important villages, towns and cities are printed in bold type. If a location or community has important points of interest, addresses, telephone numbers and opening times are listed under the headline with the name of the place.

Descriptions of the larger towns and cities, as well as historic, cultural and natural landmarks help round out the travel experience. These paragraphs are printed in italics to distinguish them from the route description.

Text printed in purple indicates that you must make a decision about how your tour shall continue. For instance, there may be an alternative route that is not included in the tour description or a turn-off to another location.

Text printed in purple also draws attention to excursion tips, interesting landmarks or recreational opportunities some distance off the main route.

List of overnight accommodations

The last pages of this cycling guide provide a list of places where travelers can spend the night. These range from campgrounds to comfortable 5-star hotels.

We should note at this point that despite intensive research efforts, we were unable to identify inns, motels or other overnight accommodations in many towns in Serbia and Romania.

Hungary

201.5 km

After the stress of navigating heavy traffic in Budapest, follow the Danube southward on its seemingly endless journey to the sea. In Ráckeve, ride past the palace of Prince Eugene of Savoy. The next highlight is Kalocsa, Hungary's pepper capital, where a unique museum reveals everything worth knowing about peppers. From Kalocsa you can also consider making a side trip to Hajós pinci, Europe's largest wine-cellar village, where you can sample locally grown wines. The main route continues through Baja, with its expansive Holy Trinity square, and then to Mohács in southern Hungary. This charming little city offers a number of noteworthy buildings and opportunity for rest and nourishment before you cross the border into Croatia. You can also visit the impressive monument in memory of the Battle of Mohács in 1526, where the Hungarians were defeated by the Ottoman Turks.

In Budapest and as far as Ráckeve you must deal with a great deal of traffic. South of Ráckeve the route frequently makes use of simple roads on dikes along the river. Some of these roads are even paved with asphalt. There are no significant climbs.

From Budapest to Ráckeve   52 km
Budapest

Telephone area code: 01

- **Tourinform**, V. Vörösmarty tér/Vigadó u.6., ✆ 4388080, www.deutsch.budapest.hu
- **Tourinform**, Lisztferenc tér 11, ✆ 3224098, www.budapestinfo.hu
- **Tourinform**, Deák Tér/Sütö utca 2, ✆ 4388080, 24-hour information office established especially for visitors to Budapest.
- **Mahart Passnave GmbH**, passenger ship line, 1056, Belgrád rakpart, ✆ 4384000
- **Museum Aquincum**, Szentendrei út 139, ✆ 4540438, Open: April, Oct, Tues-Sun 10-17 o'clock, May-Sept, Tues-Sun 10-18 o'clock. Monuments, ruins and artifacts (2nd – 4th centuries AD) from the Roman city of Aquincum.
- **Hungarian National Museum** (Magyar Nemzeti Múzeum), Múzeum körút 14-16, ✆ 3382122, Open: Tues-Sun 10-18 o'clock. The largest and most prestigious museum in Hungary presents diverse collections about the country's history and people.
- **Museum of Fine Arts** (Szépmüvészeti Múzeum), Dózsa György út 41, ✆ 3439759 Open: Tues-Sun 10-18 o'clock.

Budapest – Parliament

World-famous museum contains the largest collection of Spanish masters (Velazquez, Goya, El Greco) outside Spain. The modern gallery includes works by Monet, Pissarro, Renoir, Cézanne, Gauguin and others. Antiquity collection.

- **City historical museum** (Történeti Múzeum), Burgpalais E-Flügel, ✆ 2257809, Open: 1 March-15 May, Weds-Mon 10-18 o'clock, 16 May-15 Sept, Mon-Sun 10-18 o'clock, 16 Sept-31 Oct, Weds-Mon 10-18 o'clock, 1 Nov-28 Feb, Weds-Mon 10-16 o'clock. Exhibits covering Romanesque to renaissance periods – not to be missed by anyone interested in the city's history and especially the castle district.
- **Hungarian national gallery** (Magyar Nemzeti Galéria), Disz tér 17, Burgpalais B-C-D-Flügel, ✆ 3757533, Open: Tues-Sun 10-18 o'clock. Collection exhibits works by Hungarian painters from the 15th to 19th centuries. Noteworthy are the late Gothic altar pieces, portraits and landscapes by the painter Mihály Munkácsy (1844-1900) and the works by Hungarian impressionists, including Pál Szinyei Merse and Kosztka Tivadar Csontváry.
- **Ludwig Museum**, contemporary art, Budaer Palast, György tér 2, ✆ 3759175, Open: Tues-Sun 10-18 o'clock. Contemporary art collection of Irene and Peter Ludwig, of Cologne, provides an overview of the last 50 years of international art, and the last 10 years of contemporary art in Hungary.
- **Museum for applied arts** (Iparmüvészeti Múzeum), Üllöi út 33-37, ✆ 3759175, Open: Jan, Dec, Tues-Sun 10-18 o'clock. Wide-ranging collection with household and day-to-day items showing the history of design, housed in a handsome art nouveau building.
- **Jewish museum** (Zsidó Múzeum), Dohány u. 2, ✆ 3428949, Open: Mon-Thurs 10-17 o'clock, Fri, Sun 10-14 o'clock. Near the great synagogue, collection with valuable objects of Jewish art, information and exhibits about the deportation of Hungarian Jews during the Nazi period, and Nazi concentration camps. In 1993 the museum suffered a major art robbery.
- **Ethnographic museum**, (Néprajzi Múzeum), Kossuth Lajos tér 12, ✆ 4732400, Open: Tues-Sun 10-18 o'clock. In the large

neo-renaissance palais, exhibits focus mainly on how farmers and peasants lived. Attraction: model of a farmhouse furnished with every-day items and costumes.

- **Transportation museum** (Közlekedési Múzeum), Városligeti körút 11, ✆ 2733280, Open: May-Sept, Tues-Fri 10-17 o'clock, Sat, Sun 10-18 o'clock, Oct-March, Tues-Fri 10-16 o'clock, Sat, Sun 10-17 o'clock. Exhibits range from historic bicycles to railroad wagons to shipping on the Danube and at sea.
- **Vajdahunyad castle**, Városliget. Built between 1896 and 1908 to show the history of Hungarian architecture with examples of different styles, from Romanesque to baroque. Includes a reproduction of Vajdahunyad castle in Transylvania.
- **Castle labyrinth**, Úri u. 9, ✆ 212-0287, Open: Mon-Sun 9.30-19.30 o'clock. A fascinating presentation of the extensive system of tunnels under the castle, used as storage space in the 16th century, later as a wine cellar. It was used as German headquarters during WW2.
- **Citadel**, Gellért-Berg. The fortress "guards" the city since 1849, when it was built by the Habsburg rulers in reaction to the Hungarian revolts. Today the hill on which it is built is dominated by the "Liberation Monument," erected in 1947 in memory of the city's liberation by the Soviet army at the end of WWII. Excellent views of the castle and Budapest.
- **Great synagogue**, Dohány utca 4. The largest synagogue in Europe, with space for 3,000 people, was built by a student of Otto Wagner. A memorial plaque in memory of Theodor Herzl (born 1860 in Budapest).
- **St. Stephan basilica**, Bajcsy-Zsilinszky út. Construction of Budapest's largest church began in 1851. In 1868 the dome collapsed. The eclectic church designed by Miklós Ybl was finally consecrated in 1905. Contains as relic the right hand of the first Hungarian king, Stephan (975-1038).
- **Castle district**, Buda. This was the center of the medieval city when it was the cultural and political capital of Hungary. After the Turkish occupation, the district was rebuilt in the 18th century.
- **Margaret Island** (Margit sziget), north of the city. The island's

Budapest – Hilton Hotel with reflection of the Fisherman's Bastion

more recent history begins in the late 18th century, when Vice-king Joseph von Habsburg built a summer residence and a park with exotic plants and trees. In 1867 mineral springs were discovered, leading to the development of a spa resort. Today closed to motorized traffic, the island is a popular recreation site.

- **Western train station** (Nyugati pu.), Teréz körút. Interesting renovated classical terminal train station (1874-77), glass hall by August de Serres and iron construction by Gustave Eiffel, builder of the Eiffel tower in Paris.
- **Heroes square** (Hösök tér), Dózsa György út. Square dominated by the millennium monument, built in 1896 for Hungary's 1,000-year celebrations of their conquest of the country, in honor of Hungarian national heroes.
- **Jewish quarter**, between Dohány u.(Károly krt.) Király u. Kertész u., Rudasbad, Döbrentei tér 9. Before WWII, about 200,000 Jews lived in Budapest. Today little of the rich and colorful community remains visible, though behind the crumbling facades one can still find many interesting traces of Jewish architecture and culture.
- **Kiraly baths** (Királyfürdö), Fö utca 84, ✆ 2023688. Turkish bath built 1566 by the Pascha Sokoli Mustafa is one of numerous charming bathhouses and spas in the city. Expanded in the 18th century (baroque) and again in 1827 (classical style). The

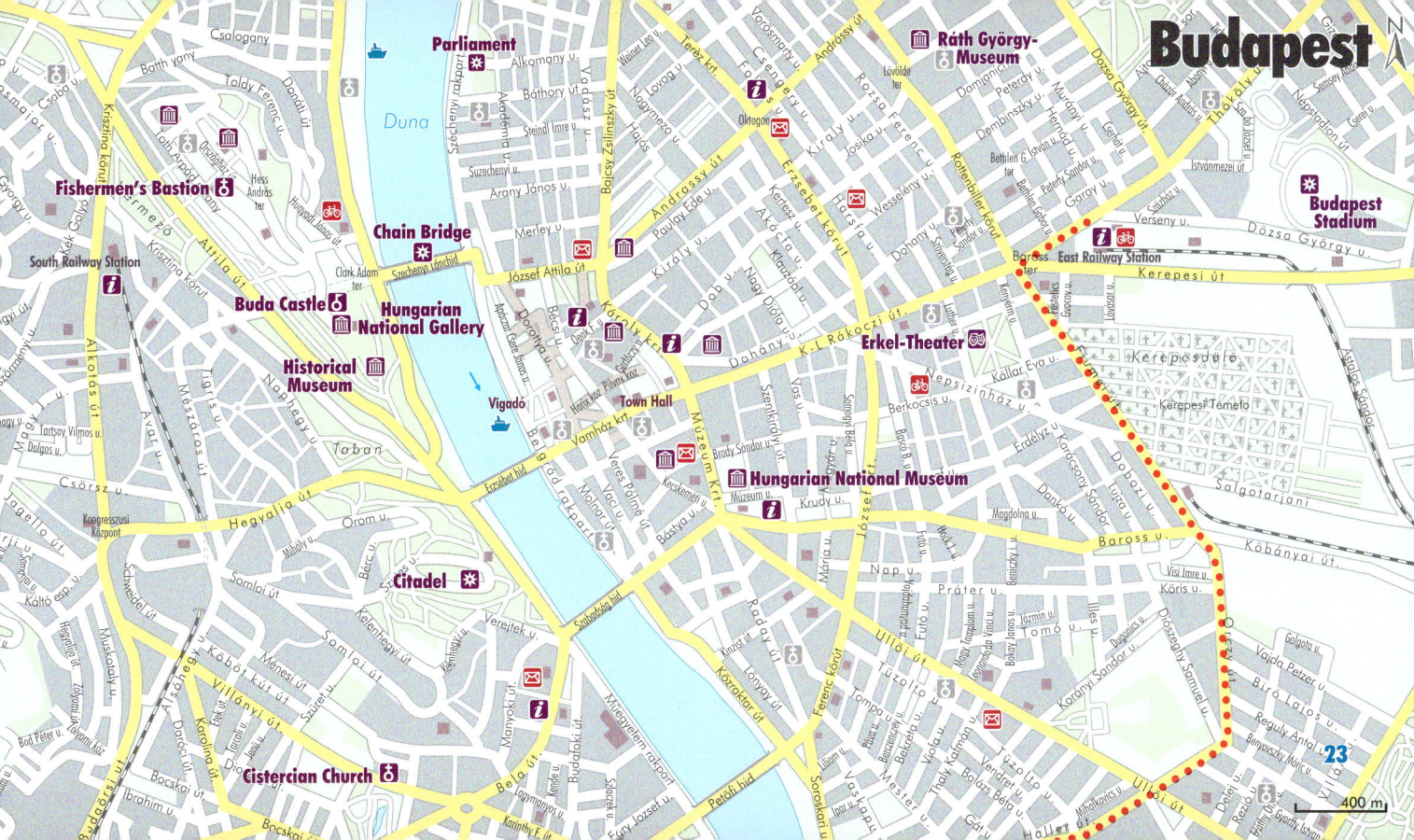

original pools and dome were retained.

- **Rudas baths** (Rudasfürdö), Gellért rakpart, ✆ 3561322. Site of a bathhouse which predated the Turkish bath built in 1566. Fed by radioactive and sulfur waters. Expanded in the late 19th century by Miklós Ybl.
- **Old metro** (Földalatti). The oldest underground railroad in Europe, built in 1896 for the millennium celebrations, it runs underneath the handsome Andrássy út avenue connecting the central Vörösmarty tér with the old Zoo in the city park (Városliget).
- **Café Gerbaud**, Vörösmarthy tér. The Budapest coffeehouse most popular among tourists, worth visiting mainly for its elaborate interior.
- **Szemlö cave**, Pusztaszeri út 35, ✆ 3256001, Open: Mon, Weds, Fri 10-15 o'clock, Sat, Sun 10-16 o'clock. Known as the "underground gardens of Budapest," Eocene cave system with magnificent stalagmites and stalactites.
- **Jánoshegy chair lift**, Zugligeti út 97, ✆ 3943764, Open: April-Sept, 9-17 o'clock, Oct-March 9.30-16 o'clock; closed Mondays of odd-numbered weeks. Total elevation difference is 262 meters. The lift covers a distance of about one kilometer and runs about 8 meters above the ground. The ride takes about 15 minutes and offers unforgettable views.
- **Széchenyi mountain train**, station at Budapest Hotel near

Budapest – Buda Castle at night

Moszkvatér. Built 1874, the 3.5 kilometer cog wheel train goes through Buda's villa district on its way up to Szechenyi Mountain.

- **Cable car to the castle palace**, Clark Ádám tér, Open: Mon-Sun 7.30-22.00 o'clock, closed Mondays of even-numbered weeks. Built 1870, historic cable car service brings passengers up to the castle in a few minutes. At the base station, near Chain Bridge, is located the "0-kilometer" stone, from which all distances to Budapest are measured.
- **Bringóhintó**, Margitsziget Hajós Alfred sétány 1, ✆ 3292073
- **László Cserny**, II, Zuhatag sor 12, ✆ 2006837
- **József Fülöp**, XIV, Gvadányi u., III, ✆ 2212192
- **Rákoskert Bike Center**, XVII, Kísérö u. 4, ✆ 2585906

Budapest! One of Europe's great cities – a capital for politics, culture and history, a city that inevitably overwhelms visitors with its majesty and elegance. It is also a city of contrasts and opposites, as well as a young city that has existed in its present form only for just over a century, yet which still exudes the faded glory of its imperial past. As the former sister city to Vienna, and one of the two poles around which the Austro-Hungarian Empire was centered, Budapest today is proud to be at the middle of a nation that was one of first to cast aside the communist system under which it was governed for most of five decades after WWII.

Budapest is the undisputed queen among Hungarian cities. Most of the country's other cities are little more than formless gatherings of houses and industry, surrounded by farmland, wide stretches of sparsely populated land where urban lifestyles never had a chance to really emerge. In the 19th century, many of the farm lads drafted to serve in the imperial armies had never seen a city hall or a market before they arrived in the capital.

That remains, in part, still true today for some of Hungary's rural dwellers, and underlines the role that the grand and dramatic cityscape of Budapest has always represented to Hungarians: a place of blinding sophistication and national self-affirmation.

Many regard it to be among the most beautiful cities in the world. Few other cities have so well understood how to wrap themselves in an aura of festiveness and brilliance.

The first people were drawn to this fertile land in prehistoric times, attracted by the shimmering waters of the river and the plain spreading eastward from the mountains. Two-thousand years ago the Romans established a city on the west bank. Legally speaking, the city of Budapest was born in 1873, when the towns of Pest, Buda and Obuda were merged. But the roots of Budapest go back to Illyrian-Celtic Avars and the Romans who lived in Aquincum.

The Magyars then built the Kurszans castle, their first center of authority. In 1241 the Mongols destroyed Buda and Pest. In 1247 King Béla IV built the first royal castle on castle hill – it soon became his permanent residence. He awarded city rights to Pest, including the stone quarry and Little Pest on the left bank of the Danube. The name Pest seems to come from the old Slavic word for oven (pesti), referring to the ovens used to treat chalk.

After the Turks conquered Hungary, Budapest became the provincial capital for a Pasha. Many of the bath-houses left by the Romans were rebuilt in this period as Turkish baths. After the

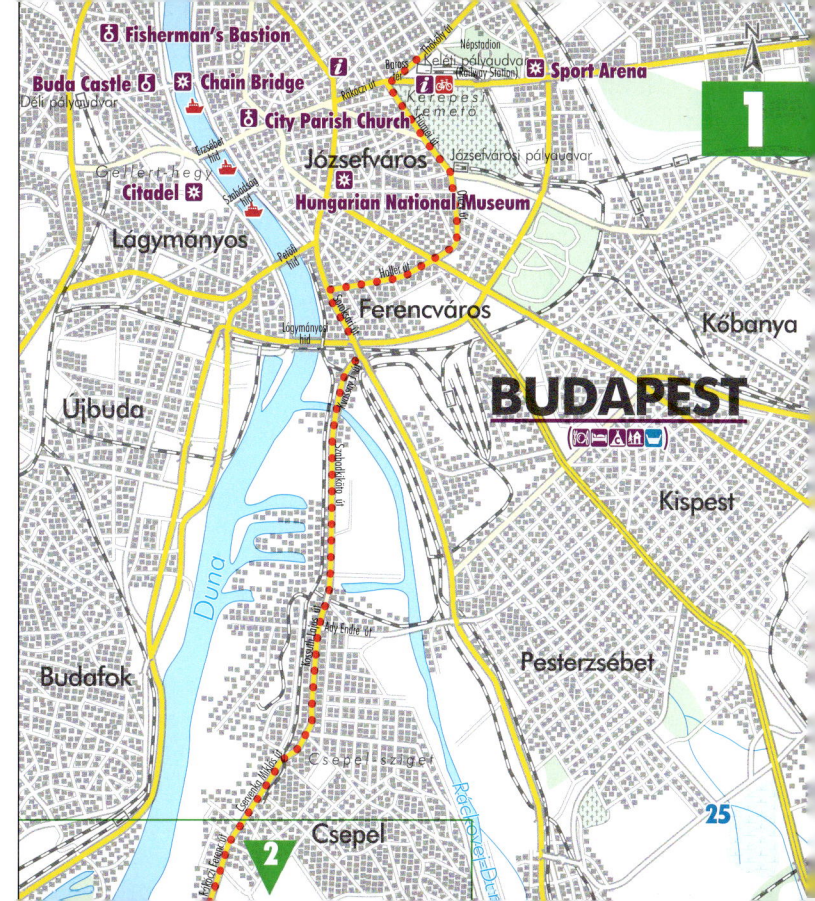

25

Turks were expelled in the late 17th century, the city began to experience a new economic and cultural boom. By 1848 the traditional main city of Buda had been overtaken by Pest as the spiritual and political center of the country. During this period the city was seized by the trend toward modernity. In 1896 Budapest became the second city in the world, after London, to open a subway. Many of the city's iron and glass train stations and market buildings were built in this period.

The wide and lazy Danube through the center of the city played a key role in every part of Budapest's history. Today 8 bridges connect the two halves of the city, and the river remains central to Budapest's character, the unifying element that make Buda, Pest and the river's islands into a harmonious whole.

Buda is the older part of the city, but its lively center today is located in Pest.

Among the many architectural edifices that dot the cityscape with a variety of styles, one of the most distinctive is the Fisherman's Bastion in the old Castle District. Behind it stands the distinguished old Matthias church and the old city hall with its renaissance windows. The Castle District is a dense maze of small streets and alleys, where handsome baroque city palaces stand next to old patrician houses, some of which are built on Gothic foundations.

Above the city on Castle Mountain stands the royal palace. It was heavily damaged by fire when the Ottoman Turks withdrew from the city. Franz A. Hillebrand rebuilt it in the baroque style and it was later modified by Miklós Ybl. In 1945 it burned again. Visitors to the Castle District should not neglect a visit at Uri utca 9. It is the entrance to a 10-kilometer network of natural caves and man-made connecting tunnels that honeycombs the mountain beneath the castle. Many of the tunnels date back to late medieval times.

Tip: If you wish to spare yourself the strenuous ride out of Budapest, simply go to the eastern train station and board a train to Kiskunlacháza. Departures hourly. The trip takes about 90 minutes and bicycles are permitted on the train. From there ride via Balbánsziget to Ráckeve and the main route.

If you choose to ride out of the Hungarian capital, the adventure begins at Budapest's eastern train station (**Keleti pu.**) ~ depart the train station main hall by turning left on **Thököly út.** ~ at the first opportunity after leaving the train station, turn left at the big 5-way intersection onto **Fiumei út.** ~ ride past the **Kerepesi temetö-cemetery** on the left ~ then past **Józsefvárosi pu.-train station** ~ and continue to **Orczy tér** ~ cross the square and go straight on **Orczy út.** ~ after the bend to the right continue straight to the next intersection with Üllöi út. ~ and straight on **Haller út.** ~ keep following this road until you get to a T-intersection and the Danube ~ turn left on **Soroksári út.** ~ and continue straight ~ first under a bridge for motorized vehicles, then under a bridge for the tram ~ just after the second bridge turn right at the first opportunity, onto **Kvassay J. út.**

Tip: Look for a sign marked Csepel-sziget. This island divides the Danube into two arms. The bicycle route stays on the island until the two arms of the Danube rejoin just downstream from Dunaújváros.

After crossing one arm of the Danube (Ráckevei Duna), the name of the street changes to **Szabadkiköto út.** ~ stay on it to the intersection with Corvin út. ~ where you cross tram tracks twice and proceed straight on **Kossuth Lajos út.** ~ this street becomes **Cservenka Miklos út.** and brings you after a small bend to the right to **II. Rákóczi Ferenc út.** ~ turn left here and continue further south and away from Budapest

Pass another cemetery ~ the street is paved with asphalt but nevertheless very bumpy.

Tip: Here the traffic volume is very heavy, with many trucks. Be careful.

Soon you come to a sign announcing the Budapest city limits ~ proceed to a traffic circle ~ then straight towards Halásztelek ~ the next town is Lakihegy.

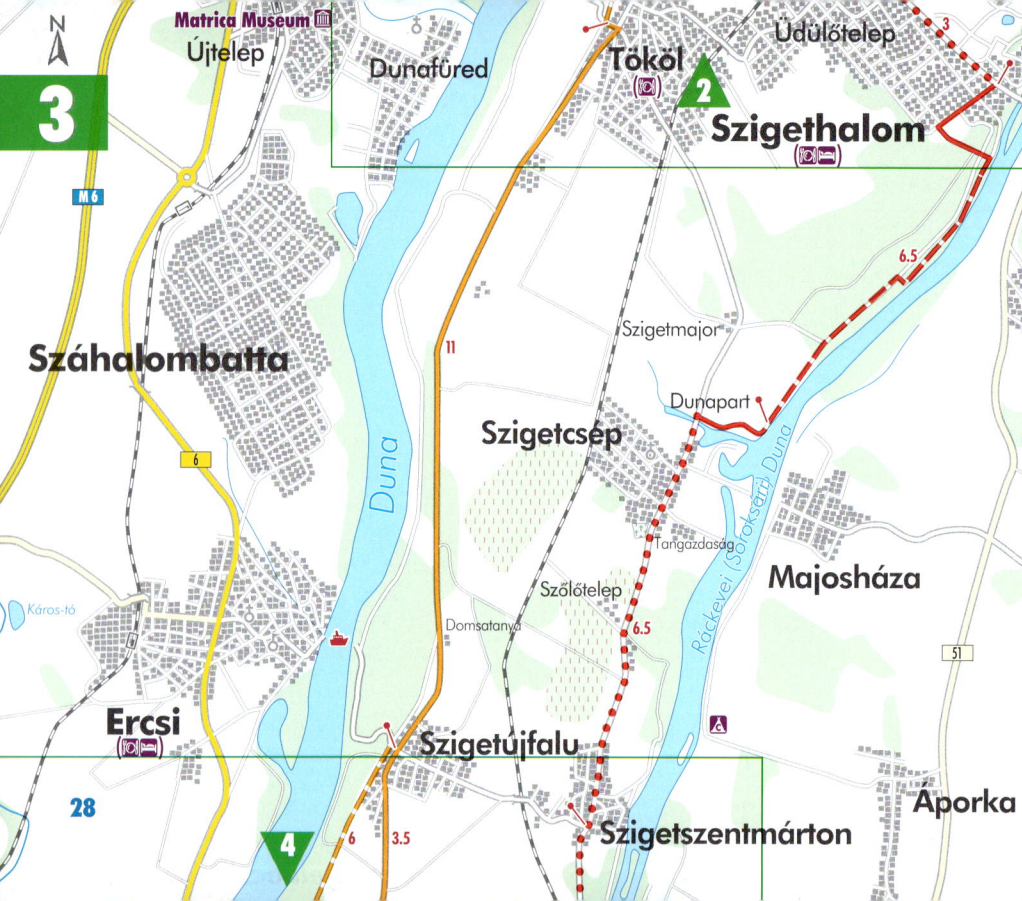

Lakihegy

Tip: Go straight to come to an unpaved small road that passes east of Halaszek and leads to Tököl. Here you then switch to a small country road and stay on it until Szigetúfalu and Ráckeve. This alternative route to Ráckeve is about 4 kilometers shorter. If you wish to just enjoy the natural landscape and bypass towns and traffic, stay on the unpaved dike-road when you get to Szigetújfalu and continue southward near the river to just north of Dunavesce.

For the main route, in Lakihegy follow the planned official route to the left ～ follow the road a few kilometers to Sziget-Szentmiklós.

Tip: This section of the route passes through a business and industry district with many large automobile dealers and transport companies. It is not particularly scenic.

Sziget-Szentmiklós

Take the road to the railroad crossing ～ and turn right just before the crossing ～ follow the road towards Szigethalom ～ go right at the traffic circle ~ at the next fork turn left ~ before the railroad crossing go right on the main road ~ at the next right-of-way road turn right ~ and straight ahead at the next traffic circle onto **Gyari útca**.

Continue straight through another industrial area. The road surface outside the town is somewhat less even ~ and proceed straight to Szigethalom.

Szigethalom

At the big T-intersection go left over the tracks ~ and follow the road through the town ~ just before the bridge over the arm of the Danube (Ráckevei-Duna) turn right ~ and ride through this small residential neighborhood.

Tip: There are inviting little restaurants directly on the Danube where you can get tasty fish dishes.

Continue along this small, well-paved road ~ past weekend-cabins, gardens and meadows ~ after the last houses the road surface becomes hardened clay that is very bumpy and leads right down to the Danube ~ after a short distance the road becomes somewhat smoother, although it is not paved ~ ride past more small cabins ~ into a curve to the right and back onto asphalt ~ at the main road turn left towards Szigetcsép.

Szigetcsép

Ride the main street through the town ~ and past a small pink church on the right.

Pass another church on the right side ~ at the edge of town pass the cemetery ~ and proceed on the country road towards Szigetszentmárton.

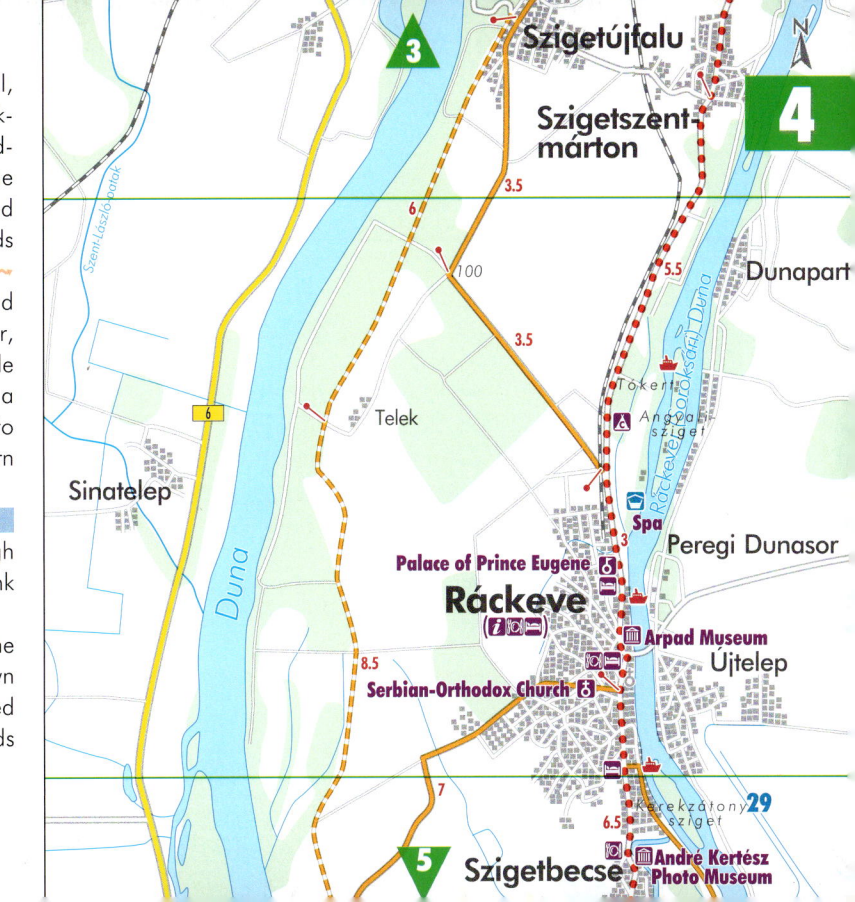

Ráckeve – Palace of Prince Eugene of Savoy

Szigetszentmárton

🚢 **Ferry to Kiskunlacháza**

Ride between the railroad tracks to the right and the Danube arm to the left.

Continue on the road towards Ráckeve.

Ráckeve

Postal code: 2300; Telephone area code: 024

- **Savoyaikastély**, baroque palace built in 1720 by Prince Eugene of Savoy, the "noble knight" who attained fame and wealth as the Austrian empire's most successful military leader. The palace today is a designated historic landmark and used as a restaurant and hotel.

- **Arpad Múzeum**, exhibits of religious art and artifacts ranging from paintings and statues to valuable clerical garments.

8 **Serbian-orthodox church.** The 500-year old church ranks among the most treasured church buildings in Hungary. Its tower stands separate from the main church building.

Tip: In Ráckeve you can choose between two routes for the next section. Either take the main road with its heavier traffic or choose a quiet unpaved path along the arm of the Danube. The distance is about the same.

Ride past the palace to the right of the road ～ and continue straight ahead.

Tip: If you wish to visit the palace or other scenic sights in the area, you may also wish to consider an excursion to Lake Velence some 40 kilometers away.

Excursion to Lake Velence   32 km

In Ráckeve follow the main road ～ at the next fork in the road turn right towards Lórév to the ferry to Adony ～ just past the ferry station you pass a small chapel on the left side a short distance off the road ～ take the ferry across the Danube (departs every hour on the hour between 8-19 o'clock). On the

other side of the river, take the main road through Adony towards Pusztaszabolcs and Velence about 30 kilometers away.

Valencei-tó

The roughly 10 kilometers long and 2-and-a-half kilometers wide Lake Velence is one of Hungary's most popular recreation and vacation spots. In addition to attracting lovers of water sports, it is also a favorite destination for bird watchers. Thick growths of reeds along the western edge of the lake provide excellent habitat to more than one hundred bird species. The wildlife can be observed from on board an excursion steamer that departs from Agárd.

Chapel near Lórév

Ráckeve to Solt   51.5 km

The main route follows the main road through Ráckeve towards Makád ~ proceed through Szigetbecse.

Szigetbecse
- Ferry to Kerekzátony island
- André Kertész Fótomúzeum

Tip: Turn left to reach the ferry to the small island of Kerekzátony Sziget. Here you also have the option of continuing on the unpaved road along the dikes, without any traffic, as far as Makád, where this alternative route rejoins the main route.

Follow the main road past the church to the right ~ across from a bus stop ~ at a small pond in the middle of the village continue through a sharp turn to the right (across from a small tavern) ~ after leaving the village the traffic becomes lighter, the road is uneven.

Pass an apple orchard on the left side and proceed to the next village, Makád.

Tip: Where the road curves to the left about 1 kilometer before the edge of Makád, there is a turn-off to the right towards Lórév, the ferry to Adony and Lake Velence.

Makád

In Makád ride straight towards the church and pass it to the right. There is a large statue in the square in front of the church ~ the road curves toward the left as you leave Makád ~ at the next larger road turn right ~ the alternate route along the Danube arm from Ráckeve

Lake Velence

rejoins the main route ~ turn right at the next T-intersection.

Pass a small birch woods on the right ~ the asphalt is in very poor condition here with many potholes ~ keep going to the barrage ~ ride across the barrage and the Danube arm and onto a better road surface ~ at the next T-intersection turn right ~ and then immediately left again towards Tass.

Tip: As an alternative you could go straight on the unpaved road on the dike next to the Danube. This route has no traffic and is the same length as the main route. It rejoins the main route at Dunaegyháza.

Tass

At the edge of Tass you meet the 51 national road ~ turn right and proceed towards Szalkszentmárton.

Szalkszentmárton
Petőfi Emlék-Múzeum

The main route continues along Route 51 from Szalkszentmárton ~ at the next main road you can go straight to enter the town ~ or stay right to continue towards Baja.

Tip: After about 4 kilometers a newly built bicycle path begins on the dike next to Route 51. Occasionally this path veers toward the heavily traveled road, but mostly it runs at a comfortable distance from the noise and exhaust fumes generated by the traffic.

Dunavecse

Follow the bike path along Route 51 through the town.

Tip: At the fork in the town you can go left and return to the unpaved, automobile-free dike road to Dunaegyháza.

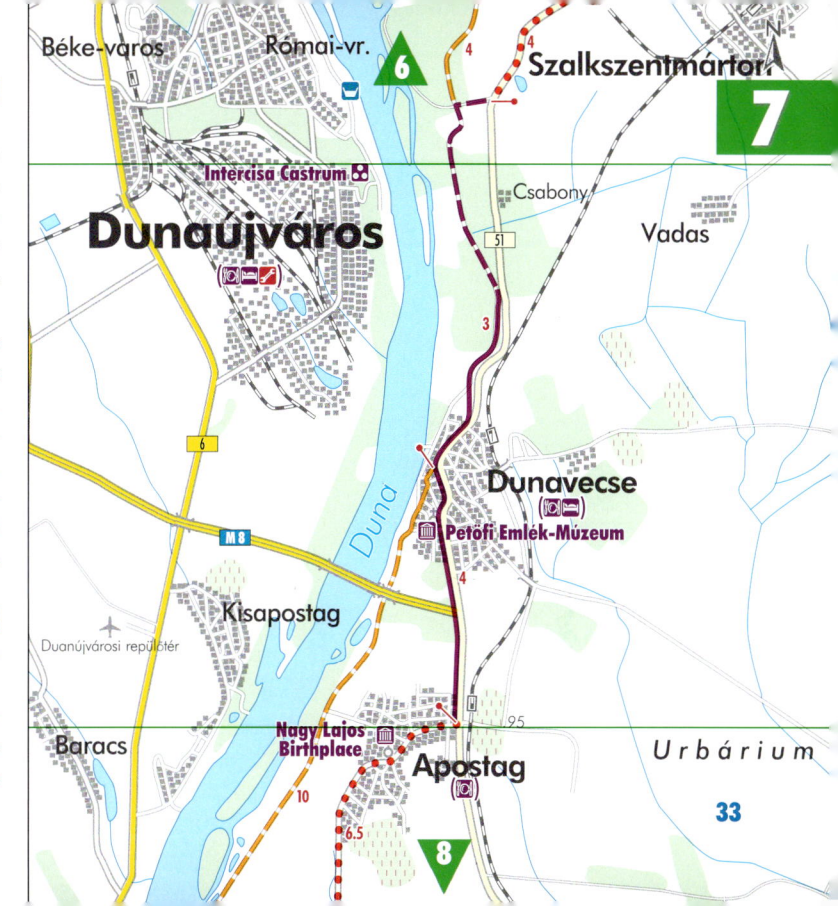

33

Ride past the church on the left ~ outside of town pass the train station and ride into Apostag.

Apostag

Follow the country road through the town and proceed to Dunaegyháza.

Dunaegyháza

Tip: Here the alternate route on the dike road rejoins the main route.

In the town proceed straight at the junction until you come to the 52 national road near Petfitelep.

Petfitelep
- Wine museum

Alternative route via Dunaföldvar   26 km

Tip: Here you have the option of riding over to the right bank of the Danube and to Dunaföldvar. This alternative route passes through pretty landscapes and is somewhat more varied than the main route. The distance is about the same. To take the alternative route turn right on Route 52 and cross the river. Dunaföldvar does not have many sights, but there are several inviting restaurants and pubs where you could take a break.

Dunaföldvar – Castle gate

Dunaföldvar
Postal area code: 7020; Telephone area code: 075
- Castle, above the Danube bridge. The 16th century tower houses a museum with exhibits on historic weapons items from the Turkish period. Changing exhibitions. (The castle grounds and advertised restaurant appear in very poor condition and may be undergoing renovations.)
- Thermal spa, indoor and outdoor pools. Open: Mo-So 10-18 o'clock

If you stay on the right bank, after crossing the bridge continue straight to the traffic circle with the fountain (built in 2004) ~ take the last exit from the traffic circle towards Bölcske ~ proceed on the country lane between the river and the E73 main road to Bölcske.

Bölcske
- Roman excavations

Take the road through the town and proceed towards Madocsa.

Madocsa

In the town follow the road through a curve to the right and then to Dunakömlöd.

Dunakömlöd
- Roman fortification

In Dunakömlöd proceed straight and across the railroad tracks ~ and keep going to the T-intersection at Route E73 or B6 ~ and turn left on the main road.

Tip: Caution – the next 3 kilometers have very heavy traffic.

Paks

Postal area code: 7020; Telephone area code: 075

- **Tourinform**, Szent István tér 2, ✆ 421575
- **Ferry to** Gederlak, 7-18 o'clock
- **City Museum**, in Cseh Vigyázá house
- **Heart of Jesus church**, Roman catholic church built in the style of a basilica.
- **Holy Ghost church** (1990), Szent István tér, designed by the architect Imre Makovecz. Unusual church design.
- **Archaeological park with a reconstructed** Illyrian burial mound that can be viewed from inside.
- **Chestnut avenue**, hundred-year old tree-lined avenue is a protected natural asset.
- **Nuclear power plant**, Hungary's first operating nuclear power station. Visitor center.
- **Spring festival on Pentecost weekend.**
- **International jazz, rock and food festival**

At the edge of Paks, just behind the Vasúti Múzeum and the train station, proceed 700 meters to the right and down to the ferry to Géderlak, where you rejoin the main route. (Ferry schedule: every hour on the hour from 7-12 o'clock and 14-18 o'clock).

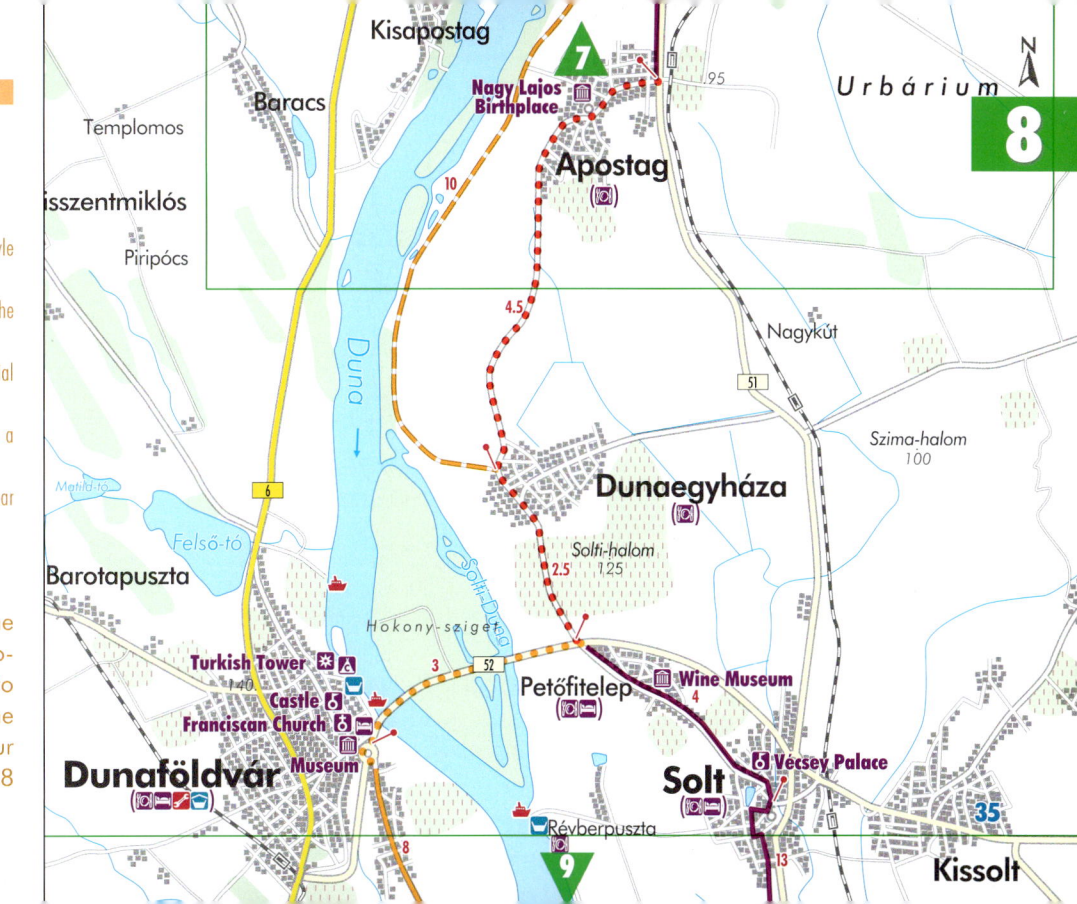

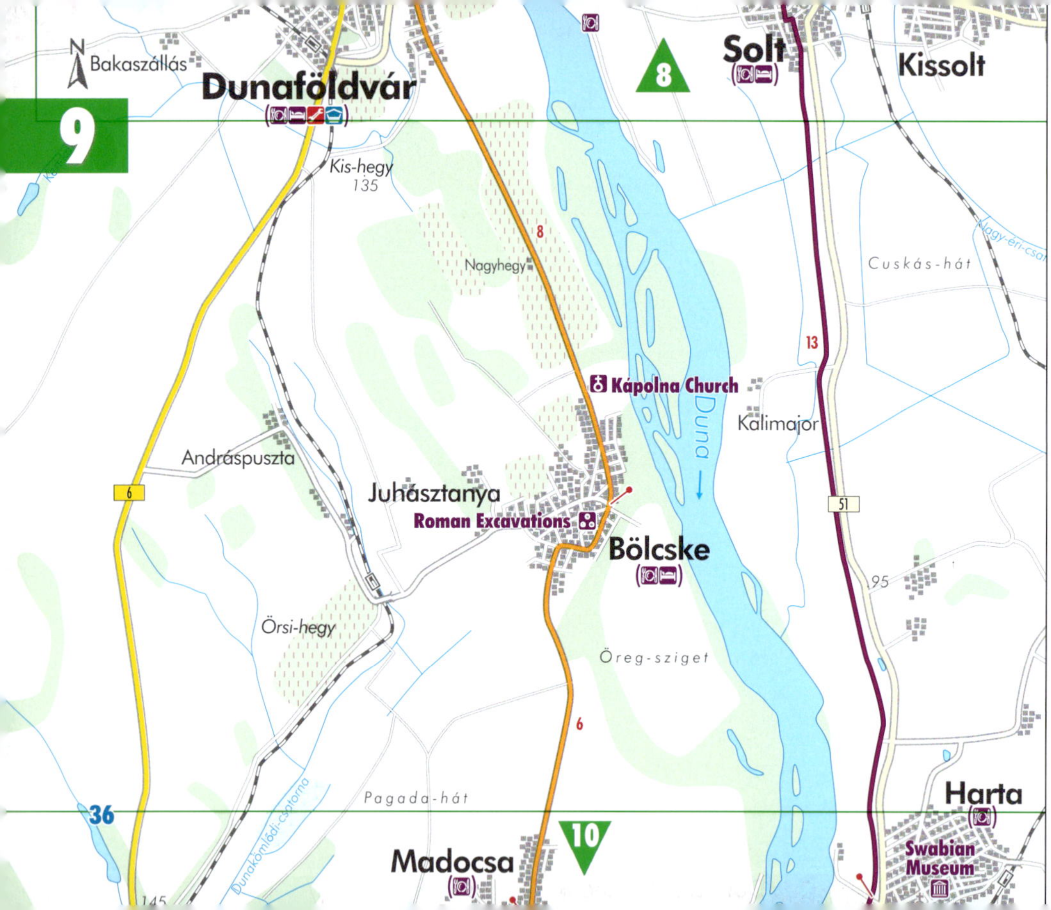

Ferry near Paks

After crossing the Danube continue on the small lane to Géderlak.

Tip: After about 500 meters you can get back on the road on the dike and follow it to Fajsz.

Géderlak

On the main route, go straight at the intersection in Petfitelep ~ the bicycle path along the main road brings you to Solt.

Solt

6 Vécsey palace

Solt to Kalocsa   43 km

Go right before you come to Route 51 ↝ and right again at the church ↝ then left at the next opportunity ↝ left again at the second fork ↝ and immediately right again ↝ and now you should be on the road out of town ↝ to Route 51 ↝ and stay on this road to Harta.

Harta

🏛 Swabian museum

Ride past the town off to the left and continue on to Dunapataj.

Dunapataj

Tip: At the edge of town you can go right on the unpaved road on the dikes or stay on the main route. The dikes alternative stays close to the river and bypasses Kalocsa until it rejoins the route just south of Fajsz.

For the main route follow the street through the town on **Ordasi út.** towards Ordas and Gederlak.

Tip: Here you rejoin the alternative route coming from near Paks.

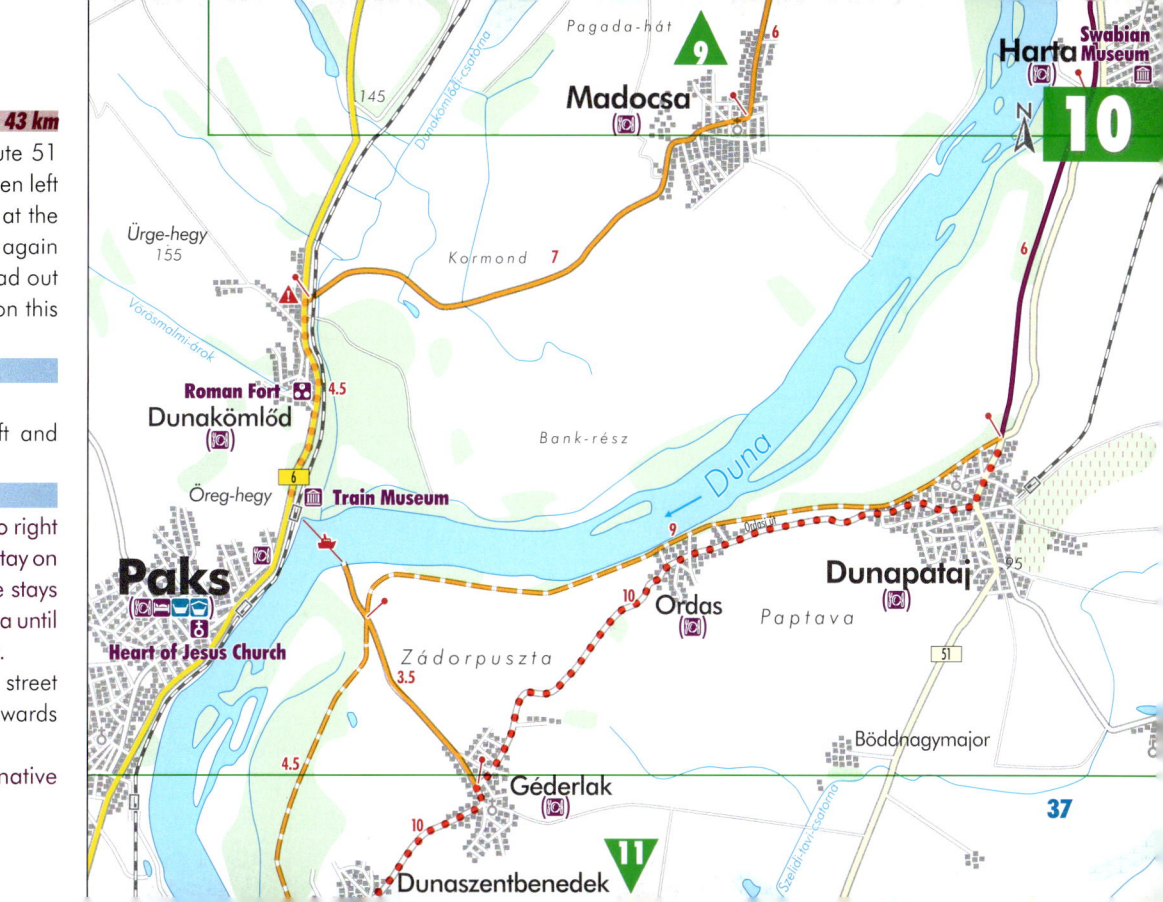

Géderlak

Turn left at the intersection ~ and them immediately right following the sign for Kalocsa ~ go through a curve to the right next to a church ~ and head to the next village, Dunaszentbenedek.

Dunaszentbenedek

Proceed on the main road ~ in a left-right combination of curves there is another sign for Kalocsa ~ directly in front of you there is a church ~ turn left at the church ~ and continue along the main road.

Tip: A marked bicycle path begins on the left side in the middle of the village. It ends at the edge of the village.

Continue to Uszód.

Uszód

Just before the edge of town there is a big shipping company, followed by a cemetery and a small church on the same side.

Tip: A posted bike path starts in the middle of the village on the right side and continues to several hundred meters past the edge of the village.

You stay on the main road towards Foktö.

Foktö

At the main road turn left towards Kalocsa ~ and proceed along the road and into Kalocsa.

In the city the road curves to the right towards the center.

Tip: Starting from the city limits sign on the edge of town there is a bicycle path on the right side.

Keep going until you reach Route 51.

When the fields are on fire...

Some Hungarians say the fields are on fire in the fall, when the paprika is ripe and ready to be picked. The blazing red colors create an unforgettable view with reds and purples evident on houses and farms where the local growers have proudly hung woven garlands of their "red gold" out to dry in the sun.

Hungary's paprika came originally from South America and it was during the region's Turkish period that farmers began planting the spicy crop along the Danube.

Around the beginning of the 20th century, Kalocsa overtook Szeged as Hungary's biggest paprika producing city, and today it calls itself the country's "paprika capital." Thirty-two villages in the surrounding areas form the world's biggest paprika-growing area. Although it was not until the 18th century that paprika gained acceptance in Hungarian kitchens, today it is impossible to think of Hungarian food without the spicy peppers. The crop is also an important export commodity.

Kalocsa

Postal area code: 6300; Telephone area code: 078

- **Kalocsa Korona Tours Kft.**, Szent István Király útca 5, ✆ 461819
- **Paprika museum**, Szent István Király útca 6, Open: Mon-Sun 10-17 o'clock. The world's only paprika museum, with exhibits on the plant, pepper mills, pickled and dried peppers, etc.
- **Viski Karoly Múzeum**, Szent István Király útca 25, Open: Tues-Sun 9-17 o'clock. Historical museum with artifacts and items from early times, the Turkish period, Roman coins as well as more recent items, including a collection of famous folk art from Kalocsa (costumes, wall paintings, embroidery).
- **Nicolas Schöffer Museum**, Szent István Király útca 76, Open: Tues-Sun 10-12 o'clock and 14-17 o'clock. Nicolas Schöffer, considered the father of cybernetic art, was born in this house on Sept 6, 1912. Contains sculptures by the artist and information about his life and work.
- **Archbishop's treasury**, Hunyadi út. 2, ✆ 461860, Open: Mon-Sun 9-17 o'clock. Exhibit includes raiment, chalices, bishops rings etc.
- **Cathedral** (1735-54), Szentháromság tér (Holy Trinity Square), designed by Andreas Mayerhofer. Old bishops graves were rediscovered here in the early 20th century. Ceiling paintings in the dome and opulent baroque decorations.
- **Archbishop's palace** (18th c.), Szentháromság tér. Frescoes and ceiling paintings in the palace chapel by the Austrian baroque

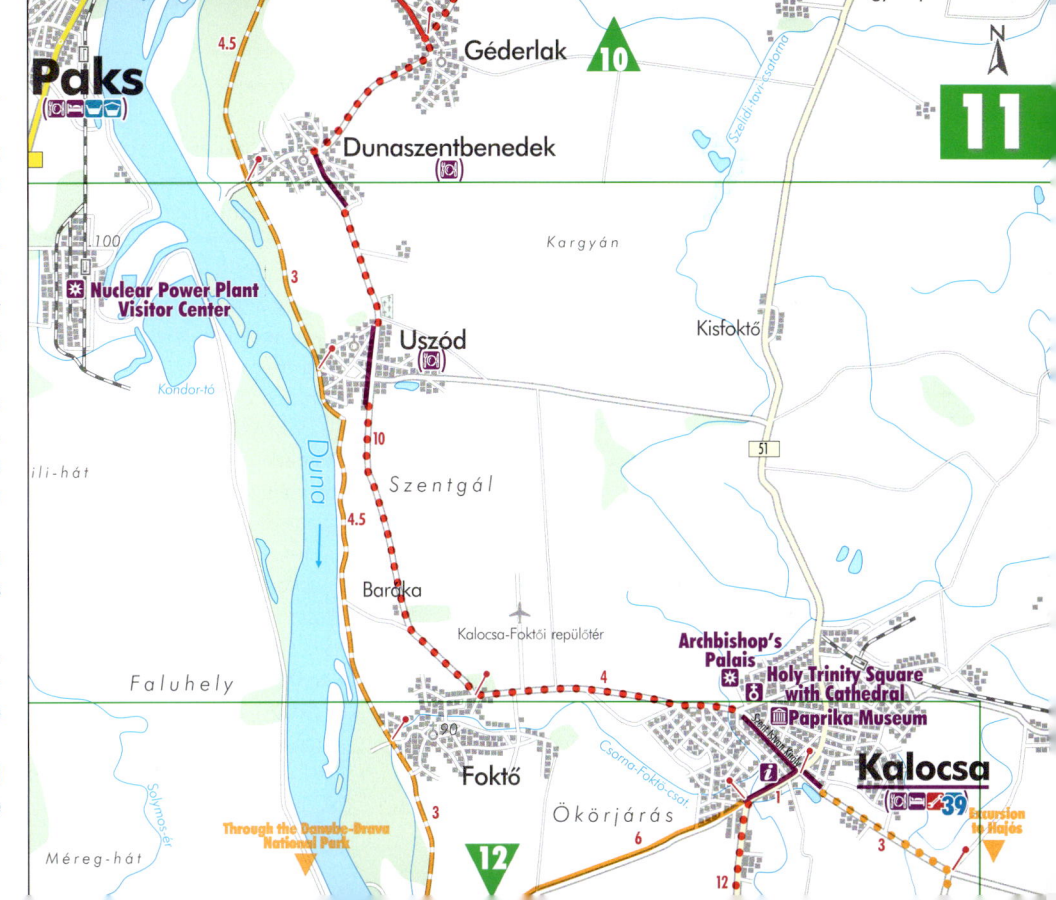

painter Franz Anton Maulpertsch (1724-96).

- **Library in archbishop's palace**, Szentháromság tér 1, ✆ 461280, Open: Tues-Sun 9-12 o'clock and 14-17 o'clock. Guided tours: every hour. World-famous library contains more than 120,000 volumes, codices and incunables. Includes a bible from 1519 with notes by Martin Luther.
- **Thermal spa**, Kossuth út. 63, ✆ 461075

Kalocsa is known not just for its paprika, but also for folk art and especially a specific type of decorative embroidery to depict old flower designs. These are much in demand for their brilliant colors and are sometimes referred to as "art of light."

Kalocsa is one of the oldest cities in Hungary, and served as the seat of an archbishop (Astrik-Anastas) during the reign of King Stephan I.

In 1529 the city was destroyed by the Ottomans, but the archbishop's castle continued in use as a fortress. The city, however, was not rebuilt and in 1686 even the castle was burned down when the Turks were expelled. Archbishop Kollonich began reconstruction by renovating the gothic chapel. It was eventually torn down and construction of a new residence began, which led to a revival of the city.

In 1784 the Archbishop Ádám Patachich combined his private collection of books with various medieval collections in the cloister to form the archbishops library, which today contains more than 120,000 volumes of old and historic books.

The palais was heavily damaged during World War Two. Parts of it still have not been repaired, but the city remains one of the most important bishoprics in the country.

Tip: At the intersection with Route 51 you must decide how you wish to continue. Go straight if you wish to undertake the excursion to the wine village Hajós, or turn right to continue on the main route to Baja or to the other side of the Danube and through the Danube-Drava national park.

Excursion to Hajós   26 km

This excursion is an absolute must for anyone who enjoys fine wine. Just about everything about the unique village of Hajós is dedicated to making, selling and enjoying wine. Plan a short stay in Hajósi pincek, where there are certain to be several wine cellars waiting to serve you their best.

Kalocsa – Cathedral

Kalocsa – Paprika museum

Take **Szent Istvan Kiraly** through the city until you come to a traffic circle ~ go straight towards Kiskörös ~ at the intersection with a traffic signal turn right towards Kiskörös, there is a bike path for the next 600 meters on the left side of the road ~ at the next fork turn right towards Miske and Hajós.

Miske

At the intersection in the town go straight ~ there is a church on the right ~ continue straight towards Hajós.

Hajós

Postal area code: 6344; Telephone area code: 078

- **Town hall**, Rakoczi utca 12, ☎ 404-100
- **Pilgrimage church** (1728), the statue of Maria in the church was brought by Germans, the so-called Danube Swabians, who settled in the area in the early 18th century. The statue came originally from the parish church in Dietelhofen in southwestern Germany.

In Hajós follow the main street. You can also use the bike path posted on the left side ~ at the next intersection go straight ~ past a fountain on the right side ~ at the end of town there is a sharp curve to the right ~

Hajós – Pilgrimage church

look for signs to **Hajósi pincék**, the largest wine-cellar village in Europe, ~ turn right here ~ past the small "Let's do it" building supplies store ~ and take the bike path on the right side to where it ends at Route 54.

Hajósi pincek

Hajós is the largest wine-cellar village in Europe, with more than 1,200 wine cellars and wine presses. The village is an architectural oddity, with small "folks-baroque" houses with their gabled roofs. Vaulted wine-cellars have been dug into the loess beneath the houses to store great wooden barrels where the region's dry red and white wines are aged.

Maria Theresia settled Swabians in the region, and it was her affection for hard work and good wine that helped make this village what it is today.

For the area's vintners, the village is a place for family celebrations and parties, but visitors are also always welcomed.

It is also possible to take an interesting stroll through the wine-cellar village as part of a folklore program. Further information is available at the Hajós town hall. The tour features songs played on Swabian accordions and dancers wearing Swabian folk costumes. Guests are welcomed with wine and salted baked goods while they listen to old folk music and dances. During a festive ceremony, selected guests are required to take an oath making them members of an "order of wine knights". In September there is an annual meeting of the order in Hajós.

We strongly recommend a visit to this

Excursion to Hajós

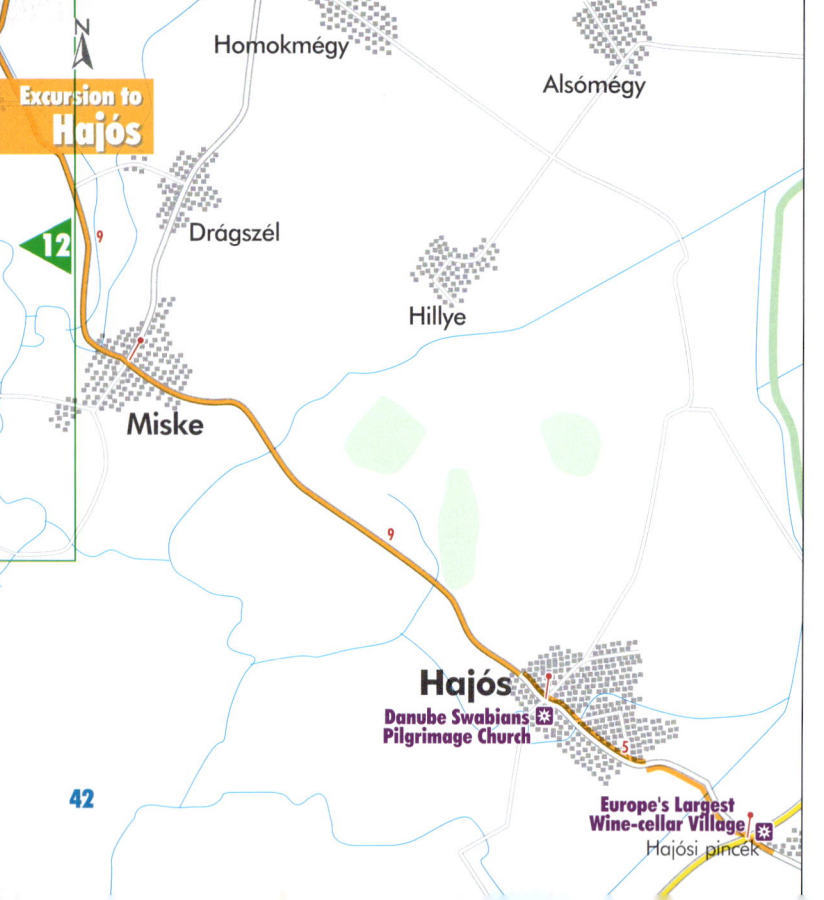

unique and interesting Hungarian village.

Tip: The route further south splits into two as you depart Kalocsa. To visit one of the most beautiful Hungarian nature preserves, go straight on the bike path next to the road. From the right side of the Danube you can then enter the Danube-Drava National Park. This detour takes at least a half-day longer and rejoins the main route in Baja.

Through the Danube-Drava National park   74 km

If you enjoy seeing fauna and flora in an idyllic nature preserve, we urge you to consider this variant of the Danube bicycle route. You will find a unique wildlife reserve and the Gemenc forest railway, which offers a relaxing and comfortable way to see the park. This variant will consume a little more time, but we are sure you will find it worthwhile.

Hajósi-pincek – Europe's biggest wine-cellar village

Hajósi-pincek – Europe's biggest wine-cellar village

Coming from Foktö, take the sharp right on Route 51 in Kalocsa towards Gerjen and follow the bike path next to the road for about 7 kilometers ~ this good asphalt road lined with handsome poplars brings you down to the Danube and the ferry to Gerjen.

Tip: There is a campground on the left bank just before you get to the ferry landing.

On the west bank of the Danube follow the road through Gerjen.

Ökörjárás
Through the Danube-Drava Park 1

Through the Danube-Drava Park 2

Tolna – Gymnasium

Gerjen
Take a left-right combination to leave the village and proceed about 9 kilometers to Fadd.

Fadd
At the next T-intersection turn left ~ and proceed straight for 3 kilometers. Turn right at the next intersection ~ the traffic is somewhat heavier now ~ past an outdoor swimming pool and into the town of Tolna.

Tolna
After the church there is a bike lane on the right side of the road leading through the entire town ~ it ends just past the railroad crossing ~ follow

the main road until you come to the traffic circle at the M9.

⚠ Caution when entering the traffic circle. Heavy traffic.

After the traffic circle continue straight towards Szekszárd ~ after a short distance ride through the village of Palánkpuszta.

Palánkpuszta

Go straight through the village and proceed to Szekszárd.

In the town follow the road to the next intersection ~ and turn right ~ at the next T-intersection turn left on **Rakóczi útca** ~ and go straight through the town until you come to the big intersection ~ turn left on **Hunyadi útca**.

Szekszárd

Postal area code: 7100; Telephone area code: 074

- **Tourinform**, Garay tér 18, ✆ 511263
- **Tolna Tourist**, Széchenyi utca 38, ✆ 418365

- **Wosinsky Mór Megey Museum**, Szent István tér 26, Open: Oct-March, Tues-Sat 10-16 o'clock, April-Sept, Tues-Sat 10-18 o'clock. Exhibits of prehistoric artifacts plus folk art items like costumes, early crafts and industry, furnishings from various levels of society.
- **House of Fine Arts** (behind the museum), in the former synagogue, Open: Oct-March Tues-Sun 9-17 o'clock. Rotating exhibitions and concerts
- **Babits-Mihály memorial house**, Babits-Mihály utca 13, Open: April-Oct, Tues-Sat 9-17 o'clock, Nov-March, Tues-Sat 9-15 o'clock. Birthplace of the Hungarian poet, writer and translator (1883-1941), contains displays of his writings and furnishings.
- **Roman-catholic church**, second-largest single-hall baroque church in Hungary.
- **Komitat house** (1828-33), Béla tér 1. Bronze wine fountain, where mostly red wine flows into ready-standing glasses. "Komitat" is a term for the Hungarian administrative district which is run by a "Gespan" (since the 11th century the highest official and repre-

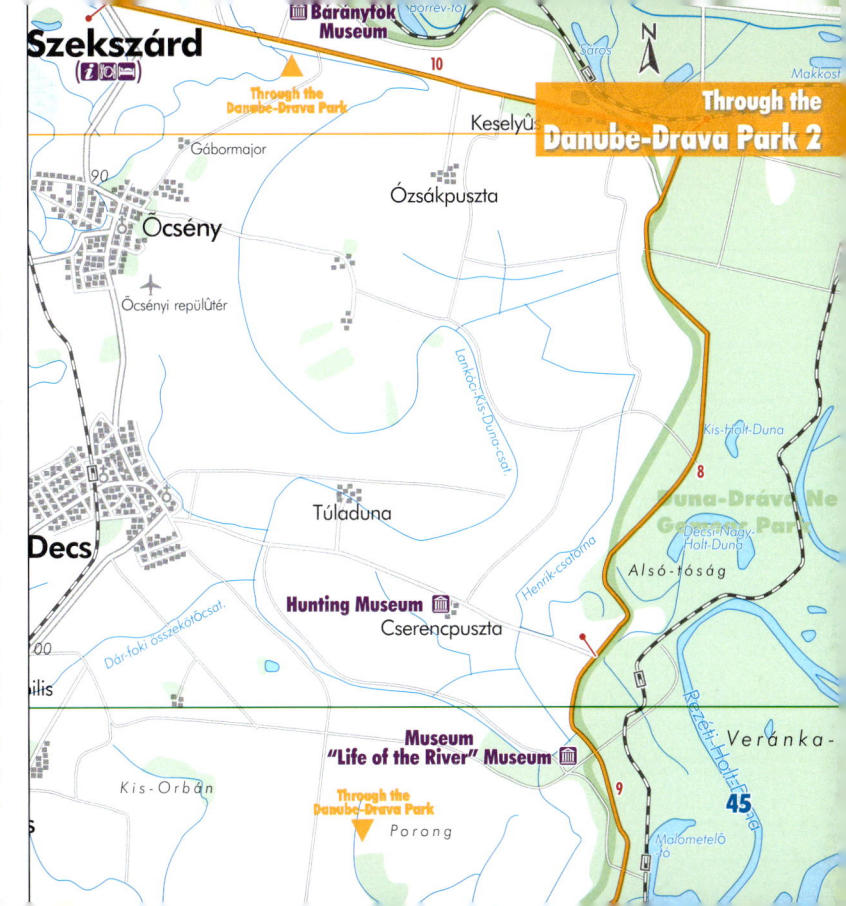

Through the Danube-Drava Park 2

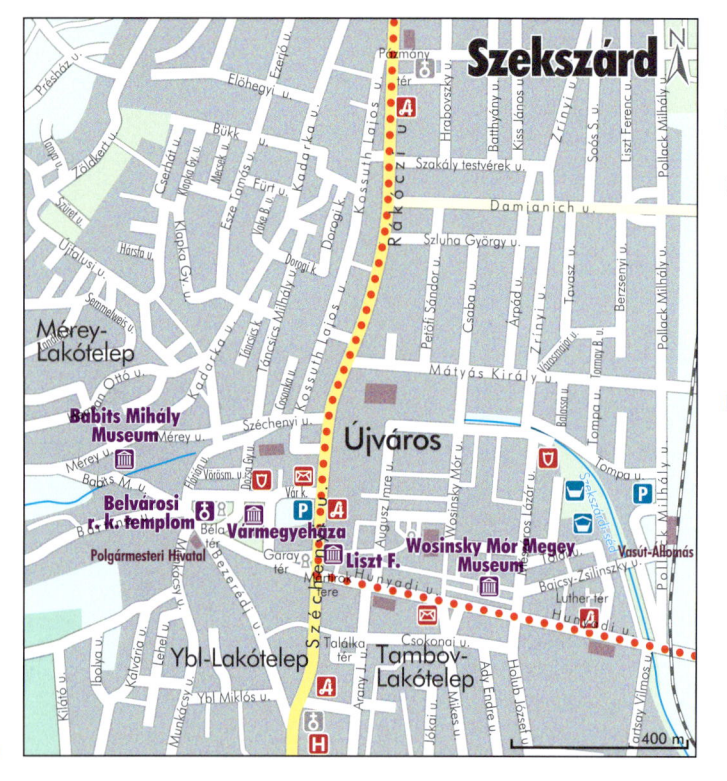

sentative of the king, since 1867 representative of the government. The office was eliminated in 1950).

- **Outlook tower** on the mountain. Excellent views of the city and surrounding vineyards.
- **Wine houses: Garay Kellerei**, Garay tér 19; **House of Wines**, Rákoczi utca 22; **Korona**, Béri B. A. utca 70; **Vesztergombi**, Béla tér 7. The city's wine-cellars contain many thousand hectoliters of excellent wines aging in oak barrels. Wine tasting and sales.
- **Gemenc Forest**, 6 km east of Szekszárd. Is part of the Danube-Drava National Park. A flood plain woods consisting of lakes and canals formed by old arms and branches of the Danube. This wildlife preserve is home to many bird species, deer and other animals. Excursions through the park can be made on the Gemenc narrow-gauge railroad (departures: May-Aug 10.30 o'clock and 15.00 o'clock, Oct-April 10.30 o'clock and 14 o'clock) or by boat (departures: May-Oct, Mon-Sun 8, 10, 12, 14 and 16 o'clock) from the park's excursion center. Tours are about 2 hours long.

Szekszard was first established by the Celts and became an important regional city during Roman times. The name Szek-szard applies not just to the city, but to the entire wine-growing area. The calciferous loess on the seven 100 to 200 meter high hills that surround the city produce grapes from which aromatic and tangy red-wines are made. They include Merlot, Blaufränkisch and, of course, the Kadarka grape which came originally from Dalmatia. White wines like Traminer and Chardonnay also are excellent.

Numerous archaeological finds in the area show that wine has been produced here for at least 2,000 years.

Go straight on **Hunyadi útca** over a bridge ~ then over the railroad tracks ~ and straight ahead. The street name changes to **Keselyusii út.**, towards the wildlife preserve ~ for 10 kilometers to Keselys.

Tip: After about 4 kilometers you pass the entrance to the museum at the start of the Danube-Drava national park and wildlife preserve. From here you can board the Gemenc forest train tour through the preserve (about 2 hours long).

After the village of Keselys follow the path to the right along the edge of the national park ~ after about 17 kilometers this route takes you into Pörböly ~ across the railroad tracks at Route B55 ~ then left towards ⚠ traffic is heavier from here to Baja.

Baja refer to page 48

Kalocsa to Baja 45 km

On the main route, follow the bike path next to Route 51 out of Kalocsa towards Baja ~ after about 1 kilometer there is a turn-off to the left. Turn left and follow Route 51.

Tip: Go straight if you wish to return to the dike road along the river from Dunapataj to Fajsz.

Take Route B51 to **Bátya**.

Bátya

At the sign for the town there is a posted bike path on the left side of the road. It switches to the right side at the next intersection.

Ride past a playground where the road curves to the left ~ after this curve the bike path switches back to the left side of the street and then ends as you leave the village of Bátya.

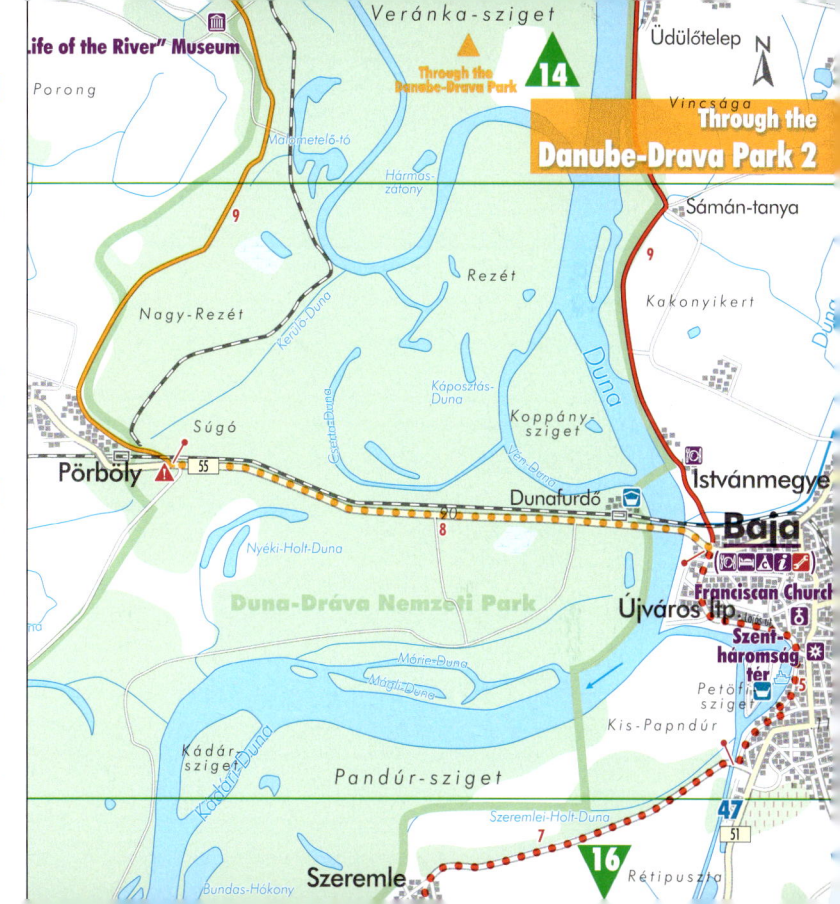

Through the Danube-Drava Park 2

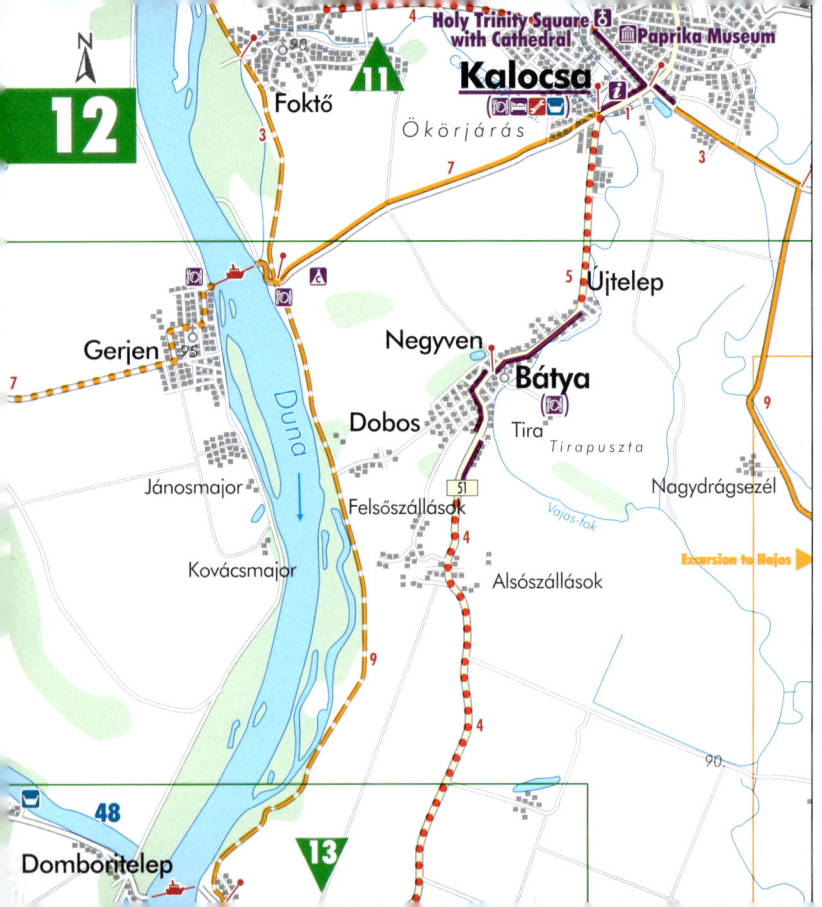

You continue straight ahead after another 4 kilometers come to a turn off to the right, towards Fajsz, away from Route B51.

Fajsz

In Fajsz, at the first larger intersection turn left and go through the village just before the end of the village turn right on the unpaved road which leads through fields of paprika to the west and the Danube.

Tip: Here the main route connects with the dike-road alternative route that started in Dunapataj.

The next 5 kilometers stay on the unpaved dike-road along the Danube until you come to the M9 motorway where the asphalt-paved dike-road is a pleasure to ride.

Tip: There is a tunnel to the other side of the motorway and after that you can enjoy the swift ride along the paved dike-road all the way to Baja.

Just before you enter Baja, the road becomes somewhat wider and is lined with weekend cabins. The skyline of Baja is visible in the distance ride past a gravel quarry and under Route B55 make a sharp left turn near the Danube, followed by a curve to the right and past a large factory with rail sidings and a huge storage silo.

Keep going until you come to a main road proceed straight and past a shopping center on the left side and continue into the center on **Lajos út.** at the next intersection turn right on **Szent Antal út.** (B51) towards Hercegsántó.

Baja

Postal area code: 6500; Telephone area code: 79

- **Tourinform**, Szentháromság tér 5, ✆ 420792
- **Türr István Museum**, Béké tér (Roosevelt tér), ✆ 324173, Open: Tues-Sun 10-16 o'clock. Largest exhibit on Hungary Danube fishery. The museum is named for Türr István (born 1825), a general under the Italian revolutionary and politician Giuseppe Garibaldi (1807-82).
- **Nagy-István-Képtár Art Gallery**, Arany János utca 1, ✆ 325649, Open: Tues-Sun 10-16 o'clock. The former Voinich manor houses paintings by 20th century Hungarian painters. Most of the artworks are by István Nagy (1873-1937).
- **Éber-Emlékház house**, Jokai Mór utca 19, Open: Tues-Sun 10-16 o'clock. Exhibits of sculptures, paintings and other works by the local artist.
- **Baroque parish church**, Ságvári Endre tér. Interior with beautiful ceiling frescoes and main altar.
- **Franciscan church**, Bartók Béla utca 1. Beautiful, richly decorated altars.
- **Synagogue**, Munkacsy Mihály utca 7-9. The synagogue today contains a library.
- **Greek-orthodox Serbian church**, Táncsics Mihály utca 21. The gold-decorated iconostasis behind the altar of this late-rococo church makes it perhaps the most treasured artwork in the city.

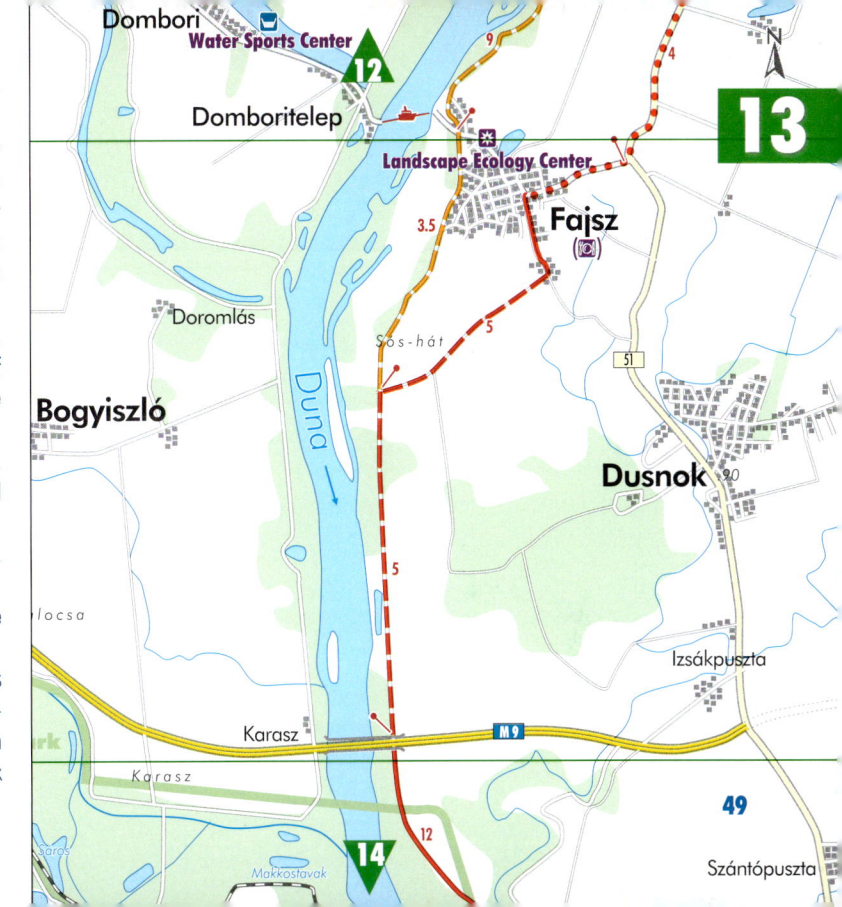

Holy Trinity column with the four Evangelists at the Szentháromság tér

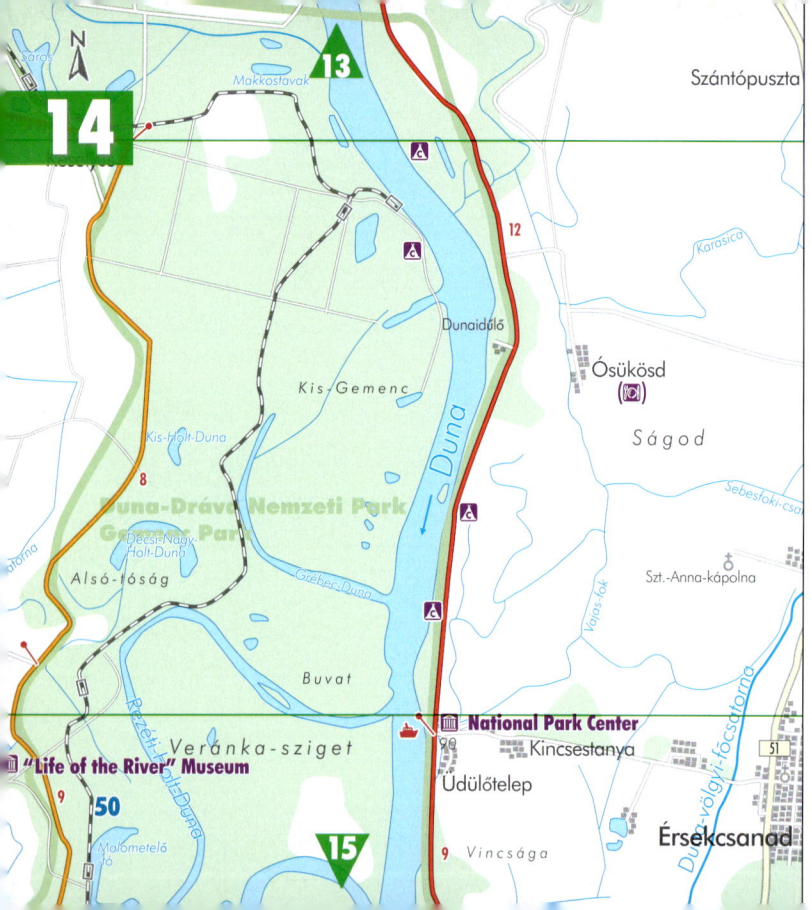

- **Szentháromság tér (Holy Trinity square)**, this large square on the banks of the Sugovica echoes with the prestige and prosperity the city enjoyed in the past.
- **Folks festival**, on the 2nd Saturday in July. Famous traditional fish-soup is cooked in more than 2,000 pots set up in the streets and tended largely by men. The soup, spiced with paprika, must be fire-red and hot. This culinary spectacle is even noted in the Guinness book of world records.
- **Marina**, directly at the campground
- **Fishing spots**, all around the Petőfi islands
- **Indoor pool**, across from Hotel Sugovica
- **Outdoor pool** directly next to the Danube

The area around Baja was already settled in the early Stone Age. Early settlers were probably attracted to the area by a wealth of fish and wildlife in the region. The town was almost completely destroyed during the Hungarian peasant wars. In 1514, peasants led by György Dósza revolted against the landed gentry and tried to free themselves from tyranny. After the peasant army's defeat, Dósza was burned on a glowing throne. The Turkish wars that soon followed prevented the population from further growth. In the 17th century, as Baja became a Muslim religious center and supply station for Turkish troops, Ottoman dignitaries started moving to the town.

Turkish dominion of the area ended after more than 170 years and Baja was granted market status. This was an important step forward in the development of local trade. In the early 18th century, German tradesmen, the so-called Danube Swabians, started moving to the area, and Baja became a conglomeration of Hungarian, German and Serbian ethnicities.

In the first half of the 19th century, Baja was an important trading center for livestock, grains and wine. A large portion of the city's buildings were destroyed in a great fire on May 1, 1840. The reconstruction that followed provided the city's current layout.

The city's development progressed only slowly until it was connected to the nation's rail networks. It was not until the 1960s and 1970s that the city became a center for industry. In addition to furniture manufacturing, Baja also has important textile and electronics plants. A huge meat processing plant is also an important employer (where more than 300,000 pigs a year are slaughtered).

Baja is also a port, serving mainly river freighters. Excursion lines between Hungary and Croatia have been closed down because they were not profitable.

Petöfi island is one of Baja's main tourist attractions, offering locals as well as visitors a variety of water recreation possibilities, including swimming, fishing and boating. But many people also visit the city simply to enjoy the full-bodied wines from Baja, Hajós or Vaskút.

Baja to Udvar
at the Croatian border — 55 km

Take Route B51 out of Baja ～ after passing the edge of the city take the first right towards Szeremle.

Tip: The dike-road is not usable as far as Szeremle.

Szeremle

The road enters Szeremle in a long left curve ～ followed by a sharp curve turn to the right ～ after

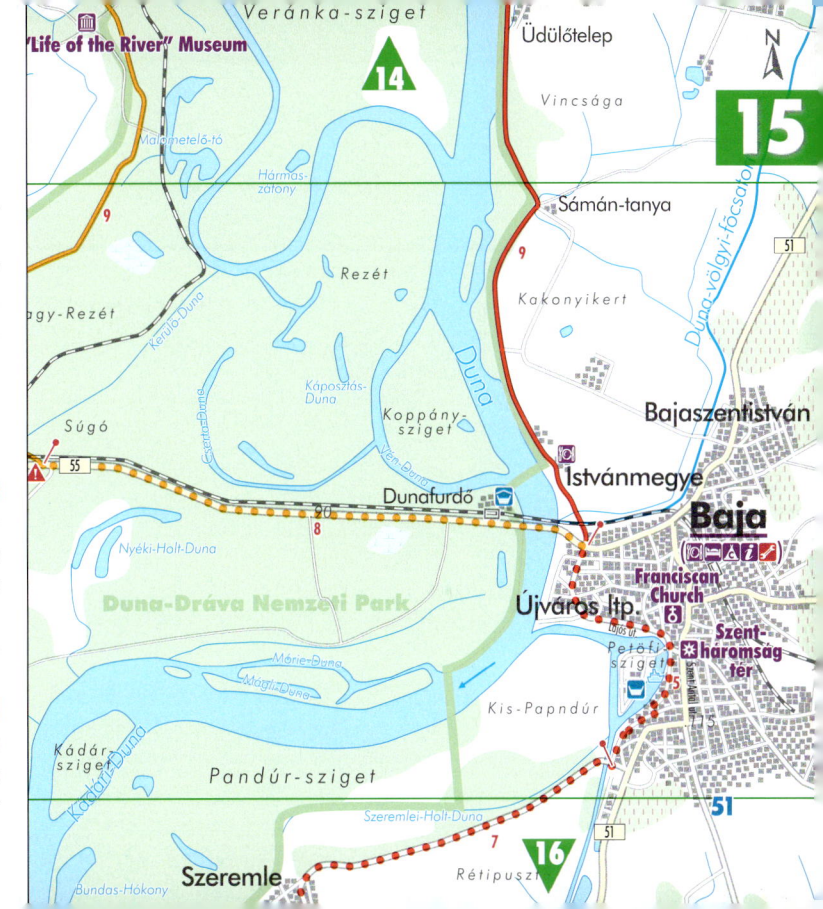

Baja – Türr István Museum

leaving the town there is a turn-off to the right that leads back to the dike-road.

After about 2 kilometers the dike-road is paved again and can be followed to Dunafalva.

Danube Swabians

The term Danube Swabians refers to German families who systematically settled in parts of eastern and southeastern Europe. The term, however, did not come

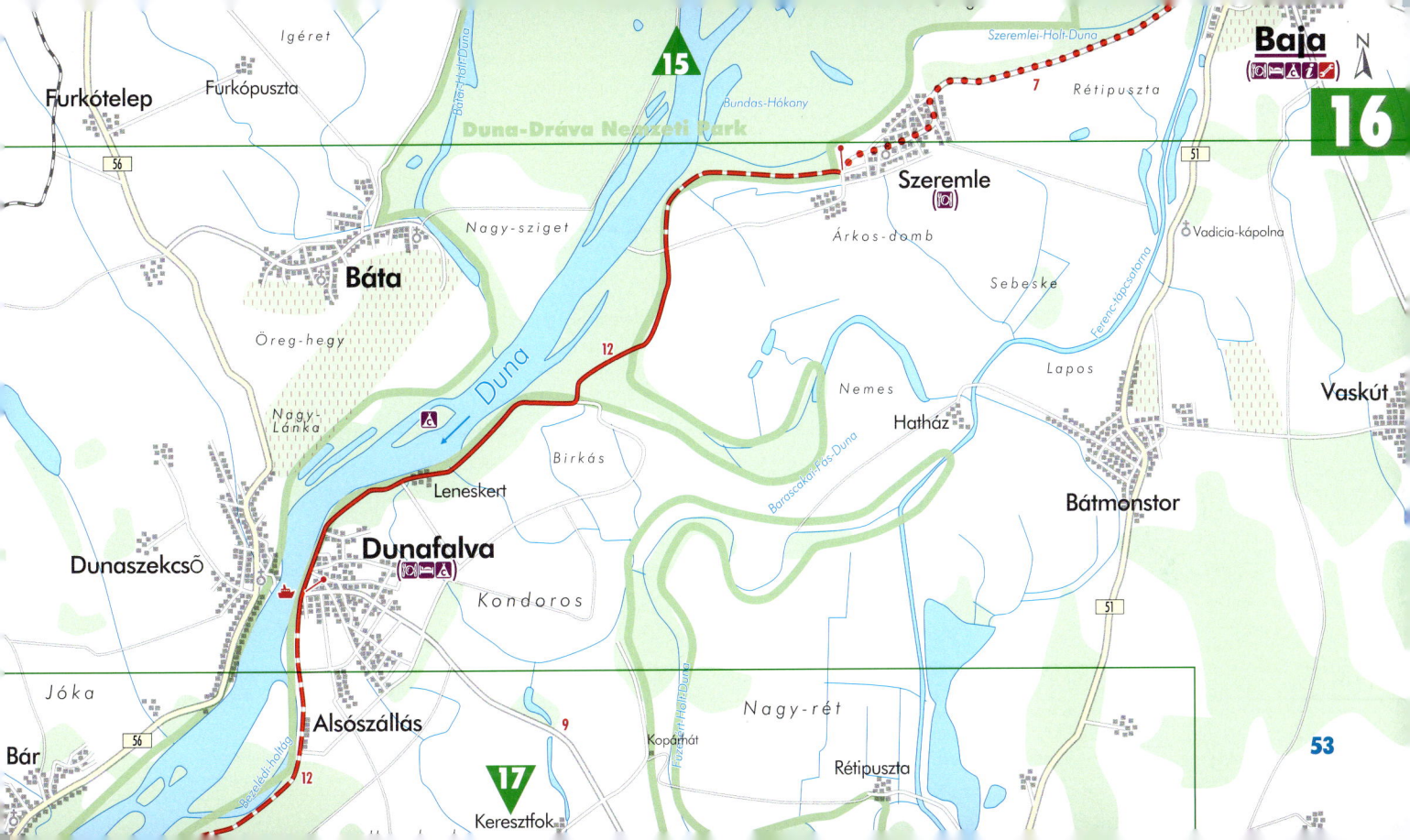

Baja

16

53

into use until after the First World War, after the Danube Swabians' settlement areas in Hungary, Yugoslavia and Romania were divided.

After the end of the Turkish wars in the 17th/18th century, the depopulated parts of Austria-Hungary were opened up to farmers and craftsmen from southwestern parts of the kingdom. Most of them came from Alsace, Lorraine, the Palatinate, Saarland and Luxembourg, and Bavaria. But many peoples from other areas, including Hessen, Switzerland, Westphalia, Prussia, Saxony, Thuringia, Austria, Bohemia, Moravia, France and Holland also looked to begin new lives in the eastern parts of the realm.

The largest settlement areas were in the Backa, Banat and Satu Mare. After the borders of Hungary were redrawn in 1920 at the Treaty of Trianon, many Danube Swabians found themselves living outside of Hungary. Much of Banat and Satu Mare became parts of Romania, other parts of Banat and Backa became parts of Yugoslavia, while the rest remained in what was left of Hungary.

At the beginning of the Second World War, there were more than 1.5 million ethnic Germans living in south-eastern Europe. During and after the war, many of these communities of ethnic Germans were broken apart by forced expulsions or voluntary flight to other parts of the world.

Today some small communities of Danube Swabians still survive, especially in Hungary and Romania. They live as ethnic minorities and struggle to preserve their language and customs.

In southern Hungary, for instance, you will occasionally spot official signs bearing both Hungarian and German names, an unmistakable indication that there are ethnic Germans still living in the area.

Dunafalva
- Ferry to Dunaszekcsö

For the main route, at the ferry landing continue straight on the dike-road toward Mohács.

At **Újmohács** go right to the ferry landing.

Mohács – On the ferry

Újmohács
- Ferry to Mohács
- Outdoor pool

Busójaros - Carnival in Mohács

Busójaros is a centuries-old carnival tradition unique to Mohács. Central to the celebrations are the Busós, local residents who wear sheepskins, cowbells and horns set above frightening carved wooden masks dyed with animals' blood.

According to local legend, the custom dates back to when members of a southern Slavic tribe, the Šokci, donned similar costumes and stormed across the river on a winter's night to frighten away Turkish troops that had occupied Mohács. A nice story, perhaps, but just a story, because it is generally accepted that the Šokci only migrated to the area after the Ottomans had withdrawn. But many residents of Mohács prefer to keep the legend alive.

Today the busójaros form part of carnival celebrations at the beginning of Lent, and the busós carry carnival pastries on the tips of the tridents instead of carved wooded heads of Turks, as was customary in earlier times.

The highpoint of the celebrations is reached when participants dance around a great bonfire and then set off across the Danube in their boats.

Tip: From the ferry you can proceed straight into the center of Mohács or turn left on the main route to Croatia.

Mohács
Postal area code: 7700; Telephone area code: 069

- Ferry to Újmohács
- **Tourinform**, Széchenyi tér 1, ☎ 505515
- **Mecsek Tourist**, Szentháromság utca 2, ☎ 511020
- **Kanizsai Dorottya Museum**, Szerb utca

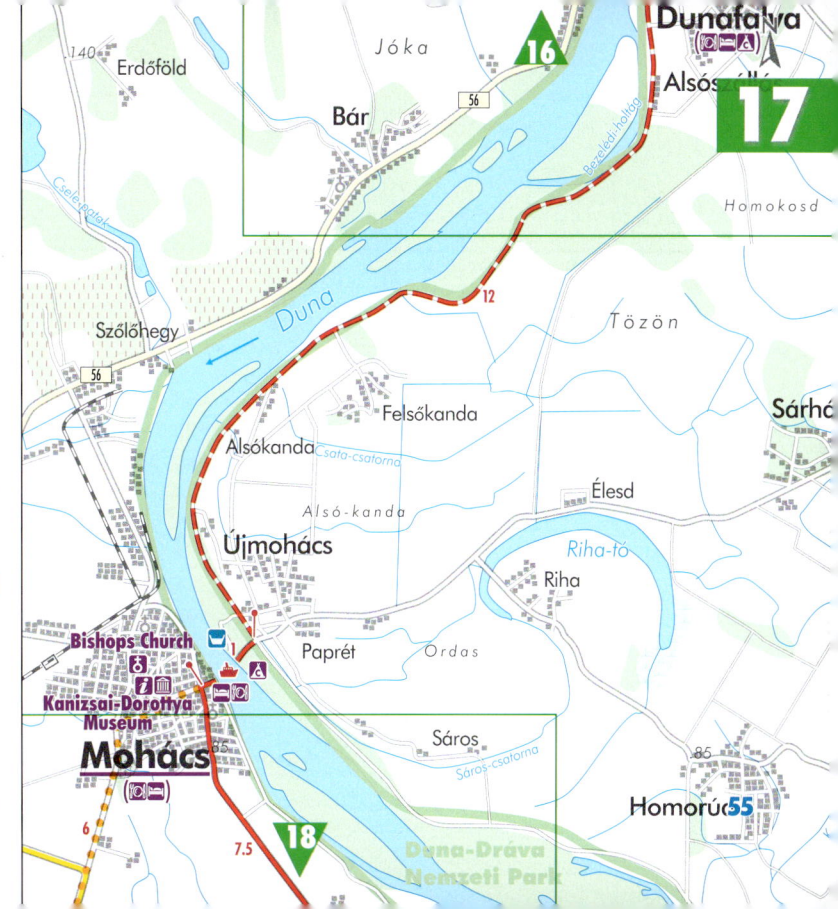

Mohács – Pedestrian zone

2, ☎ 322490, Open: Tues-Sat 10-16 o'clock. Museum about the Battle of Mohács in 1526, with artifacts from the battlefield and other related items.

- **Greek-orthodox church**, across from the museum. Interesting historic church with old and new icons.
- **Kossuth Film Theater**, Deák tér 2, ☎ 510477. Movies and changing exhibitions on other arts.
- **Historic memorial park (Emlékpark)**, Open: April-Oct, Tues-Sun 9-17 o'clock, Nov-March by appointment at Tourinform or at ☎ 382130. Memorial for the battle against the Ottomans in 1526, 6 km south of Mohács near Sátorhely. 120 wooden posts stand in memory of the 26,000 Hungarians who fell in the disastrous defeat.
- **King Lajos II memorial**, Csele-Bach. Memorial to the Battle of Mohács was erected on the 450th anniversary of the battle, at the site where the king drowned as he tried to escape the enemy.
- **Mask carving**, Kígyío utca 7, ☎ 302548. The artist and teacher Englert Antal shows visitors some of the secrets of carving the famous Busó masks. Antal received a prize for folk-art crafts in 1998 and teaches mainly children.
- **Busójaras**, three days every year for carnival, ending on Shrove Tuesday.
- **Festival of water walkers**, annually on May 16. Festival with nighttime boat procession, fish-soup competition, music and fireworks.
- **Indoor pool**
- **Outdoor pool in** Újmohács

Mohács is the southern-most Danube port in Hungary and an important traffic hub less than 10 kilometers upstream from the border to the former Yugoslavia.

Despite its significance, Mohács feels like a quiet and peaceful small city possessed of a certain contagious imperturbability. With its colorful mixture of 30,000 ethnic Croats, Hungarians and Germans the city justly prides itself as happily multicultural.

Mohács – Széchényi tér

The Battle of Mohács 1526

On August 29, 1526 the Ottoman forces under Sultan Suleiman the Magnificent inflicted a devastating defeat on a much smaller Hungarian army led by King Louis the Second near Mohács. The Turks had captured Belgrade five years earlier, and then began their preparations for an attack on Hungary to the north. That campaign came in 1526, when the Sultan and an estimated 100,000 troops marched north after the Hungarians refused to pay tribute to the Ottoman Empire. Suleiman's forces included 35,000 Sipahi mounted cavalry and 15,000 Janissaries, the Ottomans' standing army consisting mainly of Christian recruits raised as Muslims and sworn to serve the sultan for life.

The Turkish invaders were opposed by about 25,000 Hungarian troops, including 4,000 heavily-armored riders. Initially the Hungarians intended to wage a defensive battle, but the mounted nobles insisted on attacking the Turkish forces. They met with some success at the beginning, until they were stopped by the Ottoman defensive ranks and a timely counterattack by the Janissaries. The Hungarians could not hold their positions and were surrounded and captured or killed. Some who managed to escape, including King Louis II, were drowned in a nearby river.

The battle marked the beginning of the end of the Hungarian kingdom in central Europe. In the following years, the Ottoman Empire occupied and divided Hungary into three parts: the central part, including Buda and Pest, became a Turkish province; Transylvania became a semi-autonomous principality under Turkish domination, while only the western part remained independent of the Ottoman Empire.

The Turks stayed for more than 150 years, until they were expelled by the Habsburgs and the Hungarian lands could be reunited.

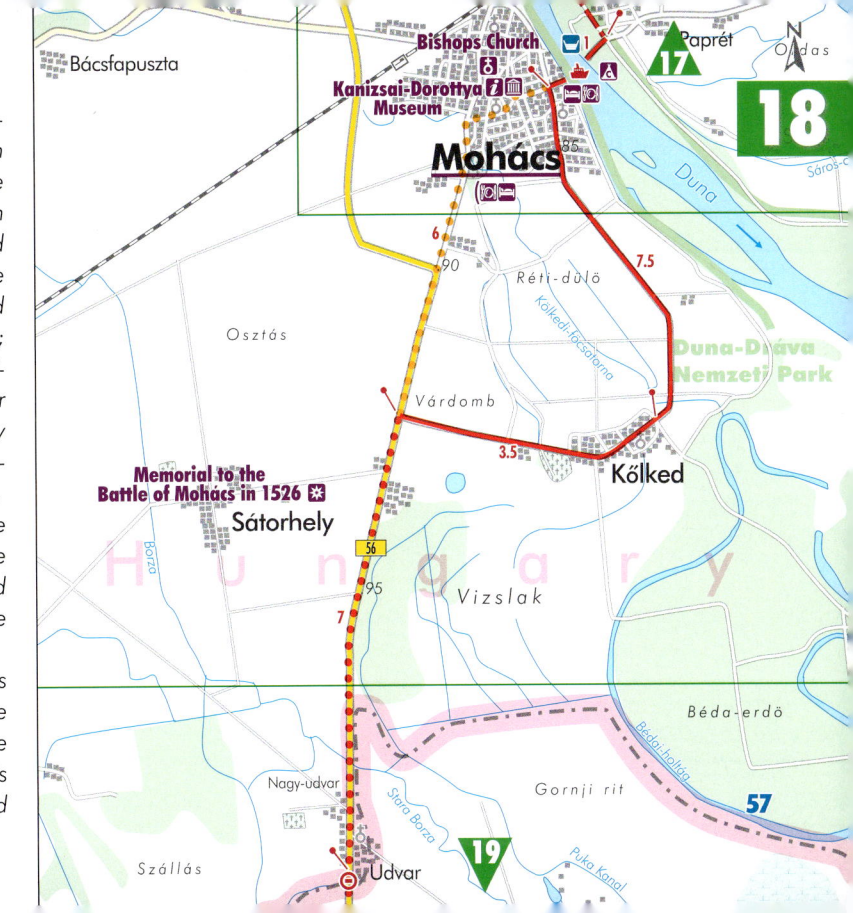

The first battle of Mohács also marked the birth of the Habsburg's Austrian Danube kingdom. Hungary's King Louis II had no offspring when he died in the battle. As a result, Hungary and Bohemia and the Hungarian crown passed to the Habsburgs, greatly increasing their domain in central Europe.

The Ottomans were defeated at the Second Battle of Mohács, on August 12, 1687, when a Habsburg army under the command of Charles the Duke of Lorraine and Maximilian Emanuel of Bavaria routed Suleiman Pasa. A year later the Ottomans were also defeated at Belgrade and completely expelled from Hungary.

Tip: If you wish to visit the center of Mohács, you can ride through the city to Route B56 and turn left. After about 6 kilometers you will rejoin the main route.

To stay on the main route, turn left at the ferry landing in **Mohács**, pass a restaurant and a small hotel ⤳ and proceed straight through a residential area and out of the city ⤳ and continue to Kőlked.

Kőlked

Follow the road through the village ⤳ and go straight to the intersection of Route B56 ⤳ turn left towards **Udvar** on the border to Croatia.

Udvar

Mohács – On the ferry

Croatia

141.5 km

The landscape through Croatia's bread basket does not offer much variety as you ride past countless meadows and fields with only rare glimpses of the Danube. It is nevertheless an exciting section of the trip. Osijek, on the banks of the Drava River, is the cultural and economic capital of eastern Slavonia. Until the civil war in the 1990, it was also an important inland port even though the Danube is almost 20 kilometers away. There are numerous other interesting sights as well, most of them on the banks of the Drava River. Less than a day's ride further you come to Vukovar, where many houses and buildings still bear the scars left by the civil war. Even so, a walk along the riverfront in Vukovar has a special charm. The tour then continues with a few climbs and descents to Ilok and the border crossing to Serbia.

Almost all of this part of the route follows a national road that is, at times, quite busy. Use care and keep a close eye on traffic coming from both directions. You will also be confronted with climbs before Batina, between Zmajevac and Kneževi Vinogradi and between Opatovac and Ilok.

Udvar to Osijek — 56.5 km

After crossing the border at Udvar continue on the minor road ~ after about 500 meters turn left towards **Duboševica** ~ just before entering the village you see the church.

Tip: Here you will see the first of the "Ruta Dunav" route signs which will serve as dependable guides as you ride through Croatia.

Before entering the village turn right at the stop sign ~ and proceed on the minor country road.

Tip: The unpaved shoulder next to the road is very rough and not suitable for bicycling.

At the large white cross and the stop sign turn left ~ and ride into the village of **Topolje**.

Topolje

Follow the road through the village ~ at the end of the village ride past farm buildings on the right ~ and towards a church that does not have a steeple on the left side of the road ~ pass the sign indicating St. Peter and Paul church (Krkva St. Peter i Pavla) ~ and then into the village of **Gajić**.

Gajić

As you enter the village you pass a river, but it is just the Tupaljski Dunav, a side-arm of the Danube ~ after the church ride across a canal ~ the road then makes a bend to the left which you follow ~ and continue to a right-left combination that then leads to **Draz**.

Draz

Ride past the "Skola" ~ you are in one of the best-known wine-producing regions in Croatia ~ cross the bridge in the village ~ and go left towards **Batina** ~ after Draž the road goes uphill through several curves ~ you ride past vineyards and orchards ~ the shade from the many trees makes the climb a little more bearable ~ at the next fork in the road turn left towards Batina ~ after about 50 meters there is a stop sign ⚠ where traffic from the right joins the road ~ proceed straight ~ downhill ~ past a restaurant on the left side.

Batina

At the edge of town the road surface becomes cobblestones which can make the downhill ride dangerous, especially when wet!

Tip: Here in Batina there is a bridge across the Danube and a border crossing into Serbia.

You follow the bicycle route sign at the 5-way intersection, just before the border station, and make a sharp right towards Zmajevac ~ ride through the flood plain forest in the cool shadows on the straight, tree-lined road.

Tip: Just before the edge of town there is

18
19
20
61
Nagy-udvar
Udvar
Gornji rit
Stara Borza
Puka Kanal
Erdöfü
Bok
Puškaš
Gerec-hát
Šarhat
Ziljevača
Labudovnjača
Telep
Mačkaluk
85
Kosutnjak
Kolut
90
Kovačica
Oraškovica
Spoljna Kovačica
Kendija
Šarkanj
Gaj
Smrkovica
90
Géta
Sirkovi
Dubośevica
Borza
E73
Topolje
Strmen Kenda
Budžak
Stari Dunav
Lorencov Dunavac
Sarkanjski Dunavac
Dunav
Baračka
Veliki Kanal
Croatia
Slatina
90
Karašica
Velike mede
Topoljski Dunav
Mali Siget
Stubanj
Ševinjak
Šumarina
Buka
Batina
Kneževo
Staro selo
Draz
Veliki Siget
Gažnja
Kruničevo kalilo
Gajić
Kanal Dunav-Hisa-Dunav
Sinor
Velika veka
Ulice
Ada
Filakovi
Trojnas
205
212
Branjina
Crni Kanal
Tavanac
200
Popovac
Karašica
Lipovo brdo
Zatoni
Daraki Fok
Mala veka
Vlaškovic
Podolje
Cibogat
Sama Surduk
Grovišče
Staro Stolo

an unpaved road that goes off to the left. This leads along the Danube through flood plain and swamp areas and is difficult to ride in wet conditions. Caution: Do not stray away from this road. There are still land-mines in the ground off to the sides! This alternative rejoins the main route just before Bilje.

Zmajevac

✽ Wine cellar

At the main road at the stop sign turn left towards **Kneževi Vinogradi**.

Tip: There is a hospital in this town.

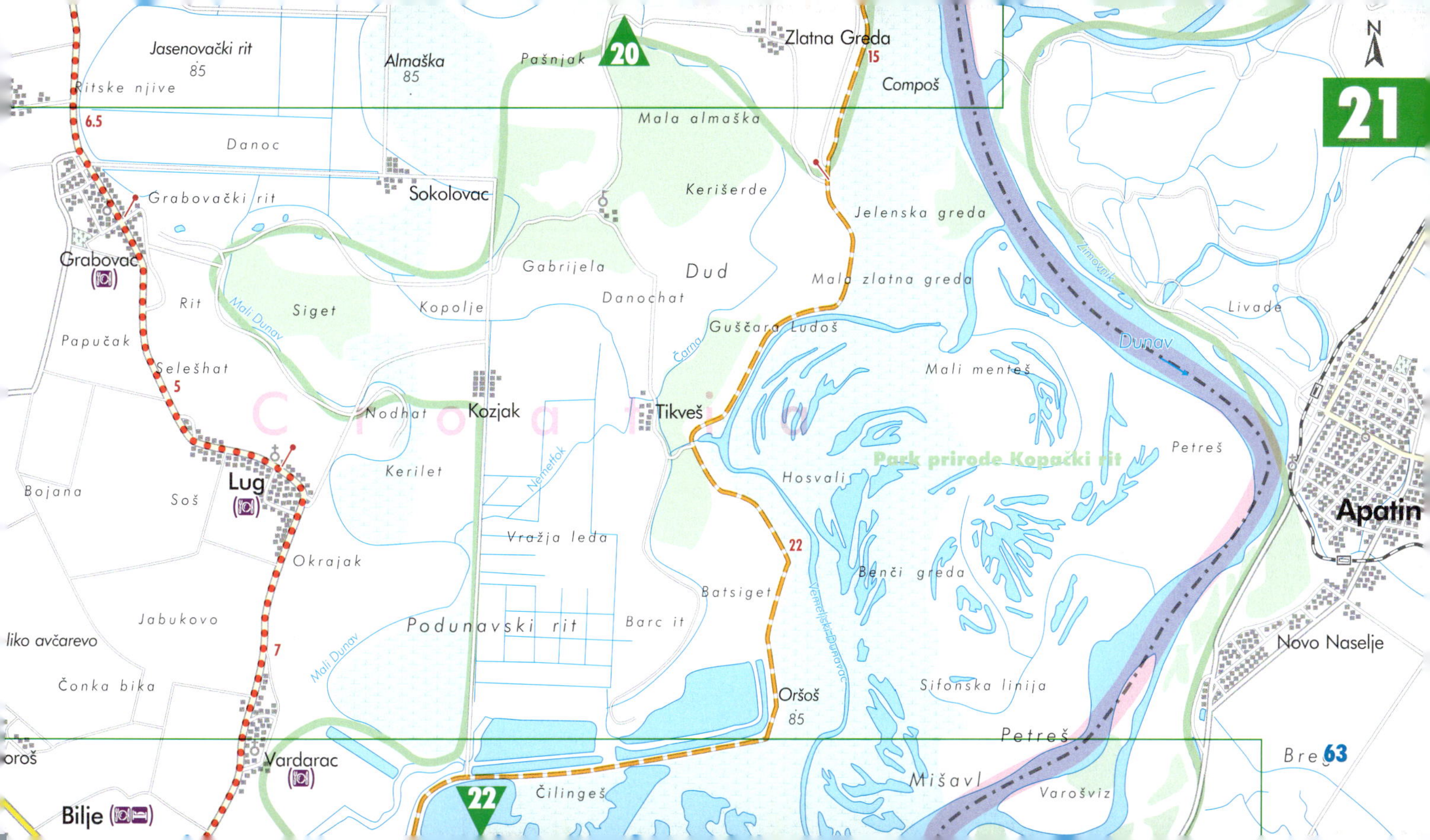

21
N
Jasenovački rit
85
Almaška
85
Pašnjak
20
Zlatna Greda
15
Compoš
Ritske njive
6.5
Danoc
Mala almaška
Sokolovac
Grabovački rit
Kerišerde
Jelenska greda
Grabovac
Gabrijela
Dud
Mala zlatna greda
Rit
Mali Dunav
Siget
Kopolje
Danochat
Gušćara
Ludoš
Zimovnik
Livade
Papučak
Čarna
Dunav
Selešhat
5
Mali menteš
Nodhat
Kozjak
Tikveš
Park prirode Kopački rit
Petreš
Lug
Kerilet
Nemetfok
Hosvali
Bojana
Soš
Apatin
Vražja leda
22
Okrajak
Benči greda
Batsiget
Vemeljski Dunavac
Jabukovo
Podunavski rit
Barc it
liko avčarevo
7
Mali Dunav
Novo Naselje
Čonka bika
Oršoš
85
Sifonska linija
Petreš
oroš
Vardarac
Bilje
Mišavl
Čilingeš
22
Varošviz
Breg
63

After the church continue on the road which heads uphill and has many curves ~ until it reaches **Suza**.

Suza
- Wine cellar

Pass a restaurant as you enter the village ~ and a sign indicating a 6% ascent ~ after the climb the road heads down to the next valley and you enter Kneževi Vinogradi.

Kneževi Vinogradi
- **Belje Wine cellar**, the oldest part of the cellar dates back to Roman times. It consists of two levels dug into the ground. Beneath it there is a reformist church, a remarkable historical treasure.
- Swimming pools
- Fishery pond with 5,000 m² surface
- Hunting and fishing tourism

After the town the road starts to climb again.

Tip: In the center of town there is a sign on the left for "Restoran Panon", which offers rooms and swimming as well.

At the next intersection turn left towards Osijek ~ at the edge of town pass a small petrol station ~ and ride with heavier traffic towards **Grabovac**.

Grabovac

Take the long straight road through the village ~ and continue on the road towards **Lug**.

Lug

Tip: This is another community with signs in various languages – Croatian, Hungarian and German.

In the town there is a sign pointing left towards Bilje 8 kilometers ~ after the church follow the curve to the right and then straight towards **Vardarac**.

Vardarac

Ride past the church ~ and up the gentle incline out of the village.

Bilje

Postal area code: 31327; Telephone area code: 031
- **Tourist Information**, ul. Petefi Šandora 35, ☎ 750855
- **Tourist Information**, Kralja Zvonimira 1b, ☎ 751400
- **Tourism Association**, Kralja Zvonimira 10, ☎ 751480
- **Public institute "Nature park Kopacki rit"**, Petefi Šandora 33, ☎ 750855

Kopacki rit nature preserve

This internationally-recognized swamplands nature preserve was created in the area around the confluence of the Drava and Danube rivers. It occupies some 17,000 hectares of floodplain which were declared protected areas in 1967 and became a nature preserve in 1976. It is one of the largest fish spawning grounds in central Europe, and home to more than 40 different fish species.

It also provides habitat to various other kinds of wildlife, including different kinds of deer, wild

Sign warning of landmines – Not to be taken lightly!

Darda
Mece
Vardarac
Bilje
Čilingeš
21
Mišavl
Varošviz
22
Švajcerova lada
Nadhat
Buda
Sakadaš
Vartibara
Kišhat
Kopačevsko jezero
Meneš
Hordovanj
Martićeva greda
Kopačevo
Kerilo
Kovačirje
Šurnsko ostrvo
Šašhat
Jelensko ostrvo
Kilšeš hat Rečje
Belo jezero
Tabak
Kristina
Hulovski kanal
Stara Drava
Tohat
Kovačke livade
Stara Drava Okruglica
Jelensko ostrvo
Kerešhat
Humka
Palvova greda
Malo rečje
Sarvas bara
Insej bara
Dombovska bara
Veliko rečje
Dunav
Beketešhat
Bikova bara
Renovska bara
Croatia
Remeta
Veliki Linjak
Dombo
Specijalni rezervat prirode
Tvrda
Davotja greda
Kanova bara
Podravlje
Mali Linjak
Gornje Podunavlje
Dunavac
Olaj bara
Crna bara
Kopacki rit Park
Donji Grad
Lanište
Mali bajar
Hulovo
Osijek
Nemetin
Drava
Veliki bajar
Opštinski rit
Staklara
Kučka
Paljevina
Bogaz
Tišna
Nemetin
Velika bara
Poličer
Tufek
Novo Naselje
Vrbak
65
Logor
213
90
Mišino brdo
120
23
Aljmas
Mitnica
Branjevine
Sarvaško polje
Sarvaš
Stara Drava
1
6
7
22

pigs and other large and small game.

More than 260 bird species also live in the nature preserve.

The beauty and variety of the area can be explored by boat on Kopacevo Lake.

Take **Ulica Sandora Tetefija** at the T-intersection, right in front of the church, there is a sign pointing left towards Osijek to the right is an inn named "Löwenbräu" and on the left a "Konzum" store.

Tip: The town offers overnight accommodations, several restaurants and it is possible to go fishing or paddling.

After about 8 kilometers you arrive in Osijek, which lies directly on the Drava river in the town there is a bicycle path on both sides of the main road.

Osijek

Postal area code: 31000; Telephone area code: 031

- **Tourism association of Osijek**, Županijska 2, ✆ 203755
- **Muzej Slavonije** (Slavonian Museum), Trg sv. Trojstva 6, ✆ 208501 or 122-505, Open: Tues-Sat 9-18 o'clock, Sun 10-13 o'clock. Exhibits about folk customs, local archaeology, history and much more.
- **Parish church Petra i Pavla** (Peter and Pauls church) (1894-98), Starevia Trg. Neogothic church built according to plans by the Bonn architect Franz Langenberg and Richard Jordan of Vienna. Many other internationally-renowned artists have also contributed to the church. They include Eduard Hauser of Vienna, who did much of the ornamentation; the Czech artist P. Novotny, who did several sculptures; and Mirke Raki of Croatia, who painted the frescoes. The church is a surviving remnant of the old Austro-Hungarian monarchy.
- **Capuchin cloister** (1710), Kapucinska
- **Croatian national theatre**
- **Holy trinity column**
- **Former military headquarters** (1724), baroque-renaissance building commissioned by Prince Eugene of Savoy.
- **Water gate** (1715) in the old city wall
- **King Tomislav gardens**, 18th century park located between the old city and the upper town. Created by Colonel Volkmann and named for King Tomislav.
- **Extreme sport**, J. J. Strossmayera 235A, ✆ 302364
- **Extreme sport2**, Županijska 16, ✆ 210660
- **Bicikli Škos**, Županijska 40, ✆ 098/252523
- **Vl. Marši Stejpan**, Vukovarska 186, ✆ 508884
- **Rog-Joma**, Jakova Gotovca 3, ✆ 200476
- **Eurobike Center**, Prolaz Josipa Leovia 1, ✆ 373605
- **Magma**, Marina Držia 1, ✆ 203377

Osijek is both the capital and largest city in Slavonia. It was established as the Roman settlement of Mursa during the time of Emperor Augustus.

In 380 AD the city was destroyed by the Goths. It then shifted between the Hungarians and the Slavs through the middle ages, until the Ottoman Turks took control for most of the 16th and 17th centuries. After the Turks were expelled, the upper city was built for Roman Catholics, while the lower town was left for people of other faiths.

Located on the Drava River just 20 kilometers upstream from the confluence with the Danube, Osijek is also a significant inland port.

This part of Croatia saw heavy fighting during the 1990s civil war. Many buildings still bear the scars of the war and have not yet been repaired. Osijek and the surrounding region have only slowly been recovering from the conflict.

Osijek to Vukovar 45 km

In Osijek cross the train tracks and go straight ~ at the next fork stay left ~ and ride across the bridge over the Drava River ~ on the right you can

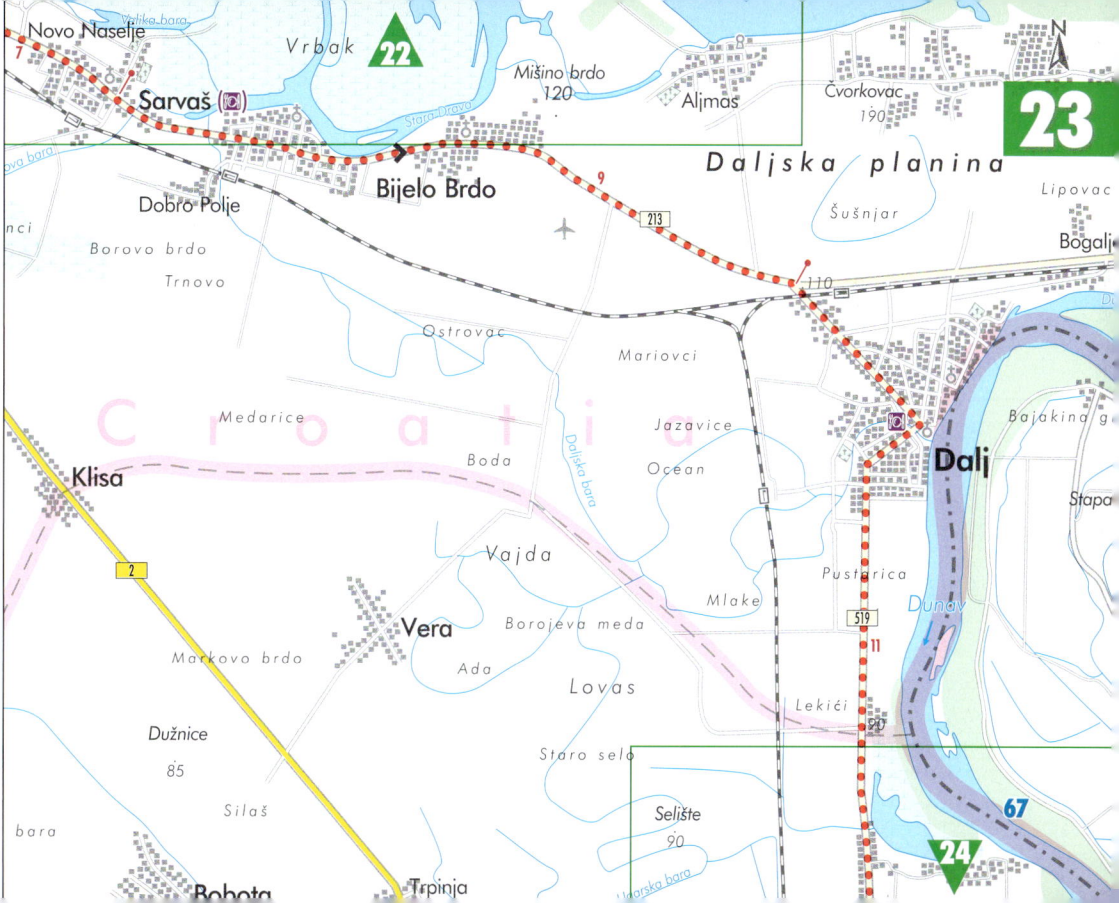

Vukovar – recently renovated church

see a fortress-like building ∾ continue to the intersection with a traffic signal ∾ follow the bicycle route sign to the left towards **Nemetin** ∾ and follow the posted bicycle path along the busy street ∾ the street has tram tracks running along both sides ∾ at the next traffic signal go straight ∾ the bicycle path ends where an industrial area begins ∾ as you leave Osijek there is another bike route sign at the petrol station.

Tip: Outside Osijek you will notice more and more signs warning of landmines. Stay on the road and do not go into the untended fields for any reason!

At the next large intersection stay left towards **Sarvaš**.

Sarvaš

The village has a small kiosk, a post office and bakery. You continue towards **Bijelo Brdo**.

Bijelo Brdo

After the village there is an 8% climb ∾ at the next fork in the road go right towards Dalj ∾ cross the railroad tracks ∾ and at the next T-intersection go left towards Vukovar.

Dalj

In the town head straight for the church ∾ and go right at the T-intersection ∾ cross a small bridge ∾ and follow the straight road for about 13 kilometers to Borovo.

Borovo

Go straight across the railroad tracks ∾ and then left at the next opportunity ∾ turn left at the T-intersection with the stop-sign ∾ at the railroad tracks go right onto **Ulica Trpinjska Cesta** ∾ and follow this street into the center of Vukovar.

Vukovar

Postal area code: 32000; Telephone area code: 032

- **Tourist Info**, J. J. Strossmayera 15, ☎ 442889
- **Orthodox parish church St. Nikolaus** (1733-37). Interior features 30 interesting icons.
- **Franciscan abbey with cloister** from 1723-36
- **City museum in the palace of the German noble-family Etz** (18th century)
- **Vucedol**, archaeological dig. The Vucedol dove was found here. It is a remnant of the Vucedol culture dating to the 3rd millennium BC.

Memorial against war – water tower in Vukovar

The earliest-known reference to Vukovar comes from 1220, and names the place as "Comitatou de Wolcou." It lies at the confluence of the Vuka River and the Danube. During the Turkish period it became Croatia's most important port on the river. Once a sparkling baroque city, Vukovar suffered grievous damage during the civil war.

Today the legacy of the conflict is readily visible in the bizarre contrasts of brand-new glass buildings that stand next to bombed out houses and the artillery-riddled water tower, which now serves as a reminder of that pointless war. The city's recovery, both economic and cultural, has been slow and faltering.

Vukovar to Ilok and the Serbian border　　40 km

At the next traffic signal in Vukovar proceed straight ~ on the left you can see what was once Croatia's largest Danube port ~ and continue straight ~ over a bridge across the Vuka ~ to the left you can see a church ~ and then a short distance later the damaged water tower, which is now a memorial to the war ~ proceed straight

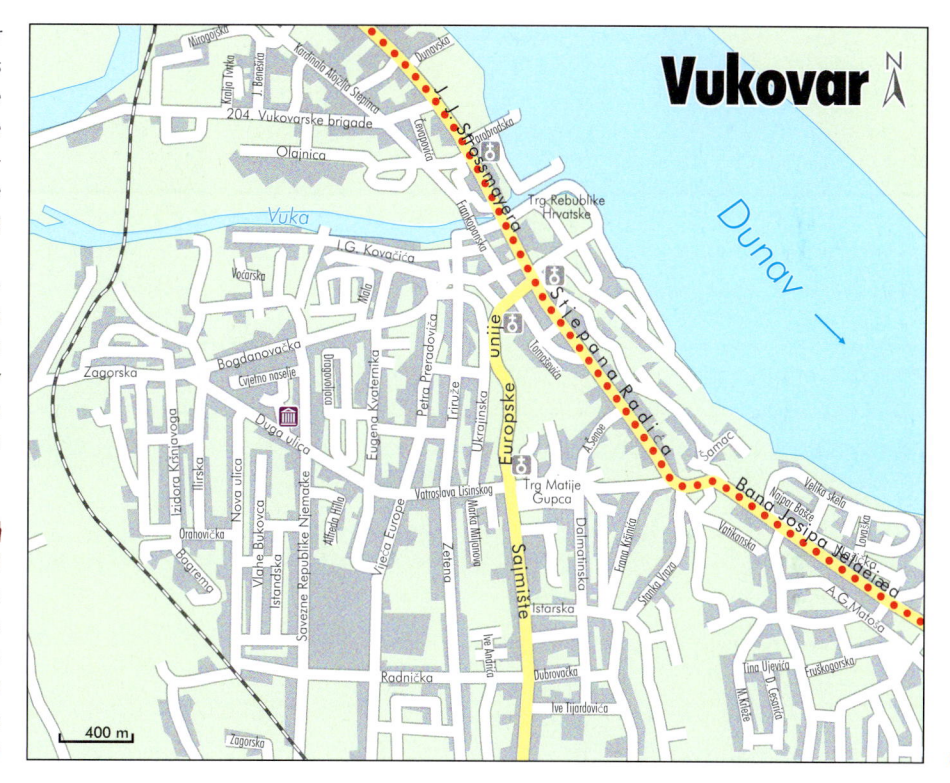

Opatovac – view to the Danube

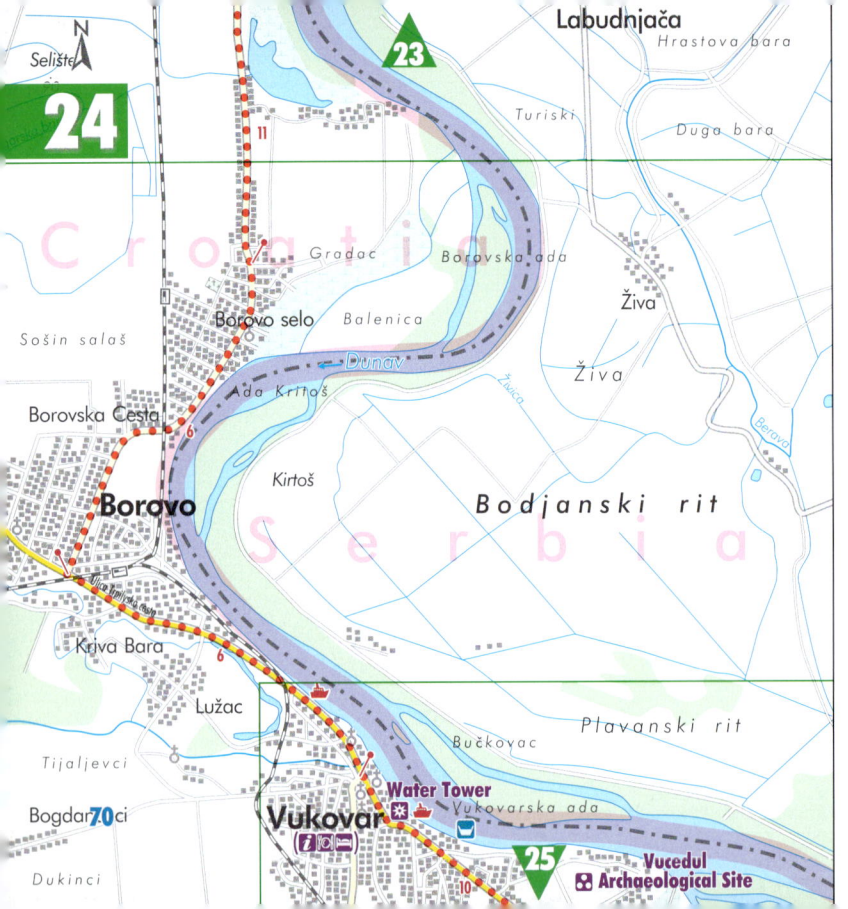

on the road out of Vukovar 〜 and continue to **Sotin**.

Sotin
Take the main road through Sotin 〜 just before you leave the village turn left on the road towards Ilok.

Opatovac
Just after the road sign for the village the road goes down hill 〜 ⚠ Caution, falling rocks! 〜 after a curve to the left you can glimpse the Danube 〜 the road curves through the village 〜 and after the church it begins a steep climb (8%).

Tip: The next 20 kilometers to Ilok are not especially fun to ride because there are many curves and hills. Some of the gradients range between 6% and 8%. You must also share the road with a fair number of trucks. You pass through the villages of **Mohovo** and **Šarengrad** before you reach Ilok.

Ilok

Postal area code: 32236; Telephone area code: 032

- **Tourism information**, Trg Nikole Ilokog 2, ☎ 590020
- **City museum** in the palace of the Odescalchi princes. The collection includes ethnographic, archaeological and cultural items of interest.
- **Franciscan church** (18th century) of St. John Capistrano, who helped defend Belgrade against the Turks. Grave stones in the church are also interesting.
- **Franciscan abbey** with richly-decorated portal and the cell of St. John Capistrano. There is also a library with 4,000 volumes, intarsia tables and a marble basin.

Ilok was also occupied by the Ottoman Turks, who used the city as a military camp. Many walls and buildings with Turkish architectural elements survive from this period.

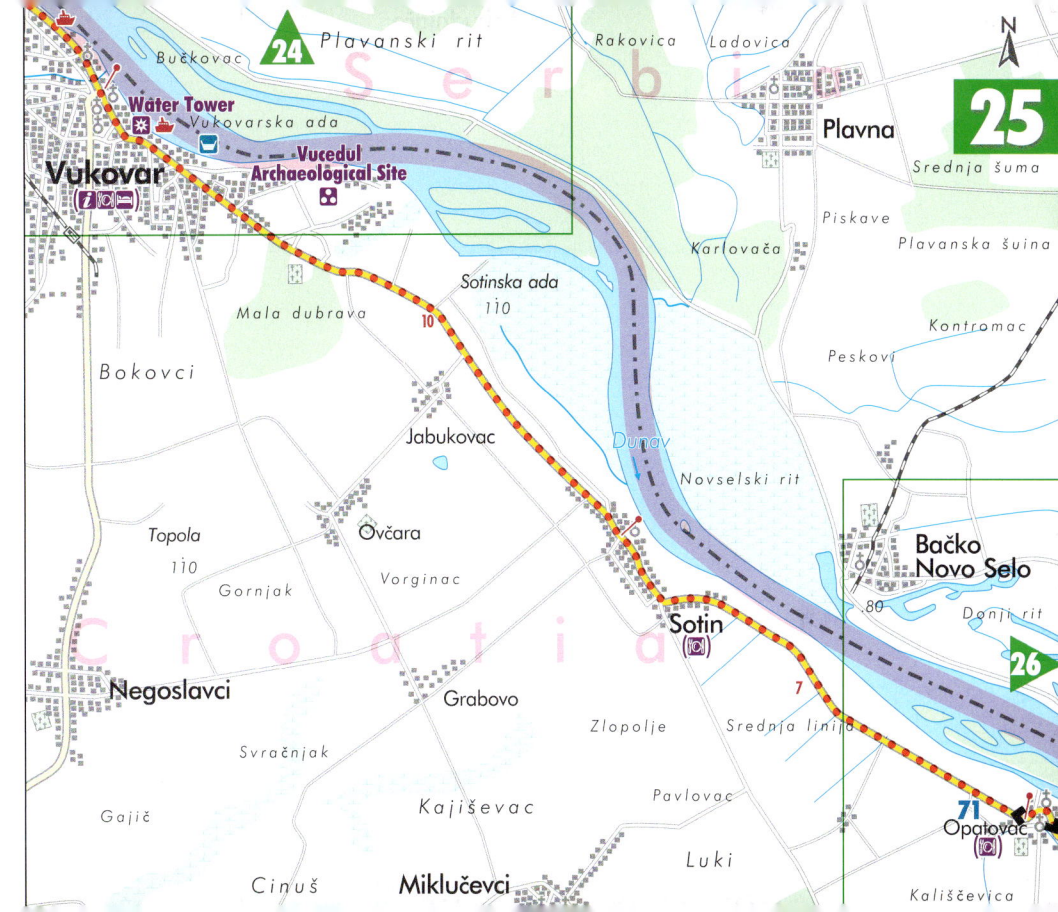

The red brick city wall rises high over the Danube and offers wonderful views on the river and the Fruška Gora nature preserve across the water in Serbia.

Ilok is also a center of one of the most fruitful wine-producing areas in Slavonia. Wines include Riesling, Savagnin and Burgundies.

You follow the main road towards **Neštin**.

At the far edge of the town there is an intersection — turn left to go to the border crossing across the Danube and into the Serbian town of **Baka Palanka**.

Opatovac

Tip: Here you can choose between entering Serbia and riding with heavier traffic on the northern bank of the Danube to Novi Sad or staying on the southern side of the river. We have decided to designate the southern side as the main route because it has less traffic and passes through idyllic small villages. However, it is also more demanding physically, with many short but steep climbs. The northern version through Baka Palanka is shown on maps 27 and 28.

At the intersection continue straight for about 3 kilometers to the border crossing towards Neštin.

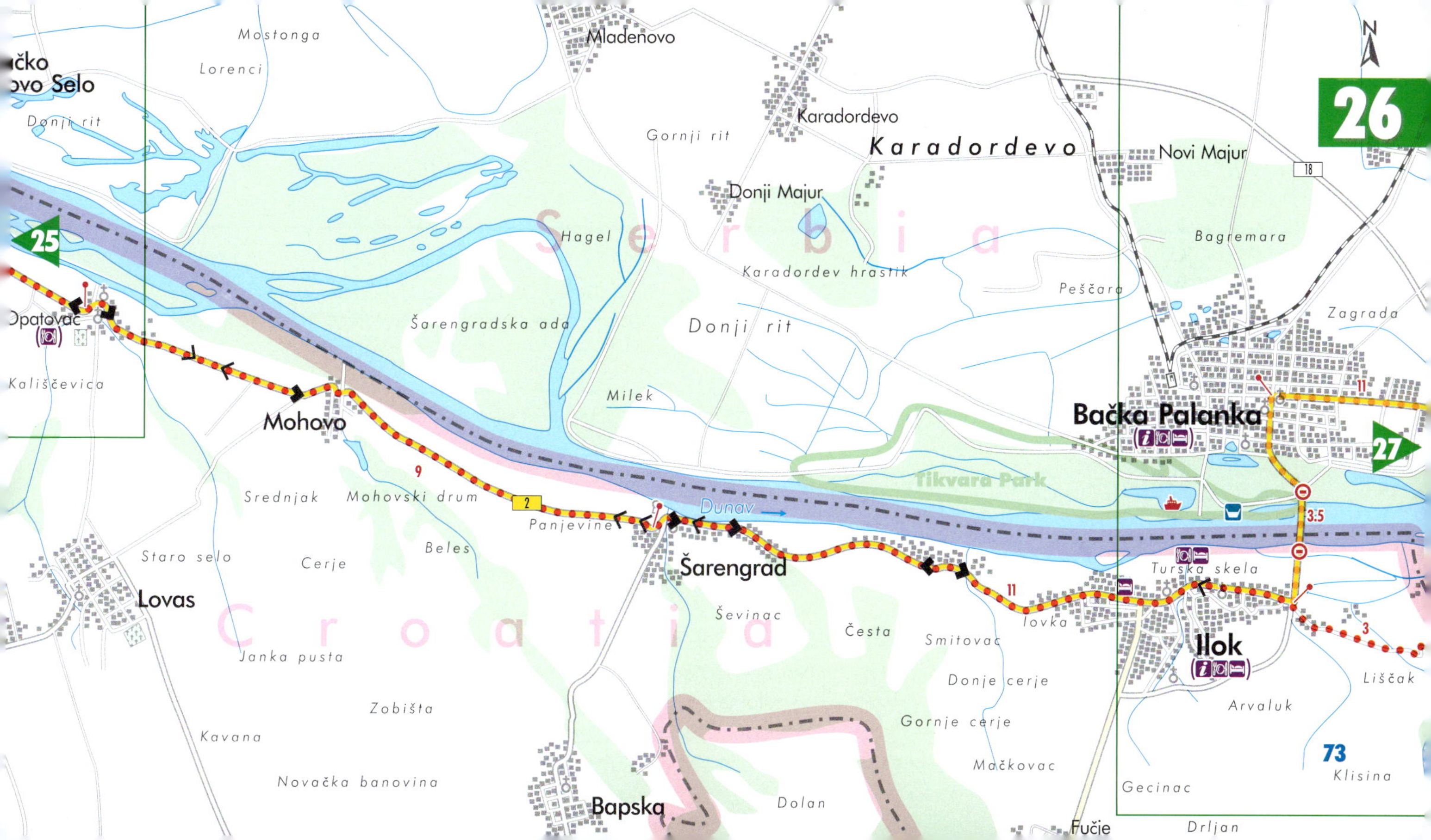

26
25
27
Mostonga
Lorenci
Mladenovo
Karadordevo
Karadordevo
Gornji rit
Novi Majur
18
Donji Majur
Hagel
Serbia
Bagremara
Karadordev hrastik
Pešćara
Zagrada
Šarengradska ada
Donji rit
Opatovac
Kališčevica
Milek
Bačka Palanka
Mohovo
11
9
Tikvara Park
Srednjak
Mohovski drum
2
Dunav
3.5
Panjevine
Beles
Šarengrad
Turska skela
Staro selo
Cerje
11
Lovas
Ševinac
Česta
Smitovac
Iovka
Ilok
3
Croatia
Janka pusta
Donje cerje
Lišćak
Arvaluk
Zobišta
Gornje cerje
Kavana
73
Mačkovac
Klisina
Novačka banovina
Gecinac
Dolan
Bapska
Fučie
Drljan
Donji rit

Serbia

241.5 km/382 km

The ride through Serbia takes you through the country's two largest cities: the capital, Belgrade, and Novi Sad. Both teem with busy traffic and noise, as well as many interesting sights. Petrovaradin fortress in Novi Sad and Kalemegdan in Belgrade cannot be missed. Outside of the cities, the route passes through numerous smaller towns on the way to the biggest highlight of this segment, the Iron Gates where the Danube breaks through the Carpathian Mountains. The higher elevations along this part of the ride offer excellent and impressive views of the landscape. One of the first sights is the mighty Golubac fortress just downstream from the town of the same name. The scenery that follows, of slopes rising steeply to both sides of the Danube, helps distract from the effort that this demanding stretch requires. Another dramatic man-made sight on the Danube is the huge dam and power station at Đerdap I near Sip, where the main route enters Romania.

In Novi Sad and Belgrade you must deal with heavy traffic. There are only a few short stretches where the route can resort to parks or promenades along the river, and even there one must pay close attention to traffic coming from or entering driveways. The rest of the route through Serbia follows country roads with moderate traffic. You will encounter more climbs, some of them quite steep, especially between Belgrade and Smederevo and through the Danube's gorge. There are also 21 tunnels of varying length and with artificial lighting.

27
Livade
Slatine
Vrške
ovi Majur
18
Serbia
Vrtlog
Bagremara
Kanal Begej
85
Prkosovo
Čelarevo
85
Gložan
13
Rit
7
Vizić bara
ačka Palanka
Pavlovac
11
26
7
80
Krstur
28
3.5
prirode Tikvara
Danube
Begeč
80
Ribnjak
8.5
Dunavac
Neštin
135
Leskovača
18
10
Jama
Park prirode Begečka jama
Susek
120
Ilok
Duboki potok
3
Lisvarski potok
Koruška
Banoštor
75
Orašje

Novi Sad

Neštin to Novi Sad — 38 km

From the border crossing at Ilok go straight towards **Neštin** ~ after passing through the village the road goes downhill into the next village **Susek** ~ and then back uphill via **Koruška** to **Banoštor**.

Banoštor
- Ferry to Bege

Tip: Here the route comes very close the Danube again and you have the opportunity to take a break and watch the river from the little inn at the ferry station.

After a few more kilometers you ride into Beočin.

Beočin
- Ferry to Futog
- Swimming places along the Danube

Cross the railroad tracks and continue straight on the main road through the village ~ the tracks run parallel to the road on the left side ~ continue through **Rakovac** and **Ledinci** ~ where you cross the tracks yet again ~ and the railroad is now to your right ~ at the edge of **Sremska Kamenica** the railroad veers away to the right and the bike route drops back down to the Danube ~ go under the bridge over the Danube and proceed on to Petrovaradin ~ and keep going to **Trg Vladike Nikolaja** at the foot of the fortress and near the Danube bridge.

Tip: To enter the center of Novi Sad turn left and cross the bridge on the pedestrian sidewalks on both sides of the busy road. Go right to stay on the main route and ride out of Petrovaradin towards **Sremski Karlovci**.

Novi Sad – Petrovaradin fortress and the Danube

A visit to Novi Sad should not, however, the missed.

Novi Sad
Postal area code: 21000; Telephone area code: 021

- **Tourist Information center**, Bulevar Mihajla Pupina 9, ✆ 421811 or 421812, www.novisadtourism.org.yu, www.novisadtourism.com
- **Excursion trips on the Danube to various sights**, April-Oct, Info: Market Tours, Bulevar Cara Lazara 55, ✆ 367612; For groups: Magelan Corporation, Zmaj Jovina 23, ✆ 420680;
- **City museum**, Petrovaradinska tvrdjava, ✆ 433145
- **Foreign art collection**, Dunavska, ✆ 51239, Open: Tues-Sun 10-13 o'clock

Novi Sad

- Klisa
- Vidovdansko naselje
- Rumenka
- Vojvodina Museum
- Petrovaradin Fortress
- Petrovaradin Museum
- Petrovaradin
- Futog
- Veternik
- Begeč
- Čerević
- N. Naselje
- Beočin
- Ledinci
- Rakovac
- Sremska Kamenica

Dunav
Mali kanal
Potklenovac
Sukava bara
Krndela
Kupusare
Ribnjak
Vizić bara

- **Museum of the Vojvodina**, Dunavska 35 & 37, ✆ 420566 or 26766. Exhibits about the history, crafts and art of the region
- **Theater museum of the Vojvodina**, Kralja Aleksandra 5/I, ✆ 613322
- **Roman-Catholic church** (late 19th century), Trg Slobode
- **Petrovaradin Fortress** (1699-1780). Details on page 80.
- Exhibition **"The Cannon boat"**, Open: Tues-Sun 10-17 o'clock. Selection of images and objects from the last 5 centuries, related to the history of Novi Sad. An original concept for presenting the development and lifestyles of the city.

Petrovaradinski sanac means approximately Petrovaradin's Ditch and was the original name of Novi Sad. In the 17th century, when it was under Austro-Hungarian control, it was called Neusatz. In 1748 the city was designated a "free royal city" and gained its current name. In the 19th century it was the cultural and spiritual center of Serbia, and known as "Serbia's Athens." It was also in this period that the city's theatre was established. It is Serbia's oldest theatre.

The original settlement started to grow during construction of Petrovaradin castle. The fortification dates back to Roman times and was extensively enlarged in the middle ages. It was here that an army led by Prince Eugene of Savoy defeated the Turks in 1716. All surviving parts of the castle date from this period.

In 1848 Novi Sad was shelled by Hungarian forces and largely destroyed. The troops were eventually forced to give up, but not before about two-thirds of the city had been devastated.

During World War Two the city again fell victim to Hungarian attack. And in early 1999 war returned yet again as NATO launched air attacks on key targets during its campaign to force Yugoslavia to end its attacks against the Albanian majority in Kosovo. NATO struck the two bridges that connected Novi Sad with Petrovaradin and Sremska Kamenica, as well as a refinery that burned for days and exposed the city to poisonous clouds of smoke. Varadin bridge and a television station in Fruška Gora south of Novi Sad were also destroyed.

The city of Sremska Kamenica lies on the south bank of the Danube across from Novi Sad. With its park and picnic areas it has long been a popular recreation destination for the people of Novi Sad. In the 1970s the city's face was changed by the construction of an SOS children's village and a respiratory clinic in the city's park. The clinic is internationally-renowned for its excellent location and top-notch medical staff and has a highly-successful heart and blood-vessel unit. In 1984 the institute's facilities and the surrounding park were extensively renovated.

Novi Sad – Danube promenade

Novi Sad
N
Petrovaradin
Dunav
Vojvodina Museum
Theater Museum
National Theater
Gradska kuca
Petrovaradin Fortress
City Museum
Sportski centar Vojvodina
Dunavski park
Trg Slobode
Trg Republike
Trg Galerija
Trg Neznanog junaka
Trg Vladike Nikolaja
Bulevar Mihajla Pupina
Bulevar Cara Lazara
Jovana Subotica
Uspenska
Beogradski kej
Kej Žrtava Racije
Kej Skojevaca
Beogradska
Strosmajerova
Preradoviceva
Marka Miljanova
Petra Kočića
Episkopa Visariona
Dunavska
Zmaj Jovina
Vladike Platona
Maksima Gorkog
Radnička
Jevrejska
Narodnih heroja
Aleksandra Ostrovskog
Arčibalda Rajsa
Koste
Nada
Šenoina
400 m

Novi Sad to Belgrade — 89.5 km

At **Trg Vladike Nikolaja** turn right on **Beogradska street**, which later becomes **Preradoviceva** and ride out of Novi Sad on this main artery.

Tip: You can also ride around the fortress if you wish to examine the complex from the outside.

To do so from **Trg Vladike Nikolaja** you must first ride under the bridge and along the river promenade on the **Kej Skojevaca** ~ continue on the street next to the railroad tracks ~ at the first opportunity turn right on **Ralačiceva street** ~ proceed to a larger square where three streets diverge ~ and proceed straight ~ at the next fork in the road stay left on **Karlovački drum**, which you take out of the city.

Petrovaradin

Fortifications have stood on the hill across from Novi Sad since Roman times. After Austria expelled the Turks from the city in 1687, it began tearing down the old medieval and Turkish fortress and began construction on the fortress that survives to this day.

The citadel occupies an area of more than 110 hectares and includes a unique and extensive system of underground tunnels with a total length of about 16 kilometers. A small part of that network, about one kilometer in length, is open to the public. The fortress has five gates and its walls contain more than 12,000 crenels and 400 artillery positions. Water is provided by a well that is 39 meters deep and 3.5 meters wide.

Petrovaradin fortress

A steep stairs leads from the dense and crowded small lower city up to the citadel, where residential buildings and a church stand amidst a complex system of fortress walls.

Of special interest is the fortress tower. Its clock was a gift from Empress Maria Theresa and came originally from France. The tower was destroyed in the 18th century and later rebuilt in its current form. All four sides of the tower have a clock-face that is 2.5 meters in diameter. The clock itself is unusual because the pointers are reversed, with the longer pointer marking hours and the shorter pointer for minutes. This was done for two reasons -- to make it easier for navigators on the river to read the clock at a distance and because the pointers move only every hour. The clock also has been called "the drunk clock" because it has a reputation for running behind during bad weather and fast during good weather.

Depart Petrovaradin in heavy traffic ~ going up the steep hill for the first kilometer ~ before a descent brings you into Sremski Karlovci.

Sremski Karlovci

Postal area code: 21000; Telephone area code: 021

🛈 **Tourist Office**, 21205, Branka Radievia 7, ☎ 882127, www.karlovci.co.yu

🛈 **National park information Fruška Gora**

🏛 **Local museum**, Patrijarha Rajacica 16, ☎ 881637, Open: Mon-Fri 9-15 o'clock. Exhibits about history, archaeology and how peasants lived at the beginning of the 20th century. There are also items from the life of the architect Svetomir Lazic.

✣ **The upper and the lower church** (Donja i Gornja crkva)

✣ **Orthodox church** (1758-62). Baroque church contains works by various Serbian artists.

✣ **Roman catholic church** (18th century)

✣ **Peace chapel** (1817), on a hill at the southern end of the city. It was built in memory of the peace treaty of Karlowitz, which was signed in 1699 to end the Austro-Ottoman war.

✣ **Neo-classical city hall** (1806-29)

✣ **Four Lions fountain**

✣ **Patriarch's court with treasury**

✣ Serbia's first public high school (1791)
✣ Annual wine festival in September

Located between the Danube and the foothills of the Fruška Gora mountains to the south, Sremski Karlovaci has a history that goes back to ancient times. In the 14th century it emerged as a cultural and clerical center. In 1713, a few years after the signing of the Treaty of Karlowitz, the city became the official center of the highest clerics in the Orthodox church. In 1791 Serbia's first high-school was established in Sremski Karlovci.

Branko Radičević (1824-53), one of Serbia's most important poets, lived here for six years as a teenager.

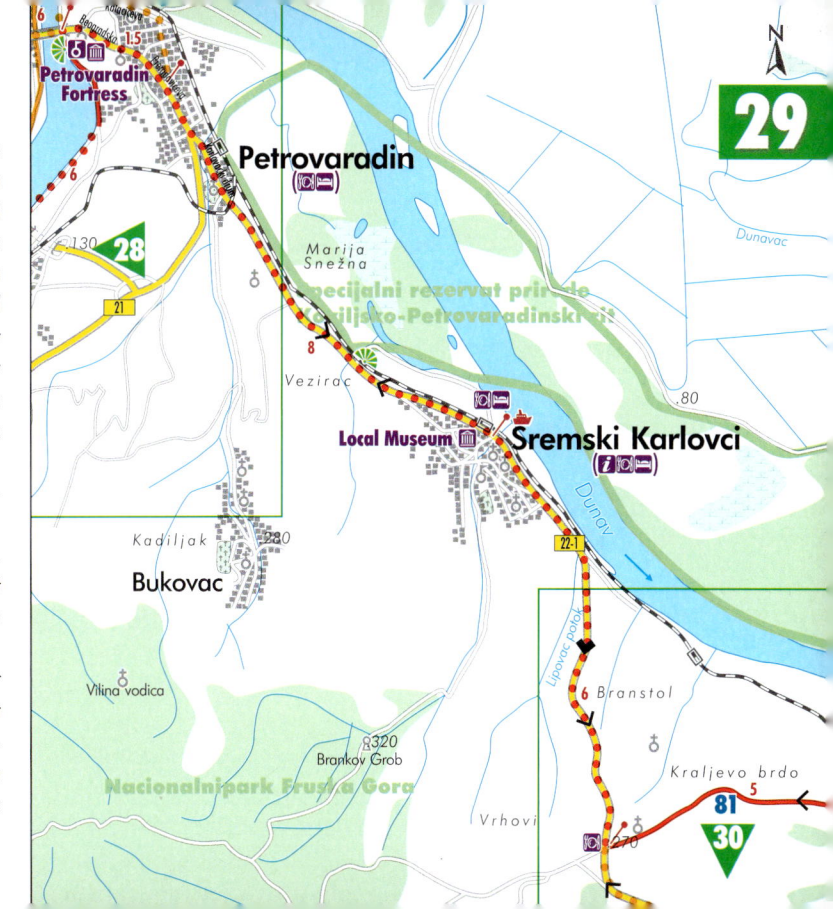

The city is not only famous for its handsome baroque center, but also for the wines that are produced on the slopes of the Fruška Gora Mountains a few kilometers

away. Some of the top wines made on "the holy mountain" can be favorably compared with wines produced in Germany's Moselle and Rhine regions. Among the most popular are Fruskogorski Rizling, Rajnski Rizling, Traminac, Frankovka, Portogizer and many others.

Fruška Gora (Holy Mountain)

South of Novi Sad lies the Crveni Cot or "holy mountain," a range of highlands that stretches about 80 kilometers from east to west and rises to a maximum elevation of 540 meters. The entire region, some 25,000 hectares, was declared a nature preserve in 1960. It is home not only to a variety of wildlife and rare plants and trees, but also to 16 medieval abbeys hidden away in the quiet scenic valleys. Most of them were built between the 16th and 18th centuries, and at one time there were a total of 35 of them. Today they form a kind of unique outdoor museum landscape, filled with cultural and artistic treasures. The best known of these monasteries include Krušedul (which was used as a prison where many resistance fighters were tortured and murdered during World War Two), Grgeteg, Hopovo, Jazak, Velika Remeta.

Tip: This section of the route offers the last views across the Danube and into the lands beyond until about 30 kilometers further. The route veers away from the river and does not return to the Danube until Slankomen.

Continue straight and up a steep climb ~ after about 6 ki-

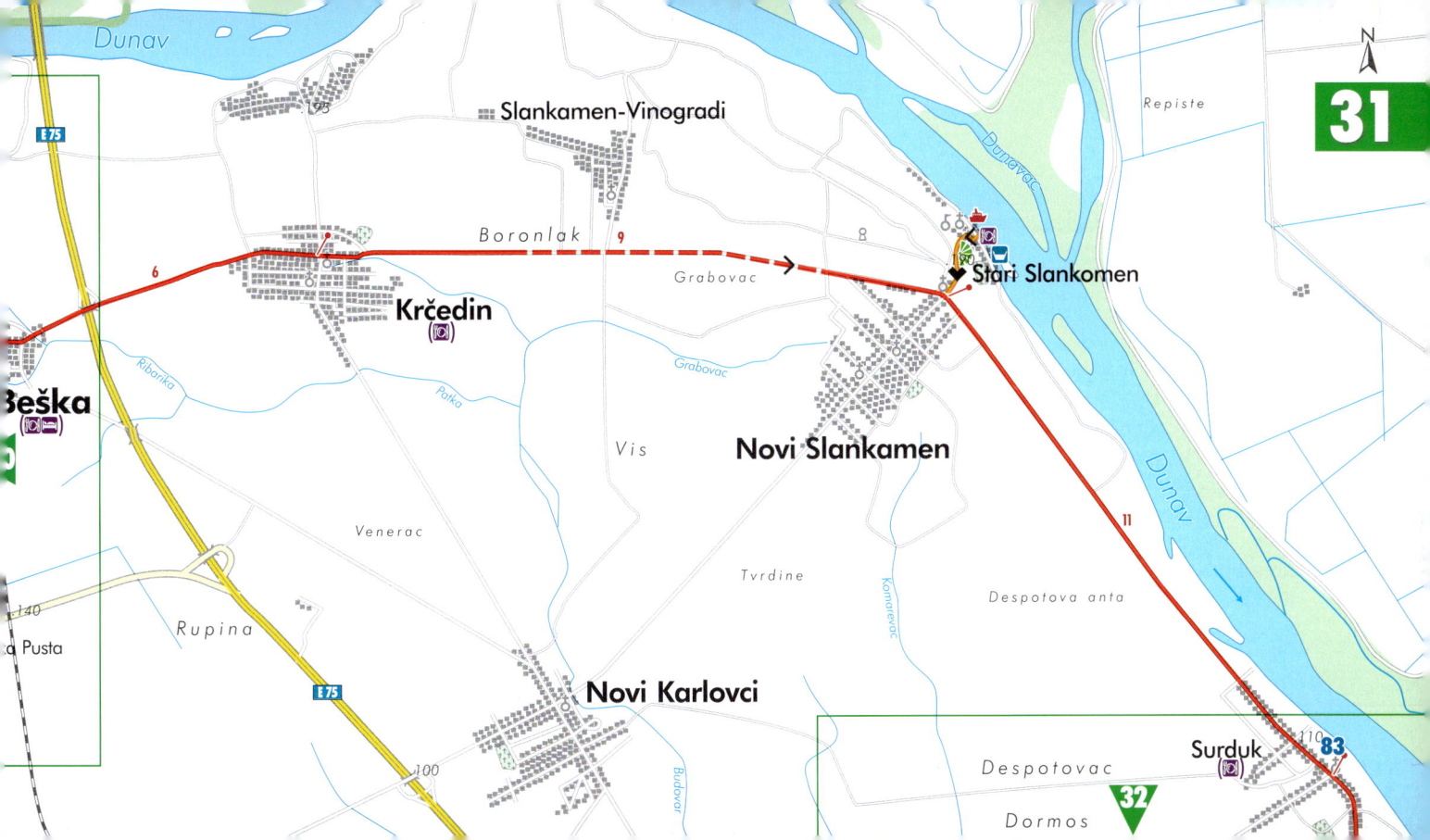

Dunav			
	Slankamen-Vinogradi		Repište
	Boronlak 9	8	
6		Grabovac	Stari Slankomen
Beška	Krčedin	Grabovac	
	Ribanka Patka	Vis	Novi Slankamen
	Venerac		Dunav
Pusta	Rupina	Tvrdine	11
		Komarevac Despotova anta	
	Novi Karlovci		
	Budovar	Despotovac	Surduk 83
		Dormos 32	

31

N

lometers there is a large intersection with an inn on the right side ~ turn left here towards Čortanovci ~ and ride downhill into the village.

Čortanovci

Proceed straight through the village ~ at the end of the village the road curves to the right and over a small river ~ go uphill to another T-intersection ~ and turn left towards Beška ~ and then downhill again over railroad tracks and into the village.

Beška

Follow the main road through Beška ~ ride past the church on the left ~ about 2 kilometers after the village the road crosses the E75 motorway ~ and then continues a few more kilometers to the village of **Krčedin**.

Krčedin

Continue on the main road through the village ~ after 2 kilometers the asphalt ends and the next 4 kilometers are unpaved ~ at the small intersection stay left and go straight ~ the road descends again somewhat ~ and

Near Krčedin

becomes asphalt covered ~ and goes past the village of **Novi Slankomen** visible to the right.

Tip: Here you also have the opportunity to go down to the river and take a rest or eat something at a pleasant little inn next to the river. To do so, however, you will have to ride down – and then back up – the short but steep slope down to the river.

Sidetrip to Stari Slankomen

From the last intersection go to the left ~ and down a steep and serpentine cobblestone road (⚠ Caution) into the village and down to the Danube. To continue on the main route you must turn around and return up that steep road.

The next kilometers run parallel and fairly close to the Danube ~ until you reach the village of **Surduk**.

Surduk

Dense flood-plain woods lie between the road and the river, which disappears behind the vegetation ~ after about 5 kilometers you ride into **Belegiš**.

Belegiš

Ride straight through the village and continue for 5 kilometers to the village of **Stari Banovci**, which lies right on the river.

Stari Banovci

Proceed along the river for a few kilometers to the town of **Novi Banovci**.

Novi Banovci

Follow the main street through Novi Banovci towards the motorway to Belgrade ~ just before the bridge across the motorway turn left at the last opportunity onto a small street ~ and continue straight to the next T-inter-

Stari Slankomen

section 〜 at the small business on the right side turn to the right 〜 outside of the village the pavement ends and the road is little more than a simple track through the fields 〜 but the surface is hard and relatively smooth with grass growing in the middle 〜 ride across the fields until you reach a large farming operation.

Tip: Caution: On the left side there is a military restricted area!

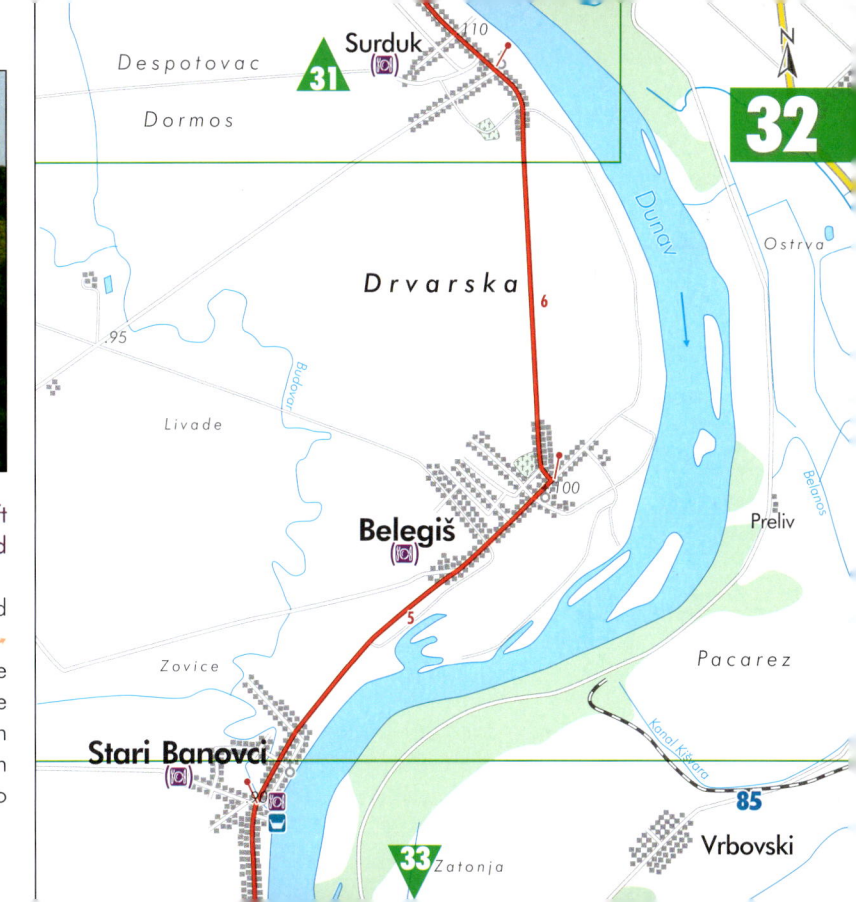

At the junction turn right and head towards the main road 〜 and proceed on the cobble-stone road 〜 you can also ride on the wide sidewalk as far as the main road 〜 after a short distance on a tree-lined avenue you come to the main road ~ and turn left towards Belgrade ~ and follow Route 22-1 right into the Serbian capital.

Alternate route via Batajnica

If you do not wish to take the simple road across the fields and do not object to heavier traffic on the main road, you can go straight on the road through Novi Banovci and across the bridge over the motorway ~ then slightly downhill and into the town of Batajnica.

Batajnica

Tip: ⚠ The traffic is already fairly heavy here, and will remain so all the way into Belgrade.

At the next fork in the road turn right on **Svetislava Golubovića-Mitraljetine** ~ proceed to the next larger intersection with a traffic signal ~ turn left on **Josipa Broza Tita** street ~ and follow this straight out of the town and through an industrial zone towards Zemun ~ outside of the town, the road is lined with trees ~ and goes underneath the motorway ~ after about two kilometers the main route connects from the left and you continue on Route 22-1.

After a short distance arrive in Zemun, a suburb of Belgrade.

Zemun

- Tourism association Zemun, ✆ 611308
- Ship tours, information from the tourism association
- Nikolaj Church (Nikolajevska), Njegoševa 43. The church beneath Gardoš fortress in the town's historic center. Built in the baroque style 1725-31. Contains valuable artworks and an interesting collection of icons, as well as purported relics of the apostle St. Andrew.

Across fields outside Belgrade

Follow the main road straight towards the center of Belgrade ~ take **Batajniki drum** until it becomes **Cara Dušana** and continue straight into the city ~ just past the cemetery on the right side the street leads into **Trg B. Radicevića** ~ turn left at this intersection, onto **Karamatina street** ~ and proceed down to the promenade along the bank of the Danube ~ and follow the promenade paths through the parklands along the river.

Tip: The Sava River flows into the Danube here. The cycle route goes along the Sava for a short distance to the first bridge.

Proceed to the "**Bratstvo i jedinstvo**" bridge.

Tip: You may wish to use the sidewalk on the bridge, but please respect the pedestrians' right-of-way.

After crossing the Sava you must plunge into the heavy traffic ~ at the first opportunity turn left on **Karađorđeva street** ~ follow the street ~ downhill to **Bulevar Vojvode Bojovića**, which curves around the famous Kalemegdan.

Tip: Here you can get away from the heavy traffic and ride through the parks beneath the fortress. It is, of course, a good opportunity to visit the fortress as well.

Belgrade

Postal area code: 11000; Telephone area code: 011

- **Tourism Organization**, Dečanska 1/II, ✆ 3248404 or 3226154, www.belgradetourism.org.yu
- **Tourist Info at Belgrade airport**, ✆ 601555 or 605555
- **Tourist Info at the main train station**, ✆ 3612732 or 3612645
- **Tourist Info Terazije**, underpass at the Albanija palace, ✆ 635622
- **Tourist Info**, Knez Mihailova 18, ✆ 2629992
- **Tourist Info at the Sava harbor**, Karađorđeva
- Ship tours on the **Danube and Sava**, April-Nov, Infos: Tourism Organization Belgrade, ✆ 3248404; "Metro na void" company, ✆ 2781027; Travel Agency "Putnik" ✆ 3242490; Yacht club Kej, ✆ 3165432
- **Belo brdo archaeological site in Vinča**, 29. Novembra 107, ✆ 8360132 (14 km from Belgrade, towards Smederevo). One of the largest and most significant settlements of the Vinča culture, a Neolithic culture which rose between the 6th and 4th millennia BC in much of eastern Europe and the Balkans. The 10-hectare site near the town of Vinča was discovered in 1908 and includes remains of houses, earthen huts, tools, implements, figures and much more.
- **Narodni Musej** – National Museum
- **Narodno pozorište** – National Theater (1868-69), Trg Republike 2, ✆ 3281333
- **Belgrade Fortress**. At the confluence of the Sava and Danube rivers. The fortifications are divided into upper and lower parts and the Kalemegdan Park.
- **Old palace** (1882-84), at the corner of Kralji Milan and Dragoslav Jovanović streets. Seat

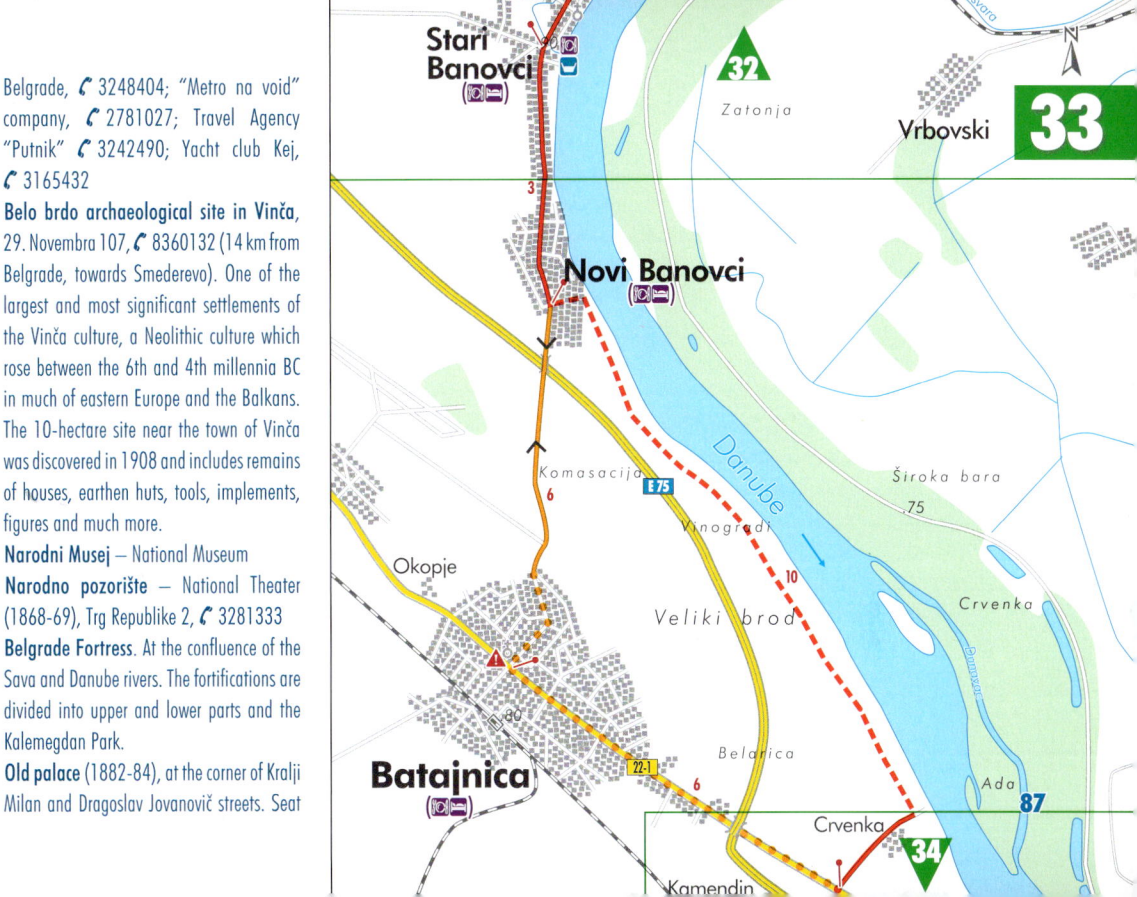

of the Belgrade city parliament since 1961. The imposing chambers serve mainly state occasions and receptions.
- **Church of St. Sava**, Svetosavski trg. Although construction began in 1894, it still has not been completed. It nevertheless ranks as one of Belgrade's landmarks, and is named after the Serbian-Orthodox Archbishop Sava (1169-1236).
- **Mother of God Church**, Kalemegdan 6. The church in the lower fortress below the Zindan Gate was used as a powder magazine in the 18th century, then as military church. Heavily damaged in World War One, it was rebuilt in 1925 and today contains beautiful icons and frescoes.
- **Chapel of St. Parascheva**, directly next to Mother of God church. Built at the end of the 19th century over a miraculous spring. Interior decorated with mosaics.
- **Church of the Ascension** (1863), Admirala Geparta 19. Built with donations from Belgrade residents. Modeled after Serbian monasteries, the church contains a large collection of icons, books and other religious items.
- **St. Alexander Nevsky church**, Cara Dušana 63. Completed 1928-29, as the larger replacement for a church first built at the site in 1877. Contains memorials to soldiers who died in the wars of liberation (1876-1918), Russian Czar Nikolai II and King Aleksandar I.
- **St. Mark's church**, Bulevar Kralja Aleksandra 17. Built 1931-40 on the site of an old Serbian-Byzantine church. The interior is not complete. Contains relics of King Dušan and the Patriarch Germančorič and a large collection of 18th and 19th century icons.
- **Prince Miloš residence**, in Topčider Park. Built 1831-34 by Janja Mihailovič and Nikolai Čorčevič. Today home of the Museum of the First Serbian Uprising. Europe's oldest plantane tree (160 years) stands in front of the building.
- **Captain Miša House** (1858-63), Studenski trg 1. Private palais of "Danube captain" Miša Anastasijevič (1803-1885). He was a ship owner and merchant and, at the time, Serbia's richest man. Today used by Belgrade University.
- **National Bank of Serbia**, Kralja Petra I. (1888-89, 1922-25). Designed by the Serbian-Austrian architect Konstantin Jovanovič.
- **Parliament of Serbia** (1907-36), Trg Nikole Pašiča 13. A monumental sculpture by Toma Rosandič stands before the main entrance.
- **Train station** (1884), Savski trg 2.
- **Knez Mihailova**, Shopping street and pedestrian zone. The oldest and most exclusive street in the city is a designated historic landmark, and features some of Belgrade's most famous and most beautiful buildings. They include the Hotel Serbian Crown, Marko-Stojanovič House, Academy of Arts and Sciences and much more. Believed to be the site of the original settlement, Singidunum.
- **Kralja Petra Prvog**. Site of Belgrade's oldest café, the cathedral, and the seat of the orthodox church patriarch. The Romans are believed to have built a Forum, baths and a basilica at the site. Later the city's first pharmacy opened at No. 8 and the city's first hotel.
- **Trg Republike** (Republic Plaza), Belgrade's best-known public square
- **Studentski trg** (Students Square), Belgrade's oldest square
- **Topčider Park**
- **Zoological Garden**, Mali Kalemegdan 8, ✆ 624526, Open: Summer 8-20.30 o'clock, winter 8-17 o'clock. Established in 1936, it is one of the oldest such facilities in Europe. Home to more than 2,000 species. Also called the "Garden of Hope".

Gizela
Ada
Crvenka
33
Stojkova bara
Ovča
34
Borča
Crkvište
Batajnički drum
E 75
Dunav
Crvenka
24-1
Mokri Sebeš
Veliko blato
Veliki kanal
Vizelj
Cara Dušana
7
Zemun Polje
Galenika
Kožara
Krnjača
1-9
Dunavac
Jojkićev Dunavac
Zemun
Karamatina
22-1
Zapis
E 70
Dunav
BEOGRAD
6
Kalemegdan
Stari grad
Višnjica
Gornje polje
Bežanija
National Theater
Palilula
Karaburma
Velika humka
105
Ledine
75
Slanci
Savski venac
Zvezdara
St. Sava Church
Orlovica
265
Novi Beograd
Sava
19
Senjak
Vračar
Mirijevo
35
E 70
11
Zmajevac

Belgrade, the White City, is the capital of Serbia and lies at the confluence of the Sava and Danube rivers. It is one of the oldest cities in Europe, with a history that goes back more than 7,000 years. Originally settled by the Celts, the Romans established a military camp named Singidunum for the IVth Legion of Flavius. Over the centuries the settlement was overrun, destroyed and rebuilt after repeated waves of Huns, Goths and Avars. The first-known mention of the Slavic name Belgrade dates to the year 878 AD.

The ebb and tide of history continued to wash across the Danube city through the centuries. For much of four centuries the Hungarian Kingdom and the Byzantine Empire fought for control of the area. The Hungarian King Stephan II destroyed the city in 1127 and then rebuilt Zemun. In 1284 Belgrade for the first time passed to Serbian rule, and became the capital of the Serbian Empire in 1403. Then came the Ottoman invasions, and in 1521 the Turks under Suleiman the Magnificent finally captured the city. The Austrians managed to recapture Belgrade several times in the 17th and 18th centuries. In 1717, Prince Eugene of Savoy defeated the Turks and began construction of the fortress, which was built between 1723 and 1736. The Turks were not completely expelled until the early 19th century when Belgrade became the capital of the Kingdom of Serbia. The monarchy was ended in 1945, when Tito became head of the communist Yugoslav federation.

It was not until 1997 that the first non-communist government was elected to run the city. During the Kosovo war in 1999, NATO bombed strategic targets in the city. Bombs also struck the National Library, however, causing the loss of numerous cultural treasures. A democratic government has been in power since 2001.

Belgrade Fortress and the Kalemegdan

The Romans built fortifications at the strategic confluence of the two rivers as early as the first century. This Roman castra served the 4th Legion levied by Emperor Vespasian. It was destroyed by the Goths and the Huns, and then rebuilt in the 6th century before being destroyed again by the Avars and Slavs.

The protection of the fortress nevertheless helped a settlement begin to take root, and by the 14th century this city extended down to the banks of the rivers. It flourished under the rule of the Serbian despot Stefan Lazarevič, who declared Belgrade the center of Serbia. He also erected a palace for himself inside the fortress and established a military harbor on the banks of the Sava River.

When Austria ruled the city between 1717-39, the fortress was expanded into one of the

Belgrade – Danube promenade

Beograd
Dunav
Sava
Veliko
Ratno
Ostrvo
Novi Beograd
Kalemegdan
Muzej Savremene umetnosti
National Theater
Park prijateljstva
Trg Republike
Railway Station Beograd-Dunav
Glavna Railway Station
Tašmajdan
Most "Bratstvo i jedinstvo"
Stari Savski most
Obala Majora D. Gavrilovića
Tadeuša Košćuška
Dunavska
Dunavski kej
Bulevar Vojvode Bojovića
Bulevar Nikole Tesle
Bulevar Mihaila Pupina
Bulevar Avnoja
Bulevar Arsenija Čarnojevića
Zemunski put
Karađorđeva
Brankova
Kneza Mihaila
Knez Miletina
Dure Dakovića
29. Novembra
Takovska
Bulevar Kralja Aleksandra
Kneza Miloša
Kralja Milana
Nemanjina
27. Marta
Ruzveltova
Višnjićeva
Čika Ljubina
Skadarska
Francuska
Makedonska
Vojvode Dobrnjca
Cvijićeva
Jaše Prodanovića
Vatroslava Lisinskog
Cetinjska
Džordža Vašingtona
Resavska
Beogradska
Admirala Geprata
Balkanska
Lomina
Kamenička
J. Bogdanova
Prizrenska
Dečanska
Terazije
Šafarikova
Hilandarska
Čarlija Čaplina
O. Đikića
Starine Novaka
Dalmatinska
Primorska
Bistrička
Zdravka
Preradovićeva
Ćelara
Vladetina
Ivankovačka
Karnedžijeva
Španskih boraca
Proleterske solidarnosti
Milentija Popovića
Vladimira Popovića
Draga Jeftića
Sadika Ramiza
Slavka Šlandera
Brodarska
Ušće
400 m

most formidable bastions in Europe. When the Turks returned in 1740, many of the structures in the complex were damaged or destroyed. The fortress attained its current appearance towards the end of the 18th century.

Access to the upper city was controlled by the inner and outer Stambol gates, the Clock Gate and the Despot's Gate. The lower city was accessed through the Vidin Gate and the Gate of Charles VI.

The Kalemegdan is the largest and most beautiful public park in Belgrade. The name refers to the plateau that surrounds the fortress, and may be derived from the Turkish words for field ("kale") and battle ('megdan").

In the year 1867 Count Mihailo Obrenović commissioned the redesign of the park, and large green spaces were laid out between 1873 and 1875. In 1905 the Kalemegdan was enlarged to include the Zoological Garden. After 1931 the park was enlarged again to reach the lower city. Many monuments and sculptures were erected. Today it includes the military museum, the "Cvijeta Zuzorič" art-pa-

Danube near Belgrade

vilion, restaurants, children's playgrounds and other sports and recreational facilities.

Belgrade to Smederevo — 46.5 km

Tip: If you wish to avoid the stress, traffic and climbs of the not particularly attractive main route to Smederevo, you may consider boarding a train out of Belgrade. There are connections to **Ralja** (about 45 minutes) or to **Mala Krsna** (about 1.5 hours). Both stations provide easy access to the Danube cycle route.

On the far side of Kalemegdan take **Cara Dušana** to the next larger intersection with 29. Novembra street ~ go straight across to **Vašingtona** ~ until you come to the intersection with Takovska street ~ continue straight ~ the street name changes to **27. Marta** ~ keep going straight to the intersection of Ruzveltova street ~ and straight to **Bulevar Kralja Aleksandra**.

Tip: Here you can only turn right or left. There is a do not enter sign straight ahead.

Turn left on the Bulevar ~ here the street goes down hill and straight with heavy traffic on the four-lane main street ~ just follow the main road out of the city ~ downhill again just before the edge of the city ~ continue to an intersection with a petrol station on the far side of the road ~ follow the larger street in a curve to the left towards **Kaluđerica** and **Smederevo** ~ you are now outside of Belgrade but traffic is still heavy and great caution is necessary.

As you pass the city of Kaluđerica off to the right the name of the Bulevar changes to **Smederevski Put** ~ continue on this highway to the next intersection.

Tip: Here you have the option of turning left and riding to the village of Vinča where you can take a break on the banks of the Danube or at a friendly inn.

The cycle route continues along the main road to Smederevo ~ after one kilometer the road begins to climb and you ride through sweeping curves up the mountain ~ after several strenuous kilometers the road descends to the next village, **Grocka**.

Grocka
Late Stone Age and Roman archaeological sites

Tip: After leaving the town the traffic finally begins to decrease and the cycle route follows a mostly well-built, wide road with little traffic. Enjoy the fine views of the flood plains and the river off to the north.

After another climb and a short descent into the next valley there is another steep climb up to the village of **Brestovik**.

Brestovik

Follow the main road through the village ~ the strenuous climb is followed after

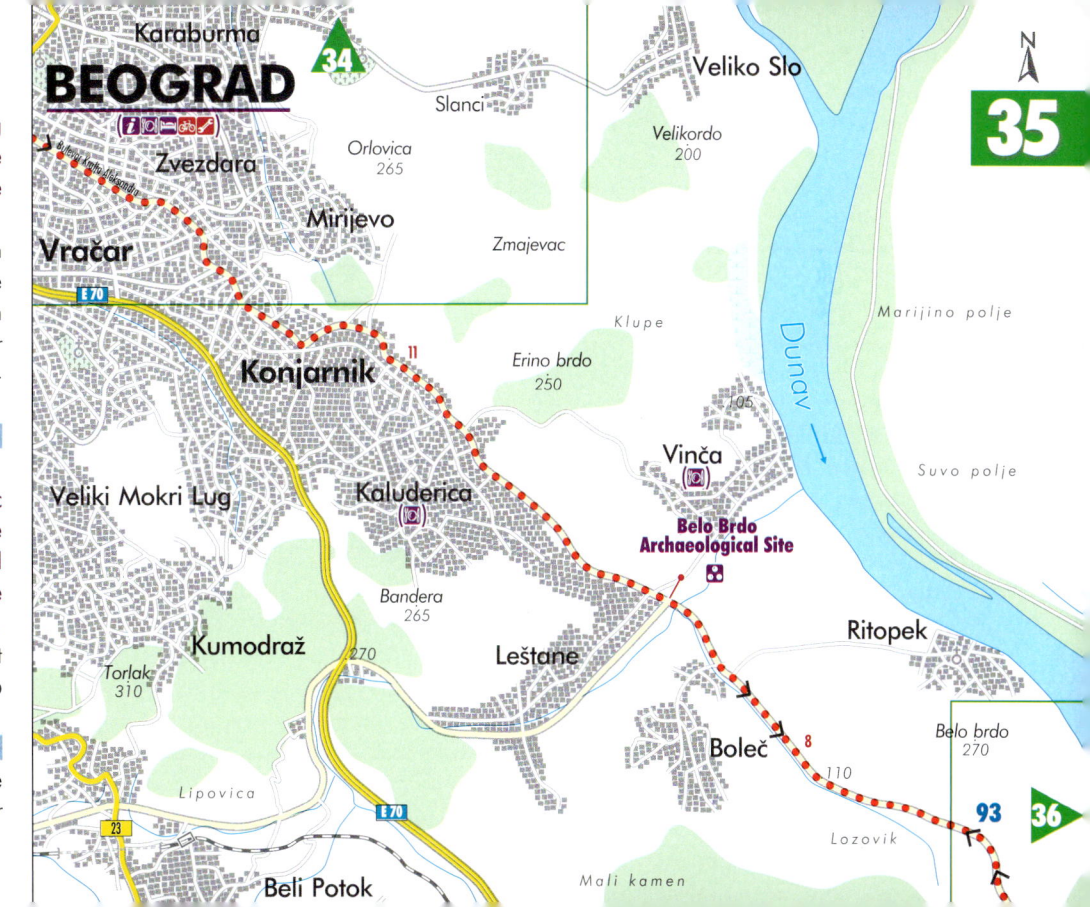

Brestovik by a long descent ~ the villages of **Orešac** and **Jugoro** whiz by in quick succession ~ as you ride in close proximity to the Danube ~ proceed downhill ~ past a harbor and the ruins of a castle ~ at the next junction follow the road through the curve to the right ~ here the road surface changes to cobblestones ~ go to the large square with the church ~ and then to the left along the spacious plaza with the nicely restored buildings and a fountain.

Tip: Time for a break? This inviting square offers a fine opportunity to rest, with shade trees and park benches from which you can watch the goings on and admire the architecture.

Smederevo

Postal area code: 11300; Telephone area code: 026

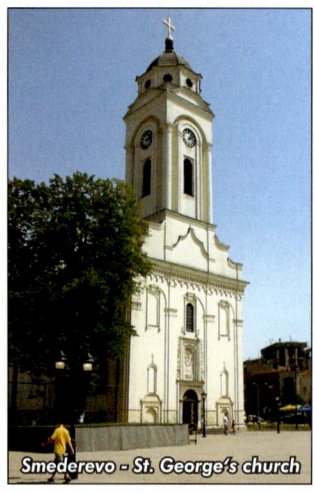

Smederevo - St. George's church

Tourism Organization, Karađorđeva 5-7, ✆ 222952

Smederevo fortress. The castle directly on the river (1429-30) has a triangular outline with 5 gates and 25 towers, double walls and a moat. On one side there is a smaller fortress consisting of a palace and citadel with its own moat and 4 ramparts. It was one of the best preserved castles in Serbia until 1941, when it and much of the town was heavily damaged in a huge explosion of ammunition stored at the fortress by the German army.

Monastery church (15th century)

St. George's church (1854) on the main square

Smederevo lies just upstream from the confluence of the Danube and the Morava rivers. From 1427 to 1459 it was Serbia's capital under the reign of the Despot Đurađ Branković, who started construction on the huge castle on the banks of the Danube. The Ottoman Turks captured the city in 1459 and held it until the 18th century.

Today Smederevo is one of Serbia's most important industrial centers, with the country's largest steelworks, a major inland harbor and other manufacturing plants. The steel works were sold to US Steel in 2003.

Smederevo to Ram — 69/67.5 km

The route into the gorge that the Danube takes through the Serbian Carpathians follows the main road through Smederevo and out of the city on asphalt.

Tip: After Smederevo the road turns south and away from the Danube until it returns

Smederevo

Map 36: Grocka – Smederevo

Rivers & Water:
- Dunav

Settlements:
- Omoljica
- Plavinci
- Banatski Brestovac
- Boštine
- Pločica
- Salašine
- Trnovita
- Badrika
- Lupoglav
- ...lopača
- Grocka
- Durdevo
- Smederevska ada
- Brestovik
- Sastavci
- Jugovo
- Jablan
- Udovice
- Cerje
- Seone
- Smederevo
- Carina
- Begaljica
- Petrijevo
- Aluga
- Vučak
- Petrijevski potok

Points of interest:
- Careva glava 160
- Stone Age and Roman Excavations
- Kozjak 200
- Smederevo Fortress
- Main Square with St. George's Church

Route markers: 35 · 36 · 37 · 95

Distances along route: 4.5, 4.5, 8, 5.5

Smederevo – Main Square

to the river near Kostolac and then the town of Ram.

The road starts to climb gently as you leave Smederevo ~ and head for **Radinac**.

Radinac

At the intersection with the Route 24 national road and the railroad tracks stay to the left and continue straight ⚠ use caution as you cross the busier road ~ and proceed out of the town ~ and head for **Vranovo**.

Vranovo

Just past the village there is an underpass for the main road (Route 24) and then you ride into **Mala Krsna**.

Mala Krsna

Follow the road through the village ~ after about one kilometer you cross another set of railroad tracks ~ and continue straight ahead towards **Skobali**.

Skobali

The smaller village lies directly adjoined to the larger town of **Osipaonica**.

Osipaonica

Proceed straight into Osipaonica ~ and turn left at the main intersection ~ the next 10 kilometers take you through pretty floodplain landscapes to an unusual bridge over the Morava River ⚠ Caution riding up to the bridge! The slope is very steep.

Tip: On the right side of the bridge there is a pedestrian walk. It is bumpy but allows you to safely cross the bridge without fear of encountering a train coming from the other direction. There is also a nice little gravel beach down to the left if you wish to take a refreshing dip in the Morava.

After this curious bridge you ride past Ljubičevo Stud, Serbia's oldest thoroughbred horse farm ~ ride under Route 24 again ~ and ride into the town of **Požarevac**.

Požarevac

Postal area code: 12000; Telephone area code: 012

- **National museum.** The second oldest in Serbia. The oldest is in Belgrade.
- **Open air museum** "Etno park Tulba"
- **Art gallery** of the surrealist painter Milena Pavlovic-Barili
- **Požarevac church** (1819)
- **interesting market square** (1827)

The name Požarevac means "fire city" and comes from the following event in the city's history. When Prince Vuk Branković and his brother were battling the Ottoman Turks, he tried to seize Smederevo. But when his attack failed, he withdrew to Slankamen. During his absence the Turk Alibeg laid waste to much of the prince's lands and palaces. There followed another battle in which Alibeg was wounded and sought refuge in a village. When the villagers did not turn Alibeg over to the Prince, he ordered the execution of 70 of the village's men. The village was henceforth known as

Udovice, or "village of widows." Alibeg fled again, into the nearby reeds. Prince Vuk Branković ordered the reeds burned down. The fire killed Alibeg and gave the area its name.

Požarevac is also famous for the treaty signed there on July 21, 1718 between the Ottoman Empire on one side and the Austrians and Venice on the other. Under the treaty's terms Belgrade, northern Serbia, Lesser Walachia and the Temesvar of Banat became Austrian territory.

Ride into the town to the next major intersection ~ and turn left towards **Kostolac** ~ stay on the larger street and ride through the city ~ at the next intersection turn right ~ and then left just before the railroad tracks ~ after about 3 kilometers you come to a 4-way intersection and then go across the tracks ~ after a short distance ride into **Ćirikovac**.

Tip: Here you enter a coal mining area with huge strip mines, conveyor systems, kilometers of pipes and railroad tracks. At times you must ride across parts of the open pits

Bridge across the Veliko Morava River near Požarevac

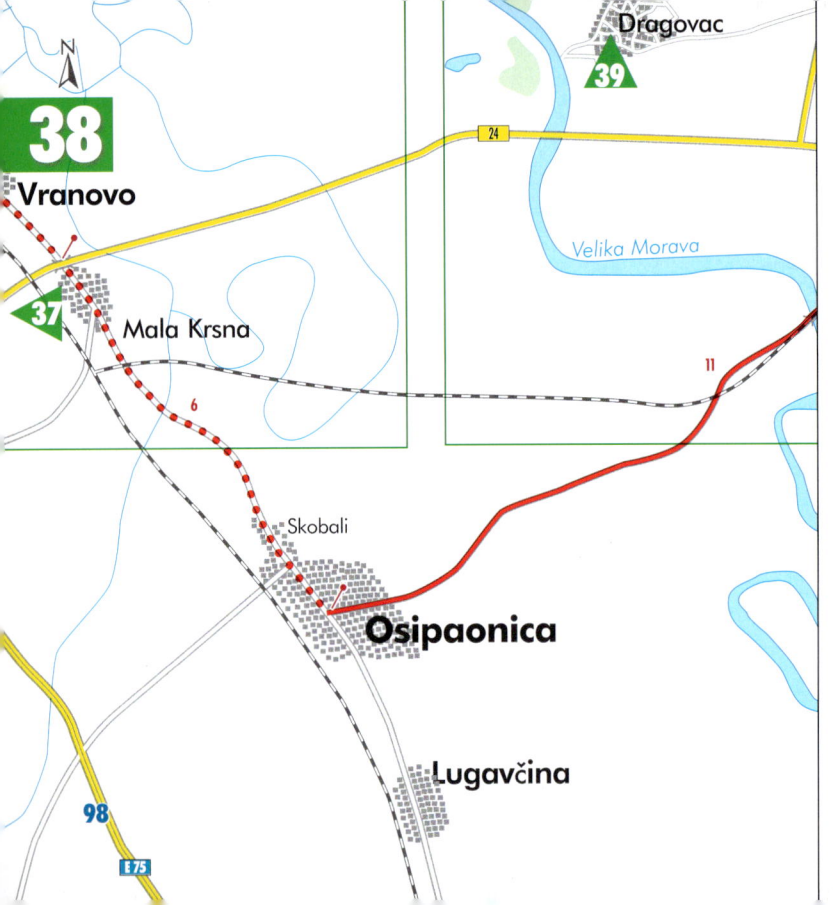

or beneath gigantic pipes and other industrial machinery.

Ćirikovac

Follow the main road straight through the town and proceed to the next village, **Klenovnik**, about 3 kilometers away.

Klenovnik

Outside of the village you can see industrial areas of Kostolac off to the left — ride past the city on the left.

Tip: Kostolac does not look very inviting, but if you wish to ride into the center, turn left at the large steel bridge and take the main street into the city.

Kostolac

Viminacium. Site of an important border town of the Roman province Moesia and headquarters of the VII Legion Claudia. More than 10,000 graves and 30,000 artifacts have been found at the archaeological digs. The largest and most interesting discovery was the grave of the Roman Emperor Hostilian. He died of plague in 251 AD after just a few months as regent. His body and burial objects were burned and buried. The remains were found in a 20-meter square grave. Researchers plan to send the bones to Australia for DNA analysis to confirm the cause of death. Because the site is relatively remote,

Church in Požarevac

it is frequently disturbed by treasure hunters who damage or destroy much of the ancient ruins in their search for valuable items.

After the bridge the road becomes narrower and leads uphill and around a hill on which the ruins of the castle Kostolac are hidden.

Tip: There is almost no traffic here and the curving road through this shady, wooded landscape provides a pleasant change of pace from the nearby industry.

Continue steadily uphill over a bridge across the Mlava ~ after about 3 kilometers ride into **Drmno**.

Drmno

Follow the road into the village ~ there is a monument on the small square to the right, across from a store ~ the road continues down hill and out of the village ~ you head south initially, but then the road turns to the east, and then to the north, as you ride around open coal mining pits ~ return to the old road about 4 kilometer before Kličevac. This road connected Drmno directly with **Kličevac** before it was closed for the mines.

Kličevac

Continue downhill into the village.

Tip: Here you can choose between two alternate routes to Ram. Either take an unpaved track across the fields without traffic or take the main road. The main road has moderate traffic and is two kilometers longer and passes closer to the Danube.

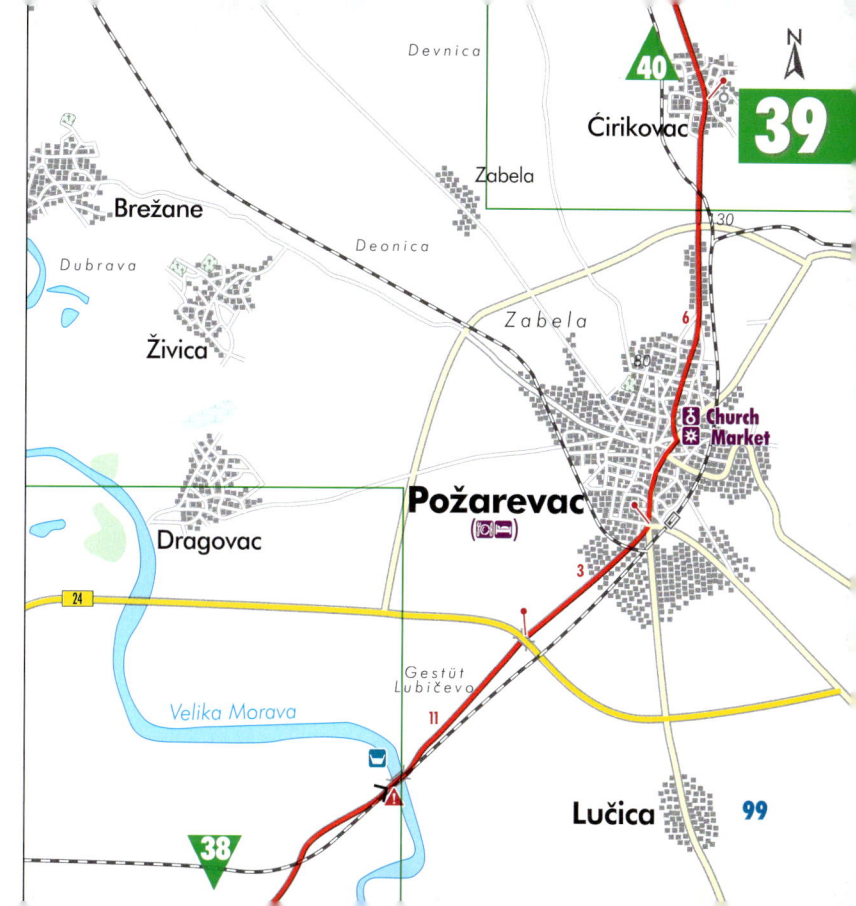

Across the fields

Ride around the church to the right and then straight on a mostly-unpaved small lane towards Ram ~ keep going until you come to a T-intersection ~ where you can turn left to get to Ram.

Main road variant

Turn left at the church in Kličevac and follow the road down to the Danube and then on to Ram.

Tip: Regardless of how you got to Ram, you now have the choice of staying in Serbia or crossing the Danube and entering Romania. If you wish to take the Romanian route, get on the ferry to Stara Palanka. The description of the route on the Romanian side of the Danube starts on page 116.

Church in Kličevac

Ram

- **Ferry to Stara Palanka**, departures at 5, 7, 10, 13, 16 and 19.30 o'clock.
- **Ottoman fortress** (15th century) with excellent views across the Danube

Tip: Right next to the ferry landing there is a restaurant where you can take a break or get something to eat while enjoying the views across the Danube to Stara Palanka and the Romanian border.

If you choose to stay on the Serbian side of the river, ride uphill out of Ram ~ and follow the main road towards **Zatonje**.

Zatonje

Follow the road into Zatonje ~ on the left side there is a small store with a snack bar ~ there is also a street that goes off to the left with a do-not-enter sign ~ go straight and look for the house on the left side with two large stone lions ~ take the next left, a small alley ~ and go down a steep grade through sandstone rocks ~ at the next T-intersection turn left again ~ where there is a great view across the Danube ~ take the dike-road next to the Danube on the left and a swimming lake on the right and head for **Ostrovo**.

Ostrovo

Take the asphalt road through the small groups of houses ~ until you reach a 4-way intersection ~ just past the intersection there is a small kiosk on the left side of the quiet street along the Danube towards **Veliko Gradište** ~ take the riverside road to a larger street ~ and proceed straight to a square with a large church ~ and turn right towards the center of the town.

Veliko Gradište

Postal area code: 12220; Telephone area code: 012

- **Tourism information**, Trg Mladena Miloradovića 1, ✆ 63161 or ✆ 62650
- **Excursion rides on the Srebrrno jezero lake**, July-Aug, Info: ✆ 064/4469045
- **Beli Bagrem recreation center**

Restaurant at the ferry in Ram

Veliko Gradište lies on the banks of the Đerdap Lake, the artificial lake created by the dam across the Danube downstream, and the mouth of the Pek, a small tributary that comes from the south. The Pek is famous as a river on which gold is panned from the gravel coming out of the mountains. West of Veliko Gradište is the Srebrno Jezero, a lake created by damming up an old bend in the Danube.

The lake is about 14 kilometers long and up to 200 meters wide, and has a recreation area entitled "Beli Bagrem".

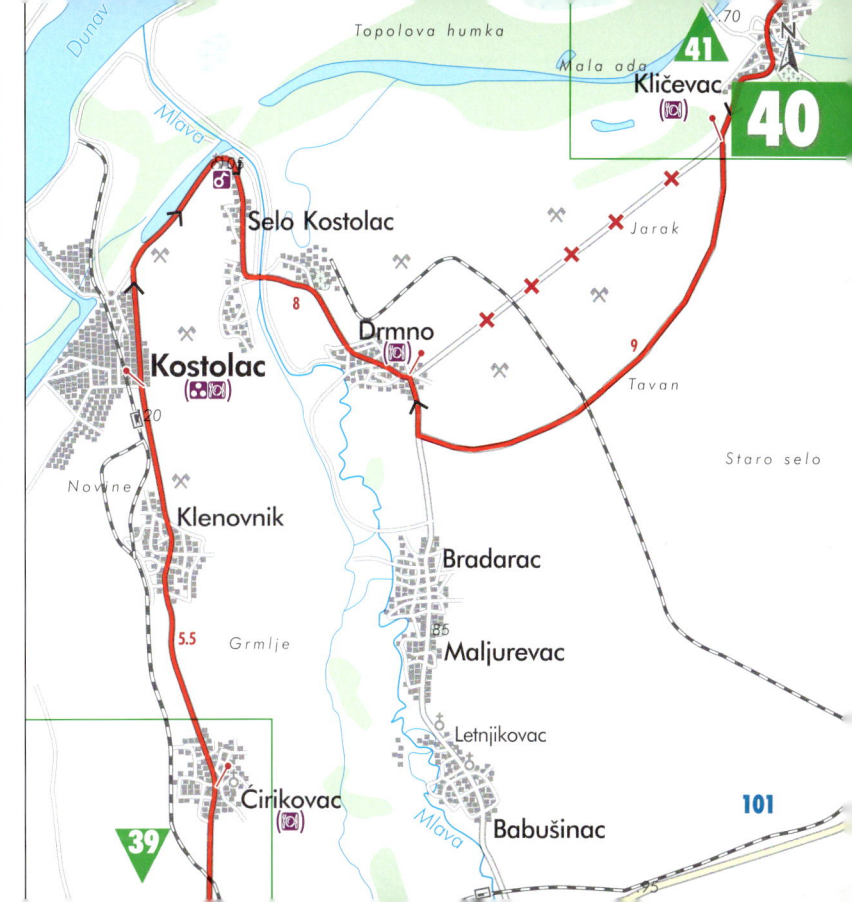

Road to Zatonje

Ram to Donji Milanovac — 88.5 km

In the town go straight until you reach the stop sign at the main street ~ turn left into the road curving to the right ~ after the curve turn left at the first opportunity, directly at the intersection with the small store with advertising signs for Bosch and Opel.

There is also a wooden sign with "Farma Sjvina" written by hand. Follow this sign ~ past the abandoned petrol station ~ follow the road as it makes a bend to the right ~ and continue straight into Požežena.

Požežena

Tip: A hand-written sign pointing to "Restaurant Alaska" shows the way towards Vinci.

Just after this sign there is a path to the left that goes to the restaurant, which is directly on the Danube ~ proceed on the small well-asphalted street ~ past an old cemetery and down the road into Vinci.

Tip: The views of the majestic Danube provide a refreshing and rewarding distraction from any aches and sores the many kilometers may have produced.

Vinci

Tip: Like most of the little towns and villages you have passed in Serbia, Vinci also offers opportunities to do some grocery-shopping or take a break in a simple inn.

After Vinci the next village is **Usije**.

Usije

In the village follow the road to a larger square with a 4-way intersection ~ turn left on the larger street heading to **Golubac**.

Tip: Here you again can enjoy excellent

Near Ostrovo

views of the Danube on its slow march towards the distant Black Sea. It curves around an island and gives the impression of a lake rather than a river.

Golubac

Postal area code: 12223; Telephone area code: 012

- **Tourist Info**, Gorana Tosiča-Macka 1, ✆ 78145, www.golubac.org.yu
- **Golubac fortress** (13th century)

The quiet town takes its name from the imposing great castle that stands about 5 kilometers downstream. Both the town and the castle were built in the 13th century by the Hungarians. The castle stands on the site of

Map 41

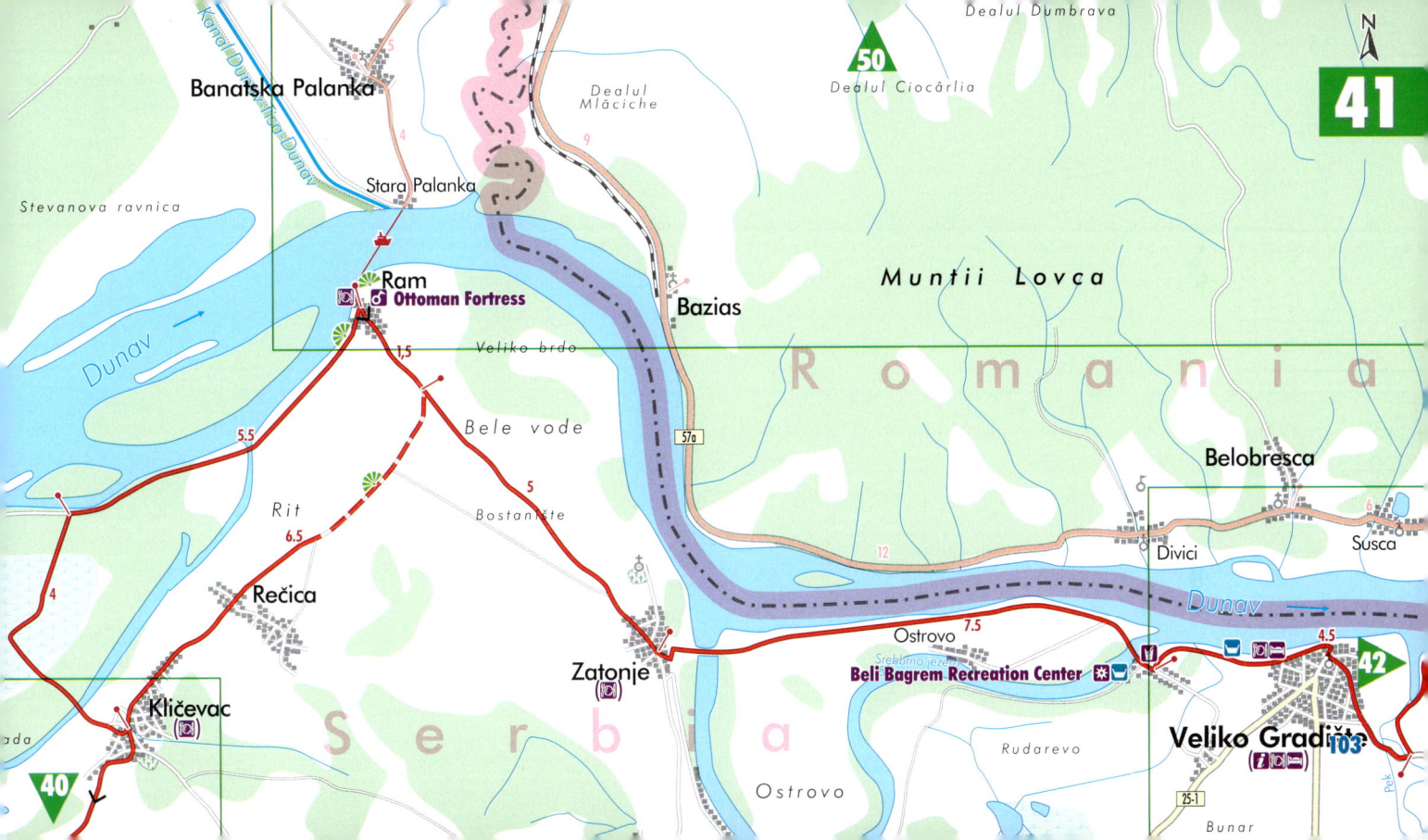

Banatska Palanka

Kanal Dunavac-Dunav

Stara Palanka

Stevanova ravnica

Dunav

Ram
Ottoman Fortress

Dealul Mlaciche

Dealul Dumbrava

Dealul Ciocârlia — 50

Bazias

Veliko brdo

Bele vode

Rit

Bostaniste

Muntii Lovca

R o m a n i a

Rečica

Zatonje

Srebrno jezero
Beli Bagrem Recreation Center

Ostrovo

Belobresca

Divici

Susca

Dunav

42

Kličevac

S e r b i j a

Ostrovo

Rudarevo

Veliko Gradište
103

Bunar

Pek

40

The ruins of Golubac castle come in to view

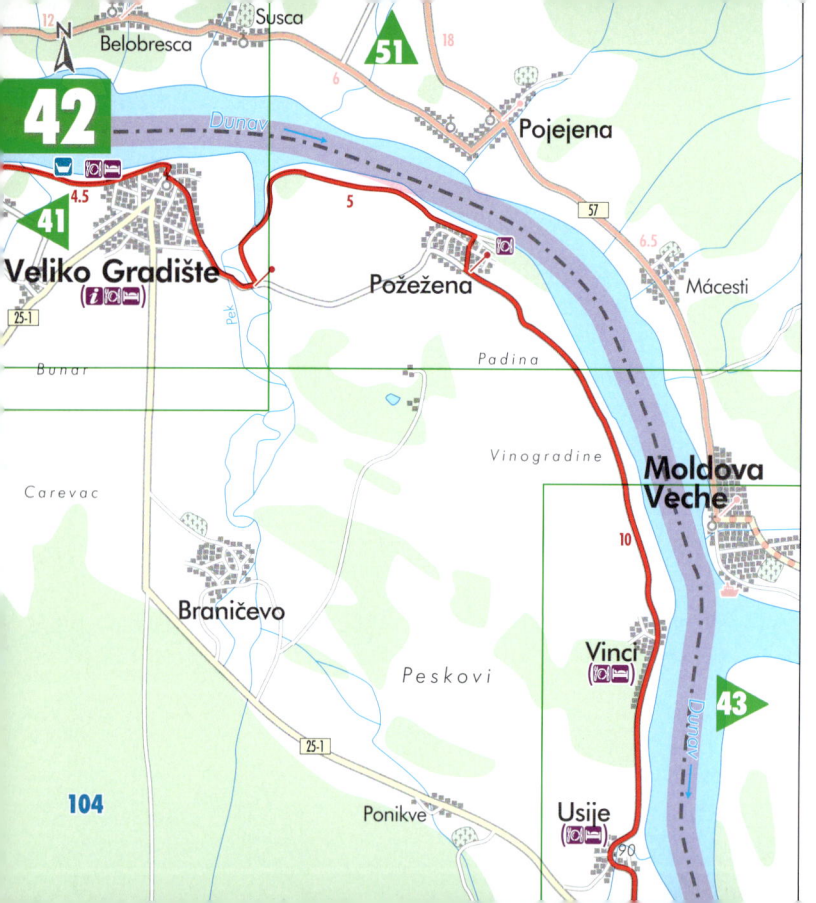

the Roman castra Columbarum. In 1389 the Turks seized control of the castle, the first of many times it changed hands until the Serbs finally took it for good in 1815.

The remains of nine towers stand up to 25 meters tall, and seem to rise from the waters of the Danube and stretch up the steep slope to the south. The road passes through two huge gates and directly along the walls. Golubac is regarded as the most beautiful and best-preserved old castle in Serbia.

Moldova Novuă
Moldova Veche
Valea Ravensca
43
42
44
V. Kamenica
57
7.5
Romania
Sichevita
210
Gornea
Cracu Sirovita
V. Liborajdea
Moldova Veche
Dunav
Sfânta Elena
Coronini
Liborajdea
Gornea
Grada Najta
305
10
3
9
6
Golubac Castle
Jerinin Grad
Dunav
25-1
11
Brnjica
Golubac
Sladinac
Golubacka klisura
Kljanc
420
Nacionalni park Đerdap
Serbia
Dublje
Kulmea del Bosi
Milojkovo
Čezana
Brnjička reka
Vojilovo
Dvorište
Crni vrh
625
Lakor

Đerdap National Park

The Đerdap National Park stretches from Golubac castle in the west to the dam near Sip in the east and comprises a total area of about 64,000 hectares. The topographical highlight of the park is the Đerdap gorge, which snakes through the mountains for a distance of more than 100 kilometers from Golubac to Tekija. It consists of four distinct sections defined by ridges of the Carpathian mountains. They are the Gornja Klisura, Gospođin Vir, Veliki and Mali Kazan and Sipska Klisura. The most spectacular stage is almost certainly the Gospođin Vir ("vir" means stream or current). The Danube here is up to 82 meters deep, making it the deepest river in the world. The cliffs of the gorge at Kazan rise almost vertically to heights of more than 600 meters. Before the dam was constructed, the river's current raced past the rocky depths, making river navigation dangerous and at times impossible. Near the Serbian village of Golo Brdo there is a Roman relief, the Tabula Traiana, chiseled into the cliff in honor of the Emperor Trajan. It was moved to a higher location in 1972 to prevent it from being submerged by the dammed up river.

The highest point in the national park is the Miroc, which reaches an elevation of 768 meters. More than 1,000 species of plants live in the park, including relics from the tertiary period like hazelnut, walnut and yew. The yew was once considered a holy tree. It can regenerate itself, growing a new tree from the stump after it has been felled. A splinter of yew buried in the walls of a house is said to assure prosperity. The woods also contain large numbers of oak, maple, elm and many other kinds of trees.

Wildlife includes lynx, bear and jackal, as well as eagles and black storks and many other birds and small animals that can live in the natural habitat.

Ride through the town ~ at the far edge of town the road starts to climb ~ and continues through many curves.

Tip: You have now reached the beginnings of the gorge where the Danube breaks through the Serbian Carpathian Mountains that start to rise from the horizon as you head east. The somewhat elevated position of the road offers excellent views across the Danube and into Romania.

The next stage of the trip takes you through 21 tunnels of varying lengths. All of

In the Danube Gorge near Golubac

44

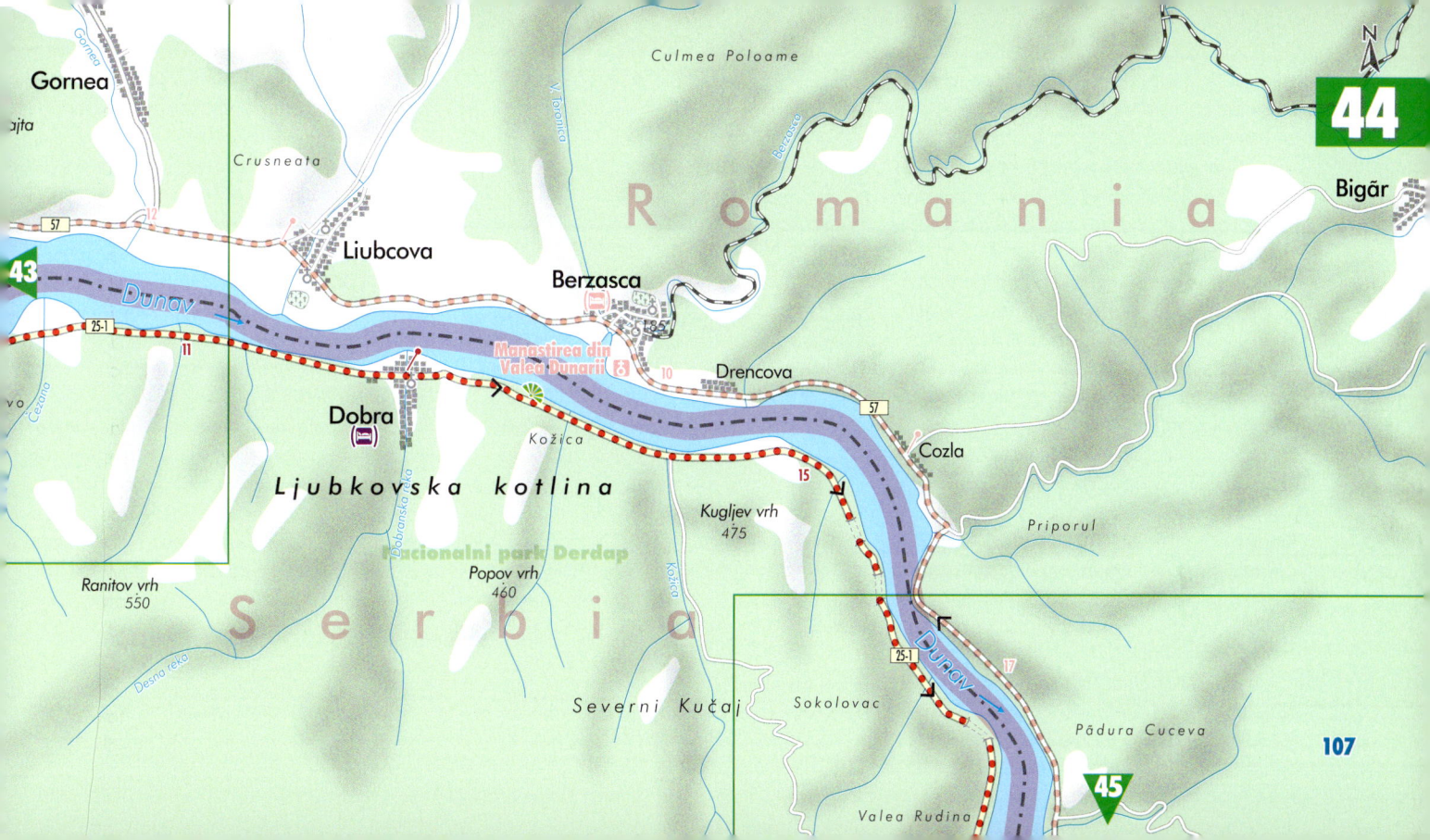

Gornea
Bigăr
Culmea Poloame
Crusneata
Liubcova
Berzasca
Romania
Dunav
43
25-1
Manastirea din Valea Dunarii
Drencova
Dobra
Kožica
Cozla
Ljubkovska kotlina
Nacionalni park Đerdap
Kugljev vrh
475
Priporul
Ranitov vrh
550
Popov vrh
460
Serbia
Desna reka
Severni Kučaj
Sokolovac
Dunav
25-1
Pădura Cuceva
Valea Rudina
45

107

them are dark and there are no shoulders. Use caution and watch for traffic carefully as you enter tunnels.

Proceed along the cliffs and under the jagged outcroppings ~ you can catch the first glimpses of the ruins of Golubac in the distance.

Tip: At the castle you ride through two gates that guard the road. On the left, mighty stone towers emerge directly from the waters of the Danube, while the rest of the fortifications cling to the steep slopes that rise to the right.

Proceed down Route 25-1, past the villages of **Dedina**, **Jerenin Grad**, and **Brnjica** on the way to **Dobra**.

Dobra

Proceed uphill to the next village, **Kozica**.

Kozica

Lepinski Vir

In 1965, during construction of the Đerdap dam, the remains of ancient settlements were found on the banks of the Danube near the

Manastirea din Valea Dunarii on the Romanian side of the Danube

Iron Gates. Two years later the discovery of Mesolithic sculptures established the location as an important archaeological site.

The evidence at the site suggests Stone Age hunter-gatherers first settled there about 9,000 years ago and reached their peak about 2,000 years later. The inhabitants built peculiar wooden houses based on a complex geometric design and equipped with a fireplace and in some cases what appears to be an altar. The floors were paved with sandstone or clay and dyed with red or white pigment. Some of the houses apparently served also as burial places. Large piscine sculptures, other decorated figurines and tools testify to a rich social and religious culture among these Stone Age Europeans. The piscine sculptures are unique to the Lepinski Vir culture and are among the oldest sculptures to have been found in Europe.

There is also evidence that the settlements were repeatedly flooded, making permanent habitation impossible, but that the inhabitants always returned to rebuild their villages.

At the same time that the hunter-gatherers lived at Lepinski Vir, other peoples also settled nearby and began farming. As the two groups started trading pottery and food stuffs, their culture changed to a more agricultural life-style.

The settlement stands across from the mountain Treskavek, which has a trapezoidal shape which seems mirrored in the footprints of the village's houses, just as swirls and waves reminiscent of the river can be found in some of the sculptures that these ancient Europeans left behind.

Here the road turns away from the Danube and starts to climb uphill as it heads south ~

Through the Danube Gorge

and past the village of **Boljetin**.

Boljetin

🏛 Lepinski Vir Museum, ☎ 063/206271, Open: Tues-Sat 10-17 o'clock, Sun 10-14 o'clock. The museum contains items found at the archeological site. There is also an outdoor museum with reconstructed houses from Porec island, which was flooded when the dam at the Iron Gates was completed.

Proceed to **Hladna Voda** where the road returns to the Danube.

Hladna Voda

Follow the street through the village ～ proceed downhill for a few kilometers to the town of **Donji Milanovac**.

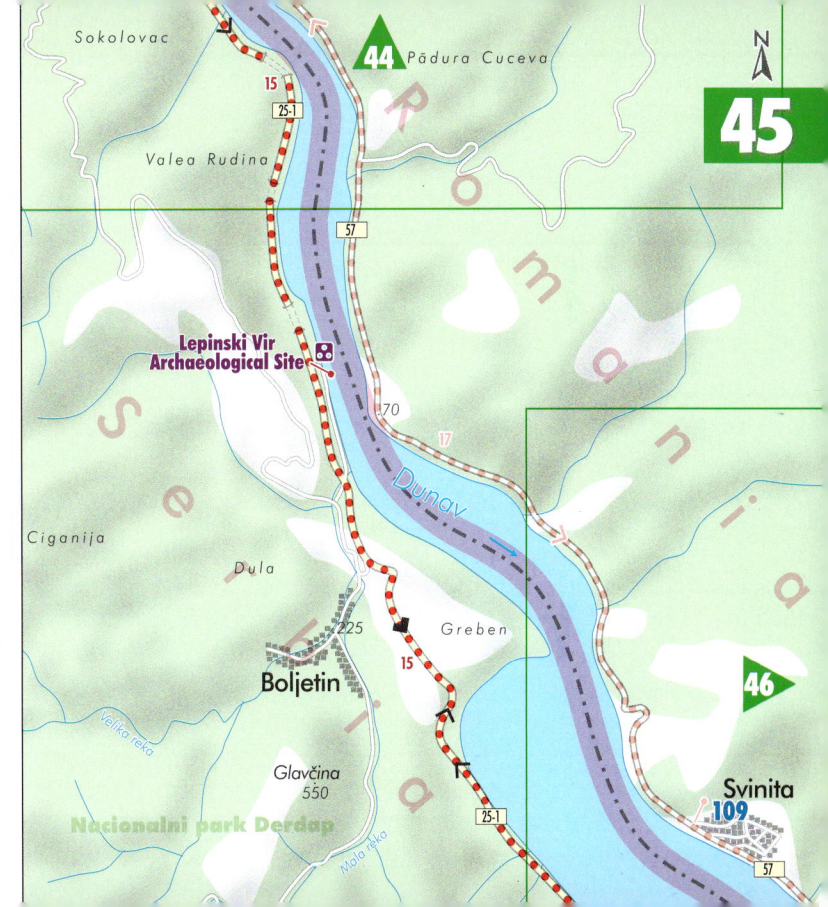

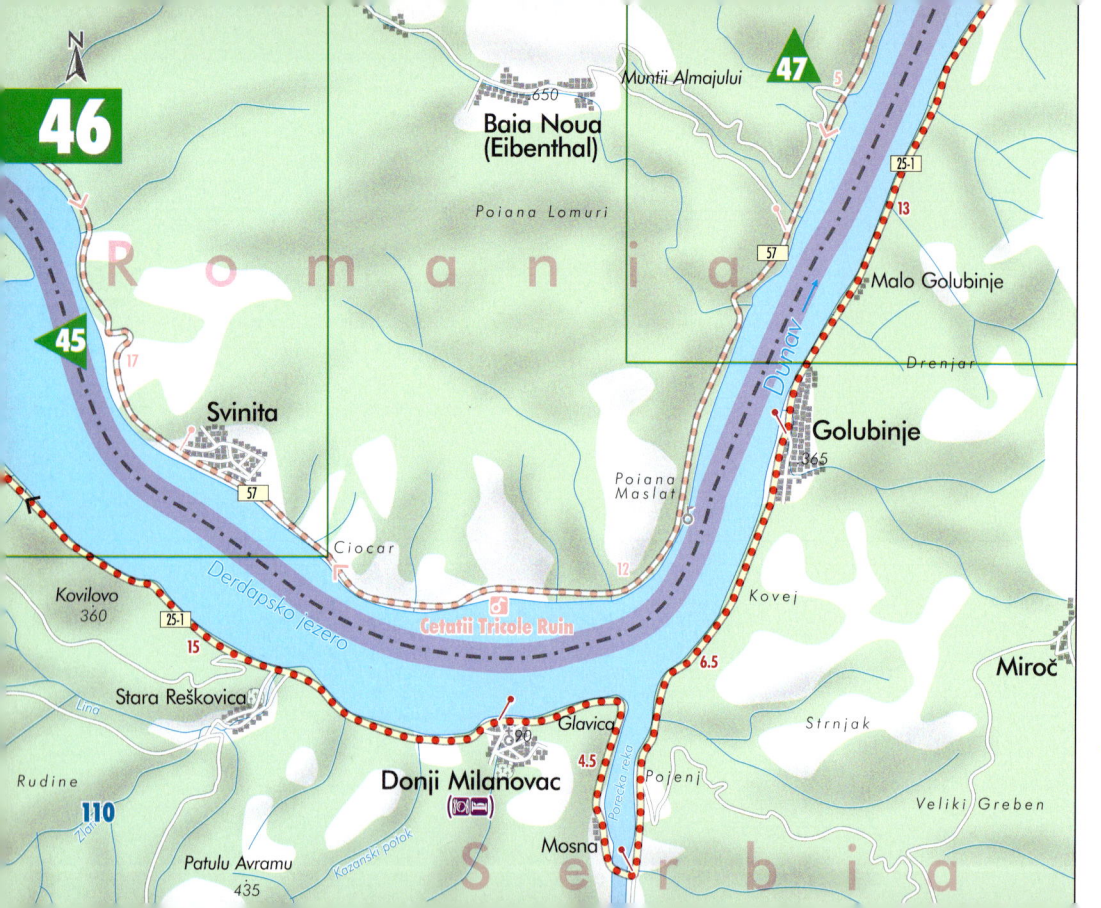

Donji Milanovac

Postal area code: 19220; Telephone area code: 030

- **Boat trips on the Danube**, between 1 and 6 hours in length, May-Oct. Information at Hotel "Lepinski Vir", ☎ 86210 or 86211
- **Museum**
- **Central information office about Đerdap National Park**, Kralja Petra 1-14a, ☎ 86788 or 86877 (across from the bus station)

The original Donji Milanovac was flooded by construction of the dam. The current village was built at a higher location for the inhabitants.

Donji Milanovac to Sip at the Romanian border — 50.5 km

After riding through Donji Milanovac the route turns to the south and winds around a tributary to the Danube 〜 the road makes a curve to the east and over a bridge over the **Porecka River** 〜 to a T-intersection 〜 turn left and return to the Danube and the road downstream.

Approaching the "Cazanele Mici"

Mosna

Follow the road through the village ↝ and proceed about 6 kilometers to **Golubinje**.

Golubinje

Just past the village pass the hamlet of Malo Golubinje on the right and ride down to the narrowest place in the gorge.

Tip: The Danube is just 150 meters wide at this point. The rugged mountains and the powerful river combine to produce dramatic and unforgettable views!

The route down river continues

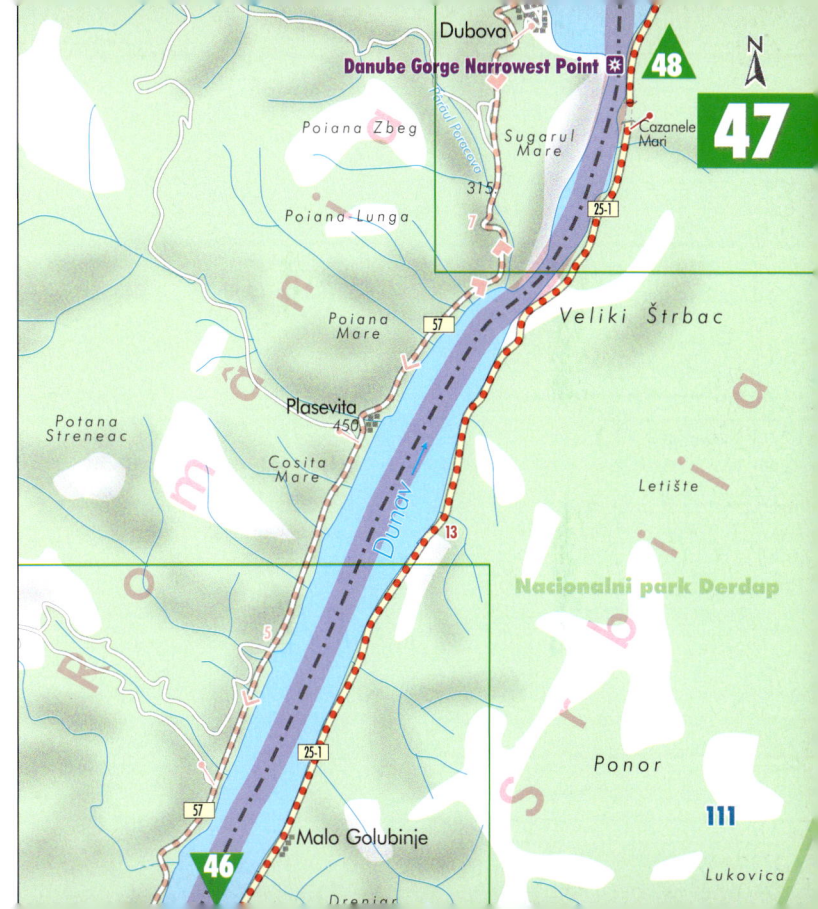

towards Golo Brdo.

Golo Brdo
✱ Tabula Traiana

Tip: The Roman monument Tabula Traiana is located near here, but can be seen only from the river.

Tabula Traiana

This monument chiseled into the rock face was commissioned by the Roman Emperor Trajan in the year 100 AD in memory of the completion of the Roman road along the Danube. The road was built mainly to serve troops and supply trains engaged in the Roman wars again the Dacians. The monument was cut out of the cliff and moved to a location 40 meters higher to prevent it from being submerged by rising waters of the Danube after completion of the dam further downstream.

The monument shows dolphins on both sides of the central inscription, and three roses with six petals each. The inscription reads: "The son of the ruling Caesar and the divine Nerva, Nerva Traianus Augustus Germanicus, Pontifex Maximus, Tribune for the Fourth Time, Father of the Fatherland and Consul, moved mountains and stream to build this road."

After construction of a bridge at Karataš near the Roman fortress Diana some 7 kilometers downstream from the Iron Gates, Trajan's way into Dacia was clear. In the second Dacian War (105-106 AD) his armies conquered the area and annexed it to the Roman Empire as the Province of Dacia.

The bicycle route continues another 21 kilometers along the river towards **Tekija**.

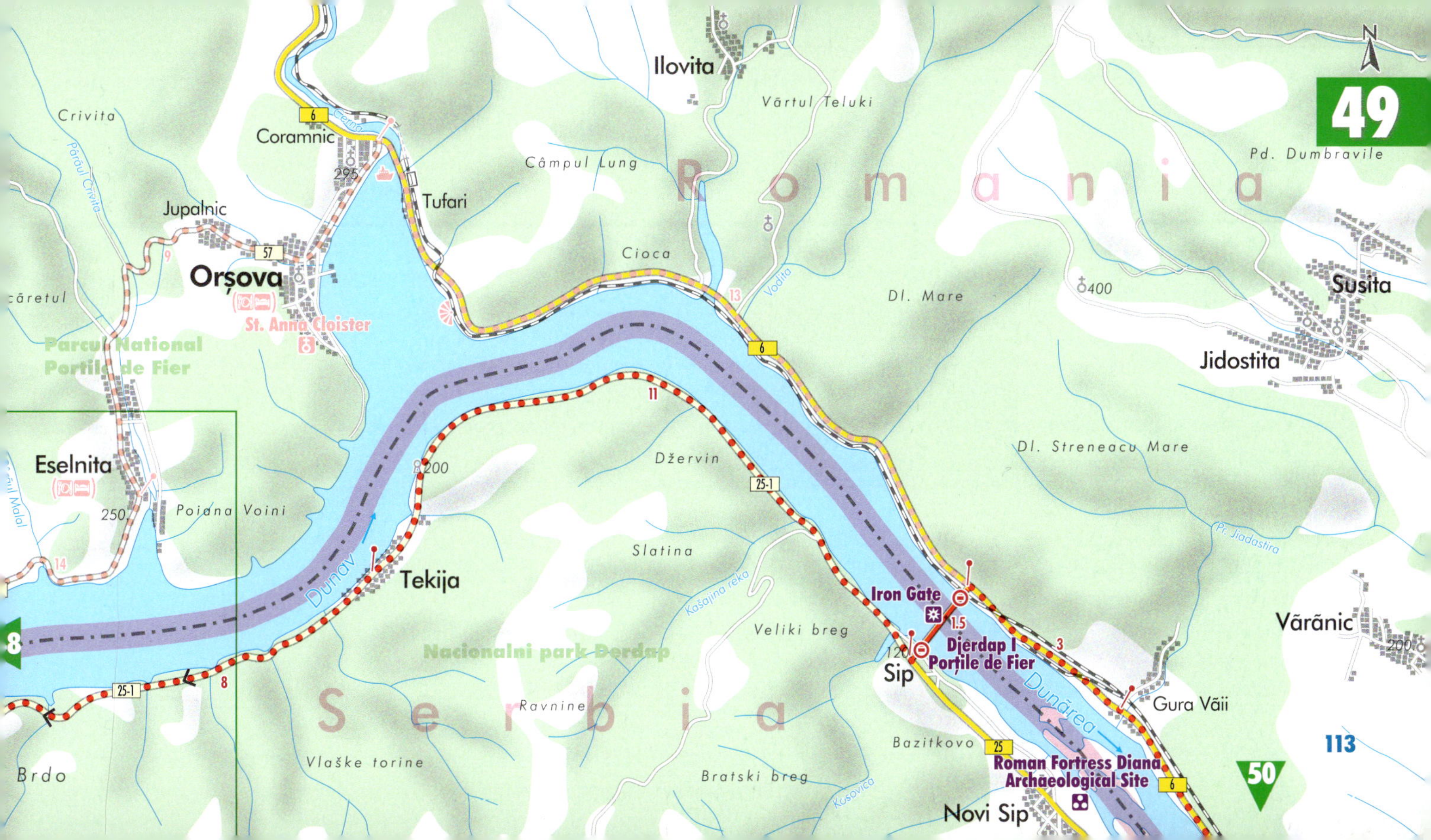
49
Ilovita
Vârtul Teluki
Crivita
Coramnic
6
Cerna
295
Tufari
Câmpul Lung
Romania
Pd. Dumbravile
Pârâul Crivita
Jupalnic
57
9
Orșova
Cioca
13
Vodita
400
Susita
St. Anna Cloister
Dl. Mare
Parcul National Portile de Fier
Jidostita
11
Džervin
Dl. Streneacu Mare
200
25-1
Eselnita
250
Poiana Voini
Slatina
Pr. Jiadastira
14
Dunav
Tekija
Kašajina reka
Iron Gate
1.5
Veliki breg
Vărănic
200
8
Nacionalni park Đerdap
120
Sip
Djerdap I Porțile de Fier
3
Dunărea
Gura Văii
Serbia
Ravnine
Bazitkovo
25
Brdo
Vlaške torine
Bratski breg
Kusovica
Roman Fortress Diana Archaeological Site
Novi Sip
50

Tekija

Tip: From here there are only another 11 kilometers to Sip (Đerdap I) and the bridge over the Danube and the Romanian border crossing.

Porile de Fier, Đerdap I, or the Iron Gate

The name Iron Gates refers not just to the hydro-electric power plant, but to the gorge through which the Danube crosses the Southern Carpathian Mountains. The name probably comes from the Turkish "Demir Kapi", which also means "iron gate." The Turks used the name for this gorge as well as for various passes through the Carpathians and in the Balkans. The narrows in the river were always very dangerous for river traffic and could be navigated only with the assistance of experienced pilots who knew the waters well. The Đerdap Dam was built between 1962 and 1974 as a joint project by Yugoslavia and Romania. Total costs came to the equivalent of 550 million dollars.

The dam is 448 meters wide at its base and more than 1200 meters across at the top. It towers 30 meters over the river, and the lake created behind the dam extends some 150 kilometers upriver. The power station produces more than 2100 megawatt.

Construction of the dam raised the river level by up to 35 meters. As a result, many villages and towns as well as the Roman road built by Trajan were flooded. Most of the communities were moved uphill and rebuilt.

Two huge locks, each of which measures 310 meters in length and 30 meters in width, can raise or lower ships by 34 meters. The locks are large enough to hold ships of up to 5,000 tons displacement, providing cargo and passenger vessels access from the Black Sea.

A road across the top of the dam connects Serbia with the Romanian inland port of Drobeta-Turnu Severin.

During construction of the dam, the river course through the gorge was cleared, in part with explosives, to remove obstacles and make the passage less dangerous to ships.

Heading across the dam and into Romania

Romania

via Bela Crkva 1,050.5 km/via Sip 874 km

Endless landscapes of small farms, meadows and pastures dominate your ride through Romania. The roads seem almost empty, with the exception of horse-drawn wagons and the rare automobile or lorry. In the towns and villages, the streets are alive with children playing under shade trees, women tending their vegetable plots or cutting hay, men sitting in front of small kiosks drinking and talking while small herds of livestock are driven from one field to the next. Outside of the towns sheep, geese and cattle graze on lush pastures under the watchful eyes of their herders who spend large parts of the summer season living in small huts near their animals. Families of Romani camp around their covered wagons in woods or are underway with all their earthly belongings from one village to the next, looking for work as farm hands or laborers.

The ride to Constanța from Romania's western borders is long. When you reach the coastal city, the view of the harbor, the smell of the open sea and the cooling breeze come as a welcome reward after all those kilometers through the Balkans. Your journey is not yet over, however. There are still a few more kilometers between Constanța and Tulcea, the harbor town in the Danube delta. There you can board a boat for the final passage to Sulina and the Danube kilometer marker bearing the zero. Having come this far, it would be reckless to skip an excursion into the delta to see the pelicans and other wildlife where the great river empties into the Black Sea.

The route through Romania follows nothing but country roads with light traffic. The only significant climbs you will encounter come between Călărași/Ostrov and Constanța.

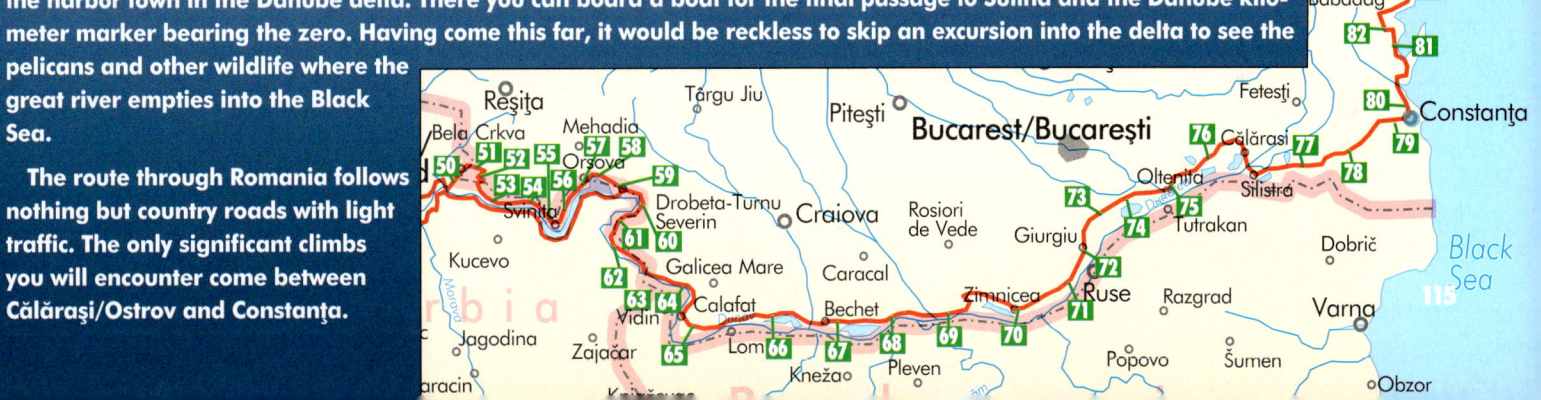

Ram to Moldova Veche — 52 km

Tip: The route along the Romanian side of the Danube Gorge is in general more idyllic and more varied than the Serbian side, with curves and small climbs and descents that help keep the ride interesting. The road occasionally passes through small woods and is closer to the riverbank with many pleasant spots where one can take a break right on the Danube. The roads on the Romanian side have less traffic, but they are also narrower and the surface is often uneven and broken. After heavy rains there is a good chance part of the road may be buried or blocked by a landslide or fallen rocks. The following pages contain a description of the route on the Romanian side. The maps are done in a scale of 1:200,000.

Ram

- Ferry to Stara Palanka, departures at 5, 7, 10, 13, 16 and 19.30 o'clock.
- Ottoman fortress (15th century) with excellent views across the Danube

After reaching the north side of the river at Stara Palanka ride past the houses and through a left curve out of the village and proceed towards Banatska Palanka.

Banatska Palanka

Follow the road through to the church and turn right to leave the village in the direction of Vračev Gaj as you enter the next village turn right at the intersection and head towards Bela Crkva.

Vračev Gaj

- Outdoor pool (at a small pond)

After the swimming hole proceed gently uphill and then downhill and onto cobblestones into the town of **Bela Crkva**.

Bela Crkva

Postal area code: 26340; Telephone area code: 013

- Tourism Organization, Mileticeva 2, 851091, www.belacrkva.co.yu

Ethnic Germans who settled in this town called it Weisskirchen, or White Church. It is a charming little baroque town with seven popular clean lakes nearby.

In the last larger community in Serbia before the border with Romania, take the cobblestone street to a fork in the road stay to the left and cross the railroad tracks proceed to the intersection with street 7-1 turn right towards Kaluđerovo and ride downhill on this lonely country road to the border.

Kaluđerovo

After the border crossing the road turns south and into a hilly region with many climbs and curves past the town of Naidaş towards **Pojejena**.

Tip: The next 20 kilometers are especially scenic and varied and can be counted as a natural highlight in and of themselves. Hills, woods and lush fertile meadows lift

50

- Šoice
- Crvena Crkva
- Vagane
- Vračev Gaj
- Bela Crkva
- Dubrava
- Kaluderovo
- Serbia
- Ornica
- Kusić
- Naidăs
- Lescovita
- Socol
- Câmpia
- Pârneaura
- Zlatita
- Nera
- Banatska Palanka
- Dealul Mlăciche
- Dealul Dumbrava
- Dealul Ciocârlia
- Romania
- Dealul Turcului
- Stara Palanka
- Ottoman Fortress
- Bazias
- Muntii Lovca
- Culmea Stramțucului

51 117 52

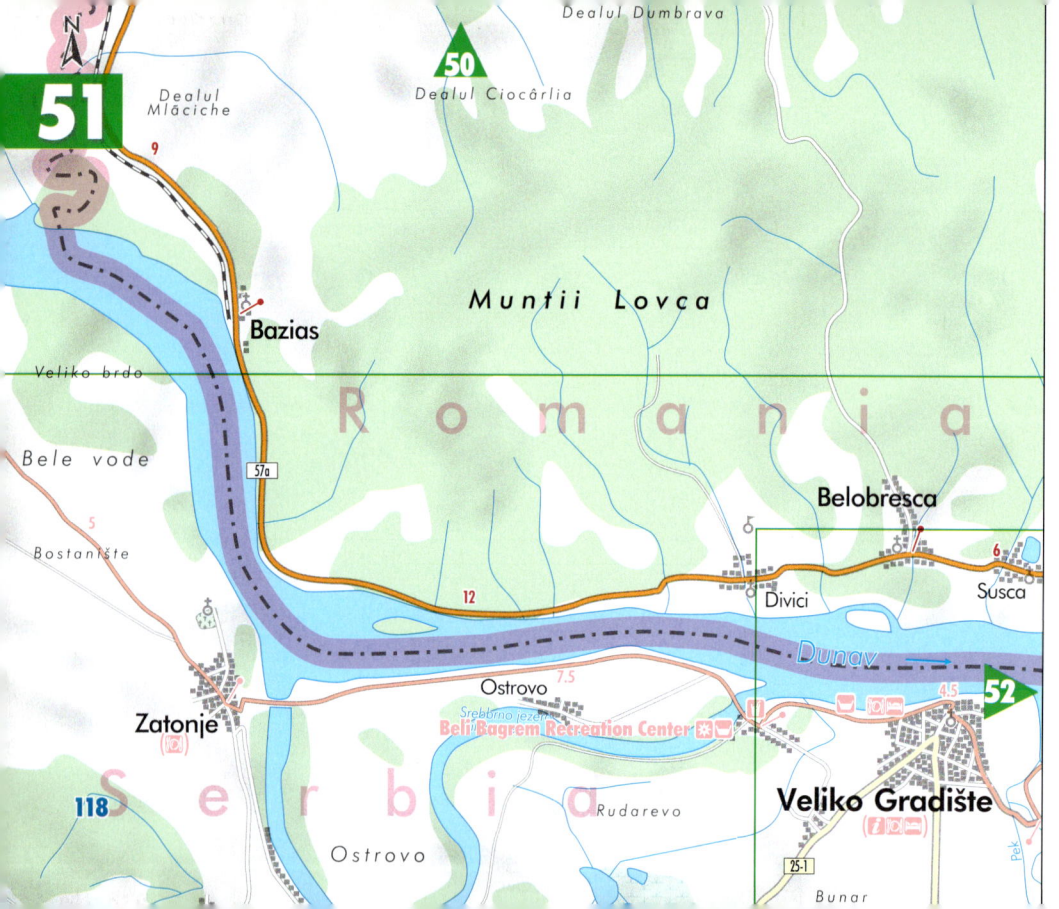

the bicycle tourist's spirit and distract from the hard work that his or her legs must deliver to power the bicycle over the numerous and steep hills.

Radimna

Just past **Radimna** there is a hotel on the left side. It is a short distance away from the road in a clearing in the woods.

Pojejena

After another 4 kilometers you ride through the village of **Măceşti**.

Măceşti

The next few kilometers present no significant climbs as you ride along the river's edge and into Moldova Veche.

Moldova Veche

Downstream from Moldova Veche the river becomes much wider and gives the impression of a large lake. The island **"Ostrovu Moldova Veche"** has a ruin.

Moldova Veche to Sviniţa — 52.5 km

Continue down the road towards **Coronini**.

Through the Danube Gorge on the Romanian side

Coronini

The route stays directly on the banks of the Danube. Just past Coronini the Danube becomes much narrower.

Tip: From here you have a great view of Golubac castle on the Serbian side of the river, and of the steep cliffs that rise from the Danube's waters.

Continue for another 23 kilometers to the village of Liubcova. Just before the village ride across a bridge over the Gornea River.

Liubcova

In Liubcova ride across another bridge ~ and proceed 6 kilometers to **Berzasca**.

Berzasca

🛈 Manastirea din Valea Dunarii monastery at the entrance to the "Cazanele Mici" Danube narrows.

Ride past the monastery and follow the road down the river.

Drencova

Ride through the village of Drencova and proceed straight to **Cozla**.

Cozla

A short distance after Cozla the road descends slightly before

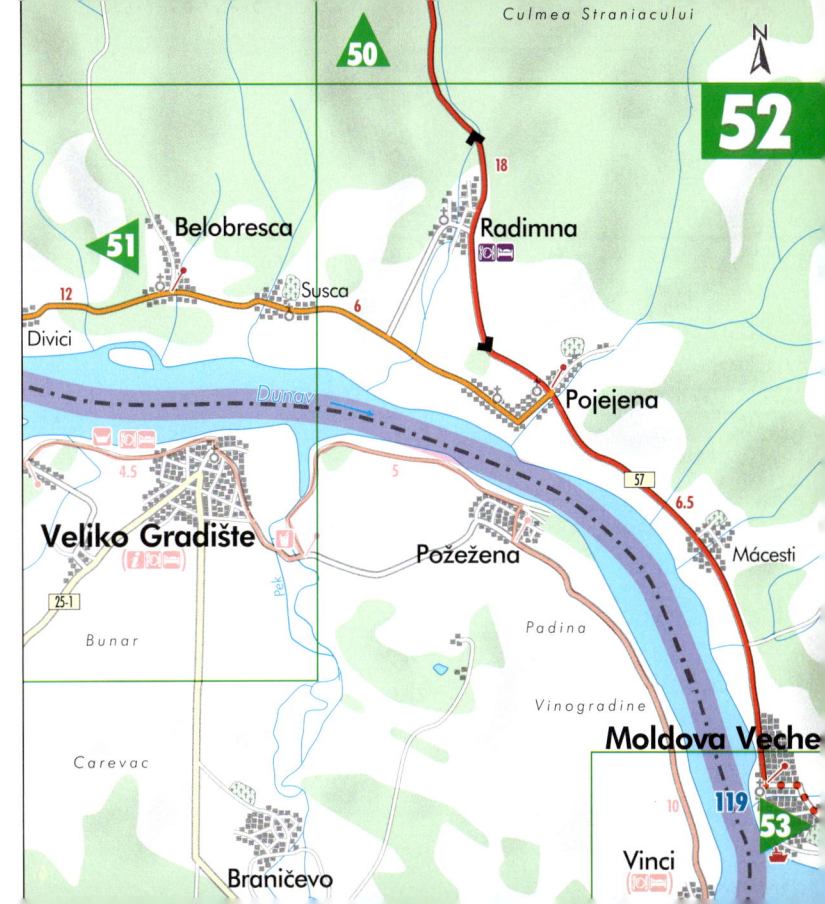

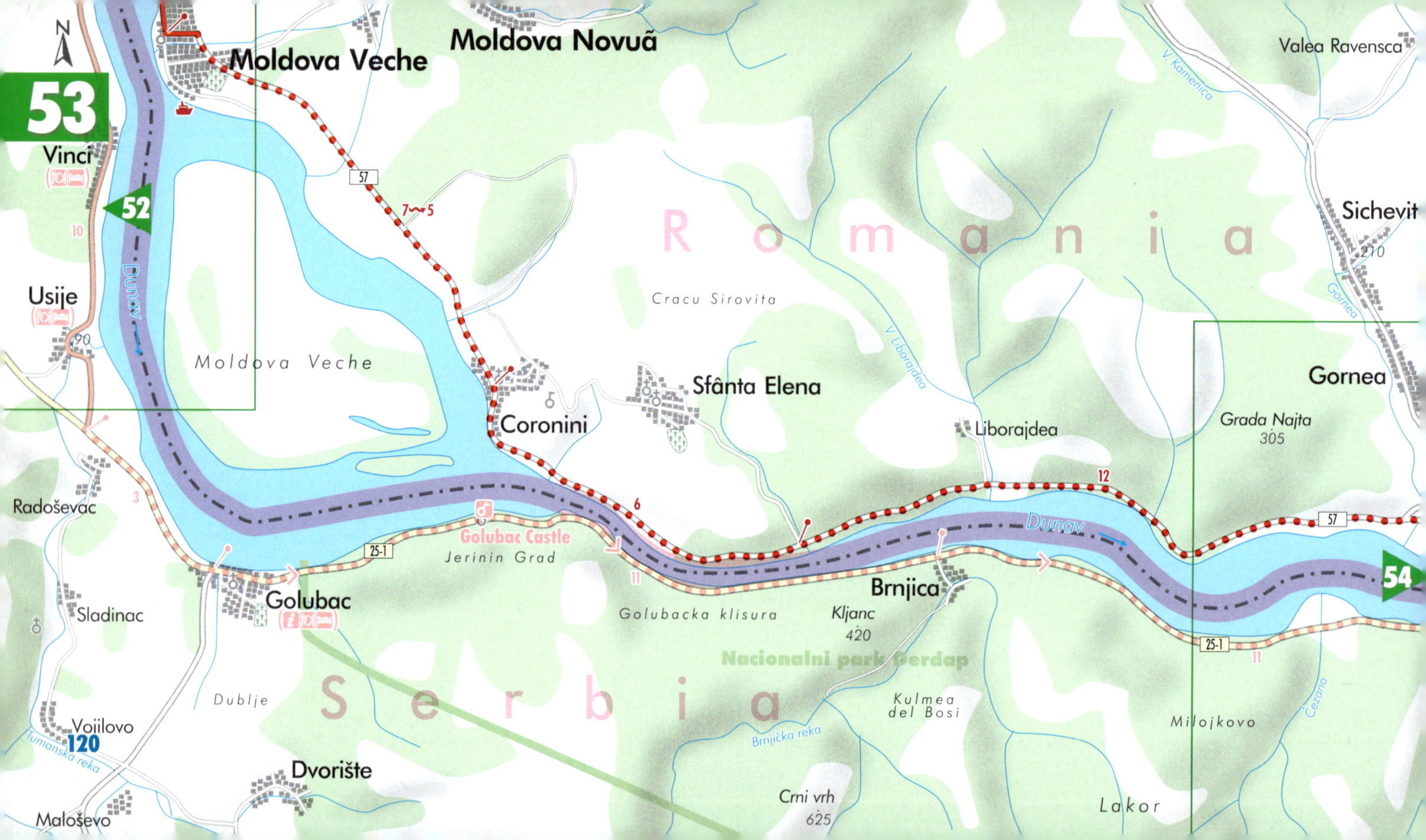

53
52
54
Moldova Novuã
Moldova Veche
Valea Ravensca
V. Kamenica
Vinci
Usije
Radoševac
Sladinac
Voiilovo
120
Tumanska reka
Dvorište
Maloševo
Dublje
Golubac
Golubac Castle
Jerinin Grad
Golubacka klisura
Brnjica
Kljanc
420
Nacionalni park Đerdap
Kulmea del Bosi
Brnjička reka
Crni vrh
625
Lakor
Milojkovo
Čezana
Coronini
Sfânta Elena
Cracu Sirovita
V. Liborajdea
Liborajdea
Sichevit
210
Gornea
Grada Najta
305
Romania
Serbia
Dunav
57
25-1
7~5
6
12
11
10
3
90

54

Romania

- Gornea
- Crusneata
- Culmea Poloame
- Liubcova
- Berzasca
- Bigăr
- Manastirea din Valea Dunarii
- Drencova
- Dobra
- Kožica
- Cozla
- Ljubkovska kotlina
- Priporul
- Kugljev vrh 475
- Nacionalni park Đerdap
- Popov vrh 460
- Ranitov vrh 550
- **Serbia**
- Desna reka
- Severni Kučaj
- Sokolovac
- Pădura Cuceva
- Valea Rudina

Dunav

53 · 55

121

starting to climb again about 5 kilometers before **Sviniţa**.

Sviniţa

- **Ruin Cetatii Tricole** (about 4 kilometers after Svinia). Flooded former Habsburg border castle. Two of the three towers still rise above the Danube's surface.

Ruins of the Cetatii Tricole near Sviniţa

Sviniţa
to Drobeta Turnu-Severin   63 km

Just past Sviniţa there is a short descent — the road surface soon becomes worse and stays bad for about 8 kilometers — then another descent — followed by two steep climbs (8% grade) and one similarly steep descent towards Dubova — the road here turns away from the Danube for a short distance and passes through a picturesque hilly area.

Tip: About 2 kilometers before Dubova you ride past the narrowest place in the Danube Gorge. Serbia seems little more than a stone throw away.

You are now in the Parcul Natural Porţile de Fier (Iron Gates Natural Park).

Dubova

- **"Monumentul Decebalus Rex"**. Paid for by the Romanian industrialist Dr. Iosif Constantin Dragan. The monument is 40 meters tall and 25 meters wide, and depicts the Dacian King Decebalus (the name means "strong as ten men"). He was the last King of Dacia in what is today Romania, reigning from 87 AD to his death in 106 AD.

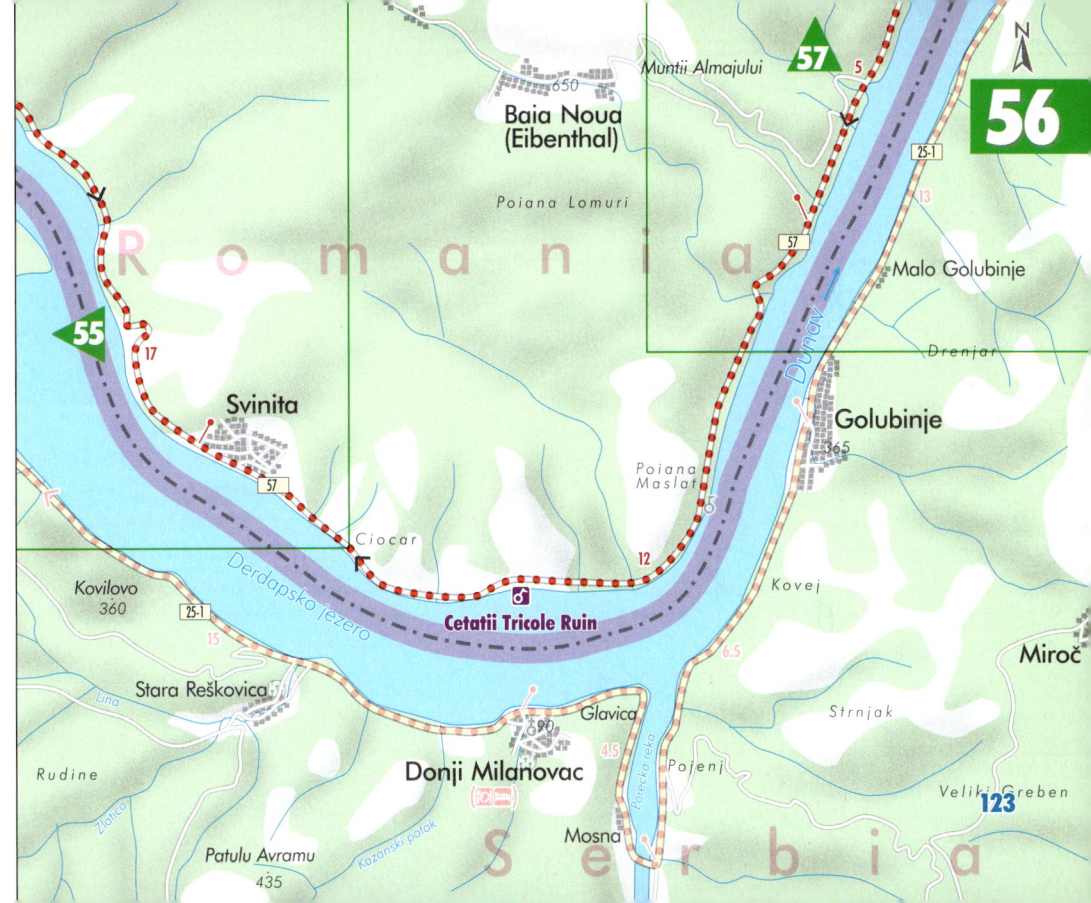

"Decebalus Rex" near Dubova

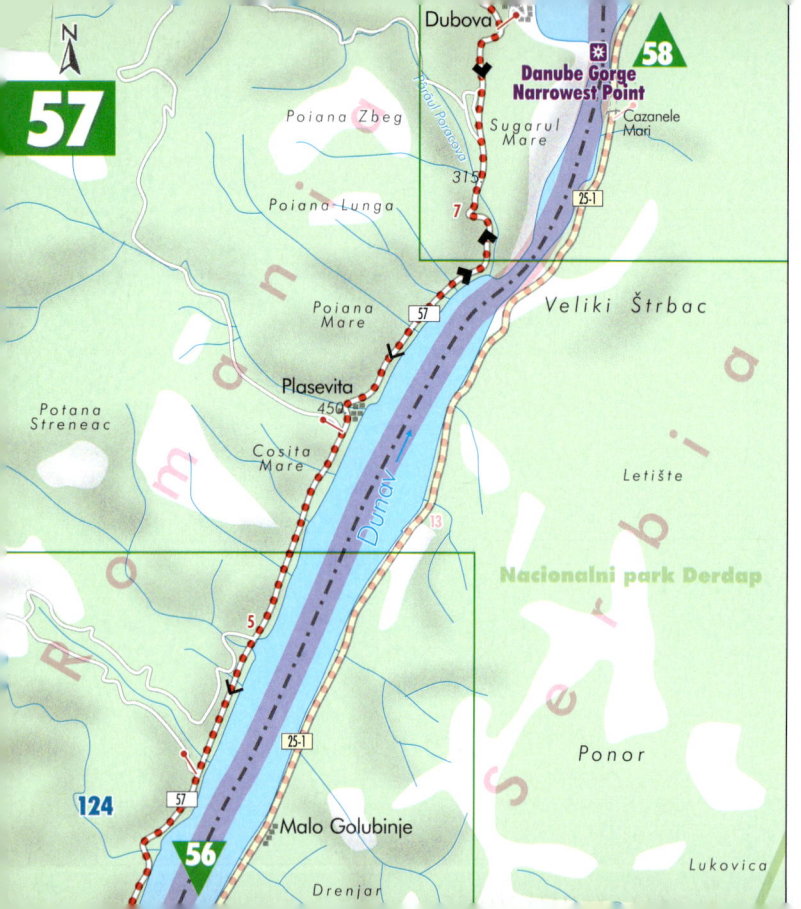

Tip: There is an inviting place for a rest here.

The road returns to the Danube ⁓ takes you to the next village, **Ogradena**.

Ogradena

The road continues through many curves and slightly downhill to **Eşelniţa**.

Eşelniţa

Outside of Eşelniţa there is a steep climb ⁓ and the road curves away from the Danube for a short distance ⁓ the road is narrow and in poor condition with many potholes and cracks ⁓ soon you must carefully negotiate an extremely steep descent (11% grade) ⁓ and then continue downhill through curves to the town of **Orşova**.

Near Orşova – with the Serbian side hidden in the morning fog

Orşova

- **Convent of St. Anna** (20th century). The convent was established after World War One in memory of the war's victims.

The small city lies near the mouth of the Cerna River on the left, or north bank, of the Danube. The old Roman city of Orşova was, like 12 other communities in the gorge, flooded when the dam at Sip was completed and the river started to rise. Orşova was an important port on the Danube before the dam was completed. This part of the river is also the location of Ada Kaleh, a small island that had been settled since ancient times and was long home to a Turkish enclave. It vanished under the water of the Danube entirely when the dam downstream was completed.

Traffic is heavier here ~ and the road is considerably wider and in much better condition ~ follow the main street through the town ~ and ride across the bridge over the Cerna River ~ at the T-intersection turn right on E70/B6 ~ ⚠ there is another steep descent and the E70 is fairly busy with traffic ~ take the national road into **Drobeta-Turnu Severin**.

Drobeta Turnu-Severin

Sip to Calafat — 152 km

Tip: Once again the following reminder: The maps showing the Romanian section, from map Nr. 60 on, of the tour are in a scale of 1:200,000.

Sip

Immediately after crossing the border from Serbia turn left on **E70/B 6** towards **Drobeta-Turnu Severin** ~ for the next few kilometers you must compete with heavy traffic before you can return to quiet country roads ~ cross railroad tracks just before **Schela Cladovei** ~ and proceed along the main road to **Drobeta** ~ the **E70** brings you straight into the city to a fork in the road.

Tip: Here you can turn right or left. The two streets come together again after a short distance and continue as the E70 through the rest of the town.

Drobeta-Turnu Severin

Postal area code: 22000; Telephone area code:

59

Drobeta-Turnu Severin

0252

ℹ **Tourist info at the Hotel Continental**, Boulevard Carol No. 2, 📞 306730

🏛 **Muzeul Porțile de Fier**, B-dul Republicii, 📞 325922, Open: Tues-Sun 9-17 o'clock. Extensive exhibits on the Danube's history, natural history, astrology and many other areas of interest. Model of Emperor Trajan's bridge and an aquarium stocked with Danube fish.

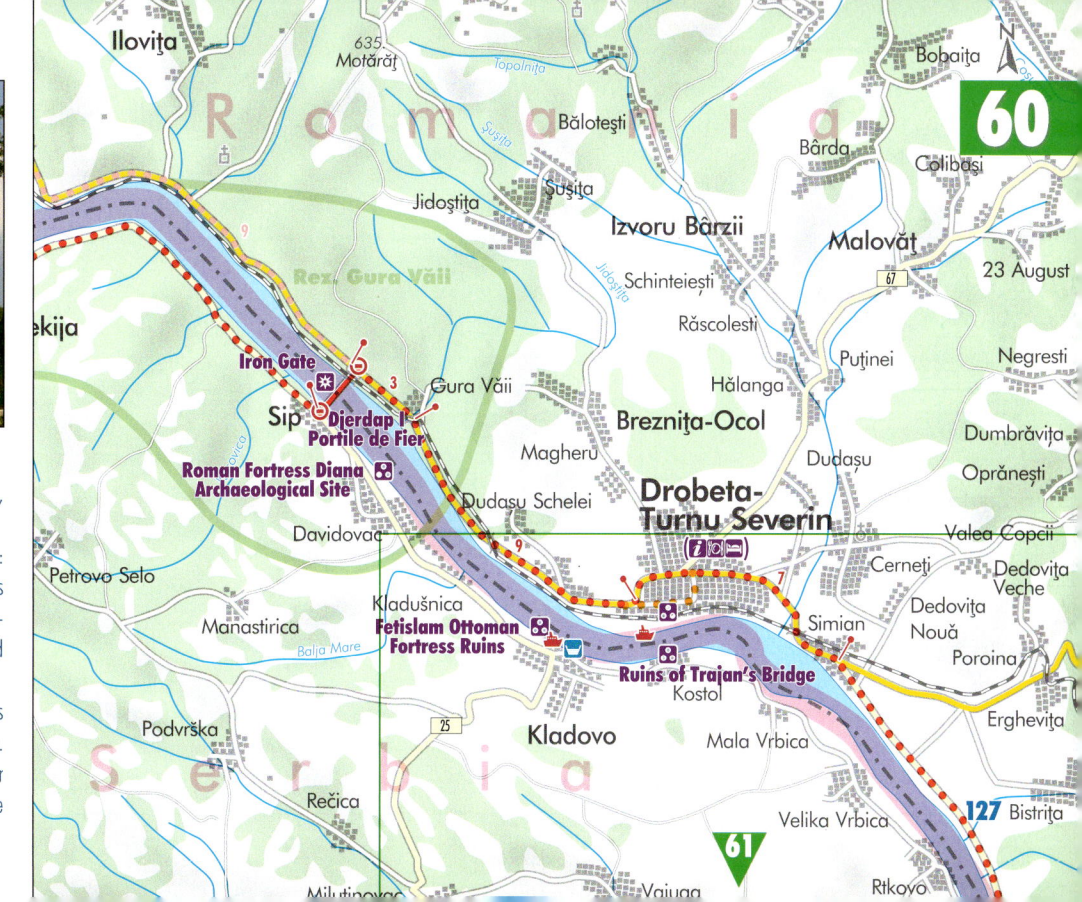

✠ **Trajan's bridge** (103). Remains of one of the longest bridges in the Roman Empire can be seen at the bridge's original site. The bridge was ordered by Emperor Trajan and built by Apollodor of Damascus, the most important architect of the time. The bridge consisted of 20 stone pillars across which a span of 19 wooden arches was constructed. Guard towers stood at each end of the bridge. It was destroyed by the Emperor Aurelian in 270 AD after Rome withdrew its troops from Dacia.

- Ruins of a 13th-16th century citadel directly on the banks of the Danube. The citadel was built on the site of Kastrum Drobeta, a Roman military camp. Today the entire area is an outdoor museum with various archaeological digs and the ruins of Trajan's Bridge.
- Severin castle (medieval)
- Roman baths and theodora
- Power station and locks Porțile de Fier I
- Water tower of Drobeta

The Romans called the city Drobotae. Its later name came from a tower built by the Emperor Septimius Severus to commemorate a military victory. Many of the names of streets and plazas in the city reflect its Roman and Dacian past.

Water tower in Drobeta-Turnu Severin

Just before Simian ride across a small river ~ then follow the railroad tracks into **Simian**.

Simian

Just before the eastern end of the town stay right at the turn-off ~ away from E70 on Route 56A towards Calafat ~ traffic is already somewhat lighter and the road has no significant climbs and a good asphalt surface that allows you to make rapid progress.

Hinova

Tip: After Hinova the next place with overnight accommodations is Calafat. Purchasing food is not a problem, however, in almost all the little villages you ride through.

At the end of Hinova turn right away from Route 56A ~ and proceed on the smaller road close to the Danube to the next village, **Ostrovu Corbului**.

Ostrovu Corbului

Follow the main street through the small village ~ then cross an arm of the Danube ~ and proceed to **Batoți**.

Batoți

At the fork in the road go right ~ and proceed to **Tismana**.

Tismana

Take the asphalt paved road out of the village ~ after about 4 kilometers the road narrows and the asphalt surface ends.

Tip: The roads are empty of traffic once you turn off Route 56A after Hinova. Occasionally you may pass a rare car or, more likely, a wagon drawn by horse or donkey. The riding is relaxed and quiet and makes it easy to enjoy the landscape.

Follow this unpaved road for the next 13 kilometers.

Vrancea

Keep going until you come to the village of **Crivina**.

Crivina

After riding through the village you come

to a curve that goes steeply uphill ~ continue to where the road is paved with asphalt again and then ride 3 kilometers into **Burila Mare**.

Burila Mare

Proceed through the town to the main intersection ~ turn right and follow the street through the town ~ and continue to Ţigănaşi.

Ţigănaşi

Keep following the road which starts to rise gently as you approach the village of **Gogoşu**.

Gogoşu

After a short distance you reach the village of **Balta Verde**.

Balta Verde

Tip: After passing through Balta Verde the condition of the road becomes dramatically worse. The road was paved with asphalt long ago but now is now so riddled with holes and cracks that you must concentrate on every meter of progress. To make things even worse, there is a climb after a few kilometers.

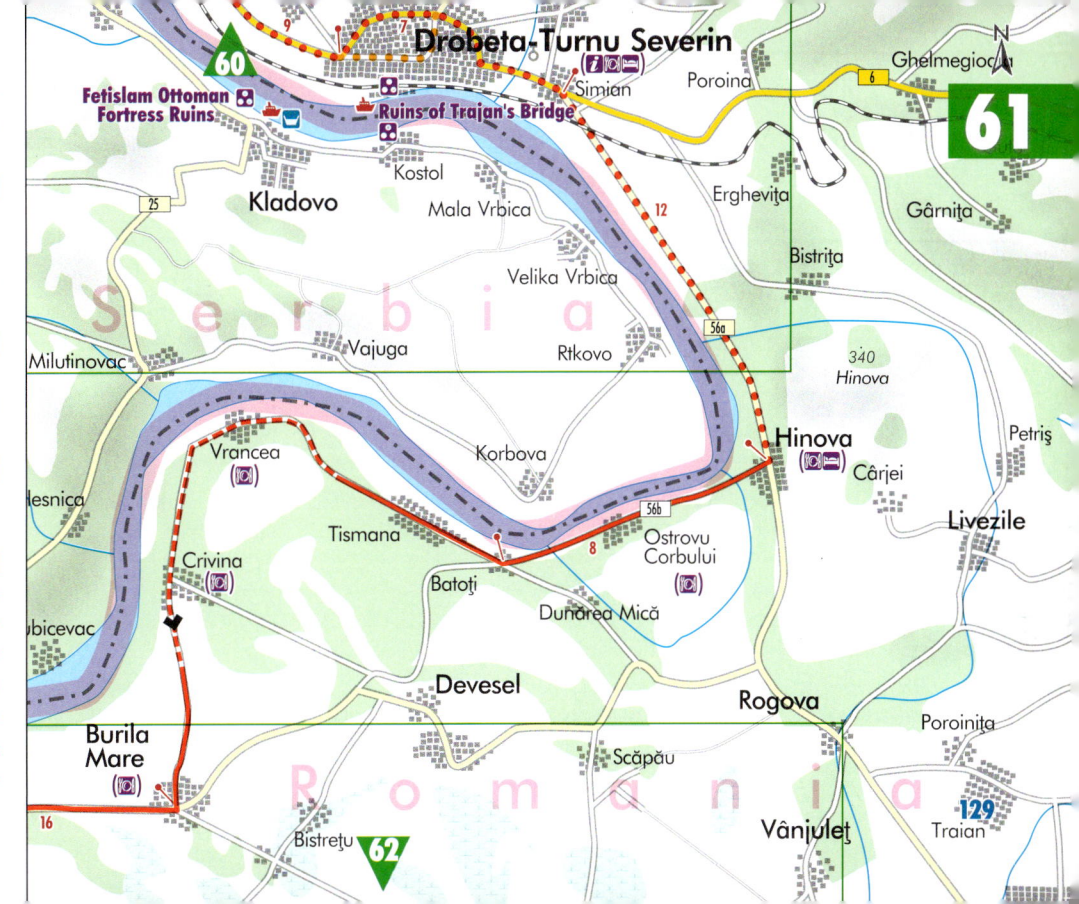

Well for drinking water near Tismana

Izvoarele
After several kilometers of rough riding you reach the village of Izvoarele where the road surface improves ~ outside of the village there is another climb before you reach **Gruia**.

Gruia
Ride past the church and out of the village ~ and to another steep climb that leads to **Gârla Mare**.

Gârla Mare
Keep going for another 8 kilometers to Vrata.

Vrata
Keep going through the peaceful countryside. The next village is named Salcia.

Salcia
About 4 kilometers after Salcia you come to a T-intersection with Route 56A ~ turn right. Traffic is somewhat heavier now ~ pass a rest area ~ after a steep climb ride into the town of **Cetate**.

Cetate
Ride past an "outdoor disco" ~ and go straight through the town of Cetate ~ the next community is **Moreni**.

Moreni
The next two villages seem to have grown together into one long cluster of houses. They are **Hunia** and **Maglavit**.

Maglavit
At the intersection in Maglavit bear to the right and continue on the larger street ~ after a short distance you come to the E70/56 national road ~ turn right on this wide and almost perfectly straight main road towards Calafat. Ride through the villages of Golenți and Basarabi on the 20 kilometer stretch to Calafat ~ follow the road towards the ferry to Vidin in Bulgaria ~ at the next intersection go straight to a second, larger intersection ~ and turn left on Route 54A.

Tip: Calafat is the last town with half-way acceptable overnight accommodations until you come to Corabia about 170 kilometers away. Even for poorly equipped rooms you must expect to pay relatively high prices.

If you do not want to camp rough or spend many hours riding across what is a fairly monotonous landscape, you may wish to consider getting on a train in Calafat for the next stage. For instance, there are trains for the route Calafat – Craiova – Corabia (about 3

Church in Gruia

hours) or Calafat – Craiova – Rosiori Nord – Turnu Magurele (about 6 hours). Several departures per day. Inquire at the ticket counter about taking your bicycle on trains.

Calafat

- **Ferry to Vidin** (Bulgaria), departures every hour
- **Muzeul de Art** (Museum of Art, Str 22 Decembrie)
- **Monument in memory of the war of independence against the Turks** 1877-78.

The city of Calafat lies directly on the Danube across from the Bulgarian city of Vidin. A bridge between the two cities is planned and may be completed in 2008. Until then, the only way to cross the river is by ferry, and the only other bridge to Bulgaria is from the city of Giurgiu many kilometers downstream. Calafat is a busy industrial city with few noteworthy sights. It was established in the 14th century by settlers from Genoa who found work in the region as "calfats" – workers who use tar to seal the gaps between the planks in the hulls of wooden ships.

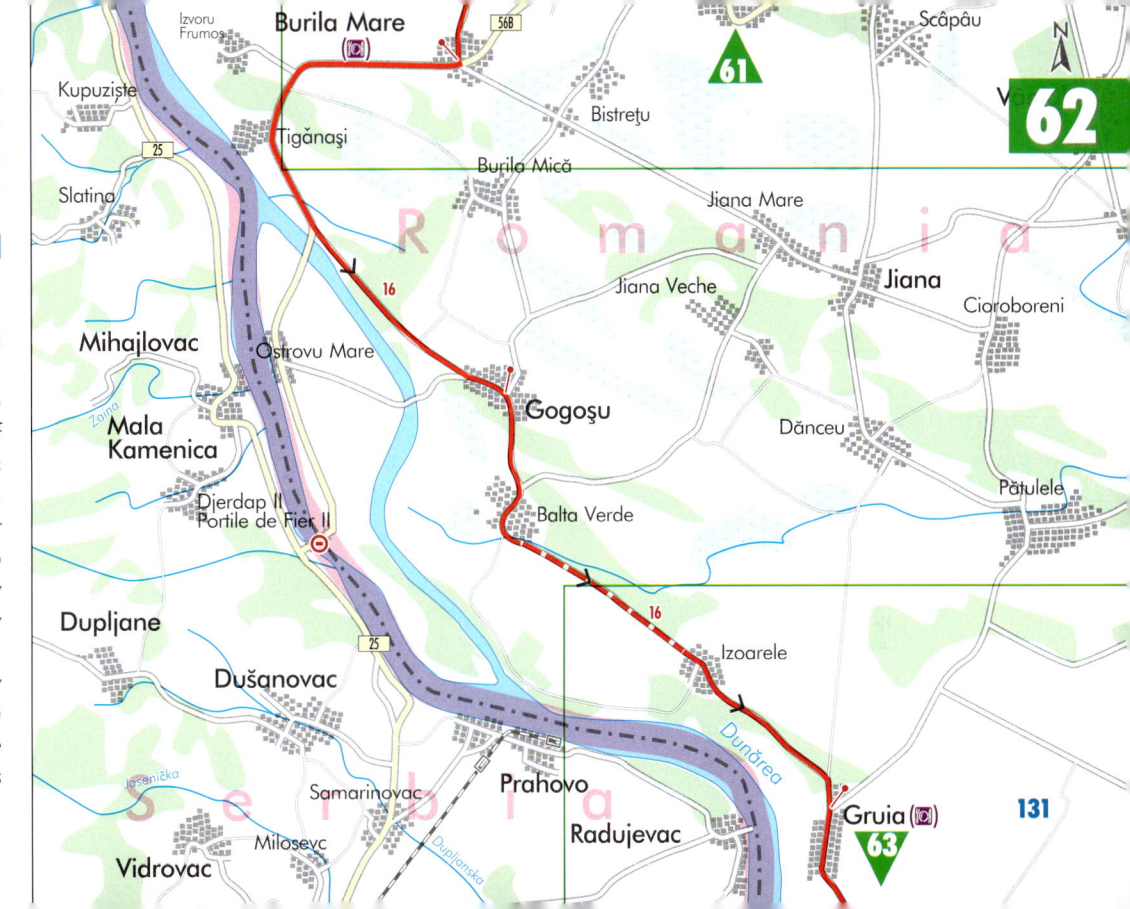

131

Calafat to Turnu Mgurele 172 km

In Calafat you must get on Route 54A ⤳ at the next junction turn left again ⤳ and after a gentle curve to the right cross railroad tracks and ride out of Calafat.

Proceed straight on Route 54A towards the next town, **Poiana Mare**.

Poiana Mare

Poiana Mare seems to merge seamlessly with the next town, **Tunarii Vechi,** and **Piscu Vechi** follows a few kilometers later.

Piscu Vechi

Southern Romania

Farmland stretches away in every direction under a vast dome of sky as you make your way down the quiet ribbon of asphalt across the flat quiet countryside of southern Romania. The villages you pass

Road between Calafat and Poiana Mare

through all look cast from the same mold, but they are alive with the smells and sounds of rural life, with inhabitants tending their vegetable plots, herding their animals, working or playing in the streets and yards around their homes and businesses.

For transport many people still use horse-drawn wagons. What they carry depends in part on the time of year. As you overtake a wagon loaded with straw or hay and an entire family, including the household dog, waving at you cheerfully you might feel as if you have been transported back to the 19th century.

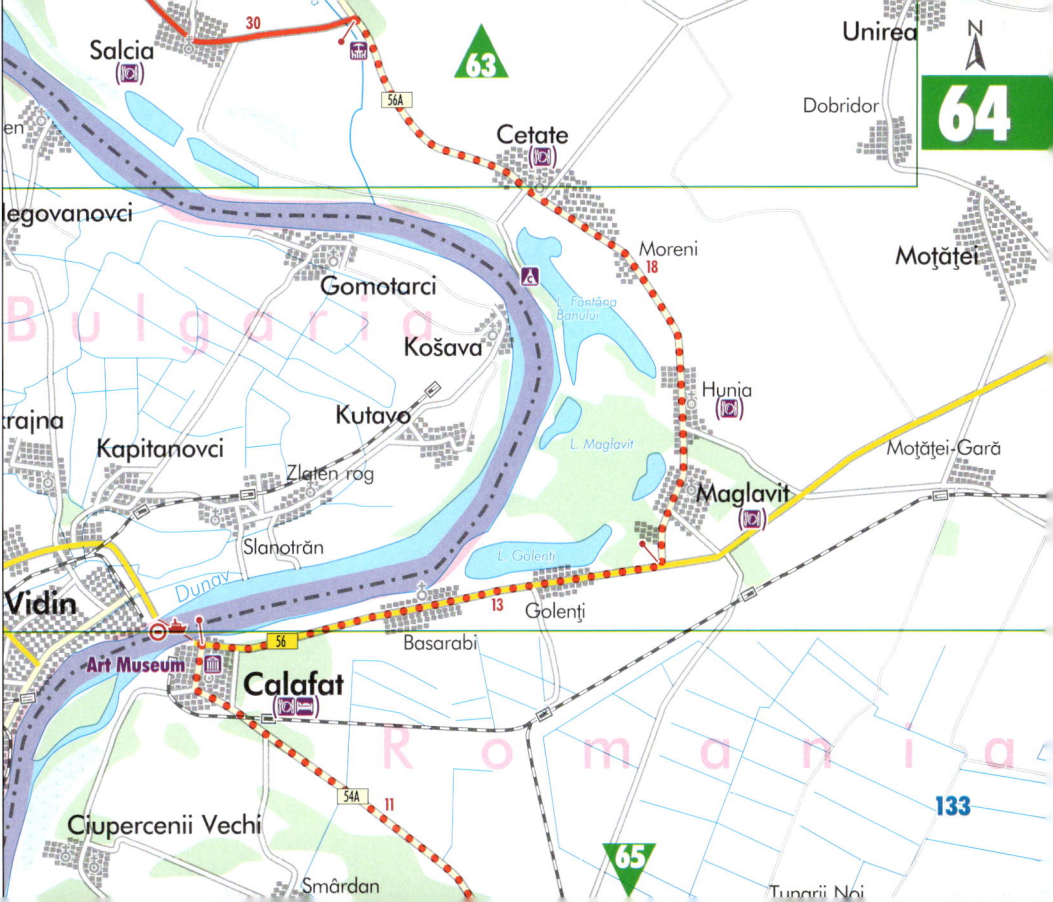

You will also pass groups of Romani, traveling in small convoys of covered wagons loaded with everything they own and need: pots and pans, pillows and quilts, tables and chairs. Sometimes they will be camped on clearings or near rivers, with children and dogs running around happily and smoke rising from a fire where food is being kept warm. It all looks peaceful and enviably simple – a kind of freedom that you may almost find yourself wishing you could share until you remember that these people also live in their wagons through Romania's cold winters.

Between villages the view down the endless-seeming road in front of you may be interrupted by the occasional flock of geese or a herd of sheep being driven down the road by the shepherd and his dog. Most of the herders spend their entire summers living with their livestock, sleeping in simple huts improvised from whatever was at hand. They live a simple life we can no longer imagine, without radio or television, newspaper, computer, internet or even a mobile telephone.

The villages pass slowly by, one after the other, with their little kiosks where you can buy water or food or take a break in the shade of a tree among the people going about their routines as they have for decades, if not centuries.

Keep riding through **Ghidici**, **Rast**, **Negoi**, **Catane**, **Bistreţu Nou**, **Bistreţ**.

After the last town a large lake, **Lacul Bistreţ**, appears on the right and stretches along the road until you come to Cârna. Ride through the villages of **Plosca**, **Cârna**, **Sapata**, **Maceşu de Jos**, **Nedeiha** and **Gighera**.

Gighera

After leaving the village the road starts to climb towards the next village, **Zaval**.

Zaval

 Outdoor pool

Tip: In Zaval there is also a swimming place along the Jiu River.

Time for a picnic...

Proceed to the bridge over the small river and continue to the next junction, where you turn right towards **Ostroveni**.

Ostroveni

Follow the main street through the town at the edge of the next town, Bechet, Route B55 goes off to the left towards Craiova.

Bechet

In the middle of the town there is an intersection with a road that goes 4 kilometers south to the ferry to Orjahovo in Bulgaria and to the harbor.

Tip: If you wish to take another look at the Danube, turn right at this road.

After Bechet the road becomes Route 54A and there is a little more traffic. But aside from a few more vehicles on the road, little else changes as you ride across the countryside through the communities of **Calaraşi**,

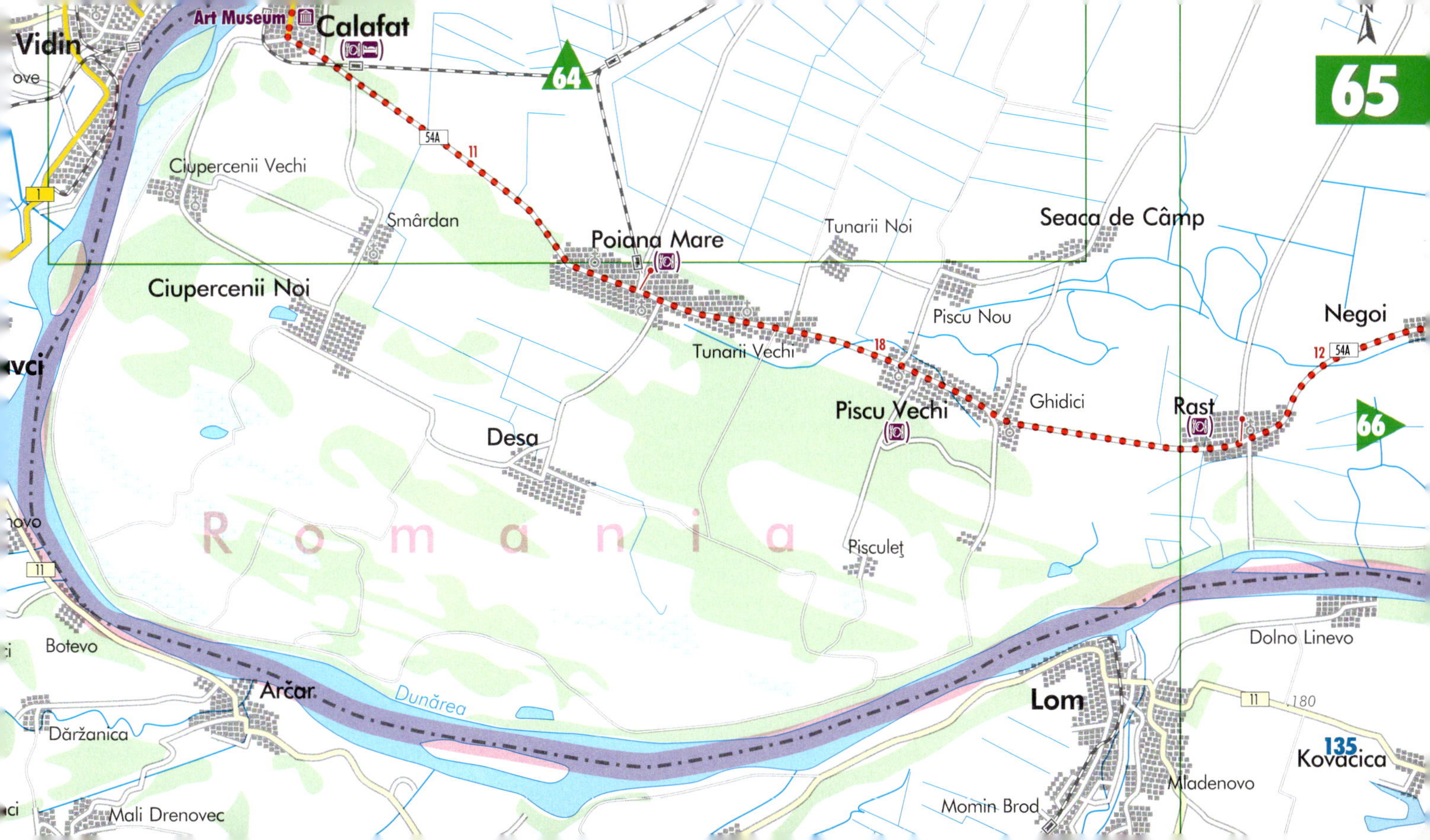

Art Museum
Calafat
Vidin
64
65
54A
11
Ciupercenii Vechi
Smârdan
Poiana Mare
Tunarii Noi
Seaca de Câmp
Ciupercenii Noi
Piscu Nou
Negoi
18
Tunarii Vechi
12
54A
Ghidici
Rast
Piscu Vechi
66
Desa
Romania
Pisculeţ
Botevo
Arčar
Dunărea
Dăržanica
Mali Drenovec
Lom
Dolno Linevo
11
180
135
Kovacica
Mladenovo
Momin Brod

Dabuleni, Grojdibodu, Gura, Padinii and Orlea.

Life of the Romani

Romania has a large population of Romani, the name given to various ethnic groups of semi-nomadic peoples that include the Sinti, Roma, Lovari, Kalderash, Lalleri, Manush and others. They are also often called gypsies in English, or similar words like gitanos, which stem from the mistaken belief that the Romani originally came from Egypt. Today the term gypsy is usually considered derogatory. Another mistaken belief is that most Romani still live as nomads, constantly on the move in caravans or wagons. In fact, the vast majority today live in permanent housing.

Linguistic and genetic evidence shows the Romani came from India. They can be divided into three main groups:

The Calé, or Gitanos, live in southern France, Spain and Portugal. The Roma live mostly in the Balkan countries and in Hungary. Some of them also emigrated to central

Bei Cârna – Lacul Bistreț

Europe and North America. The ancestors of the Sinti have been living in central Europe and Germany since the middle ages.

Roma and Sinti are related ethnic groups, but have distinct cultural and linguistic traditions.

Their language, Romani, is spoken but not written, and is divided into various dialects. They have an oral tradition of laws that cover both civil and criminal codes and are administered by respected members of their communities. Violations of these codes may even be punished by banishment from the group. The Romani do not have an own religion.

The earliest known written references to Romani date to the year 1407. In the Holy Roman Empire they were seen as pilgrims and were allowed to travel under the protection of the emperor, living from alms collected from the general population. But they were also persecuted. In the middle of the 15th century some were driven from cities and even, at the end of that century, outlawed.

Their unusual appearance, unfamiliar lifestyle and lack of ties to the land often fostered suspicion among many of the peoples the Romani lived among. They have been accused of crimes ranging from thievery to black magic to stealing children, and have suffered rejection and persecution as a result. In many European countries the Romani still suffer a quiet discrimination even today.

Romani should not be confused with the Yeniche, who live mainly in Germany, Austria and Switzerland. Their origin has not been adequately explained, but parts of the Yeniche language suggest ancient ties to Europe. Some Yeniche claim to be descended from the Celtic

66
65
67
Romania
Afumaţi
Baboia
Balasan
Curmătura
Covei
Bârca
Catanele Noi
Catane
Negoi
Goicea
Brânduşa
Mâceşu de Sus
54A
Bistreţu Nou
Bistreţ
Plosca
Cârna
Sâpata
Mâceşu de Jos
Lacul Bisteul
Dunav
Ostr. Gâtanului
Nedeia
Gighera
Dolno Linevo
Stanevo
Kovačica
Dolni Cibăr
Gorni Cibăr
ovo
11
12
16
20
50
35
30
60
25
55
180

tribes that thrived across much of Europe during the Iron Age. Yeniche are sometimes refered to as "white gypsies" because of their lighter skin and the red hair many have.

Corabia
- Ferry to Zagražden in Bulgaria
- Ruins of the Roman castra Cetatii Sucidava
- Archaeological Museum with large collection of Roman pottery
- Orthodox Church of the Holy Trinity. One of the largest cathedrals of this kind in Romania.
- Monument on the main square, in memory of the Romanian war of independence.

The name Corabia, which means sailing ship or galley in Romanian, refers to the settlement of the community by the survivors of a Genoese ship that wrecked here. At the end of the 19th century Corabia developed into a significant inland harbor.

The communist regime tried to develop Corabia as an industrial center, building factories for furniture making, sugar production and leather tanning. Today many of these factories have closed and the city's population has declined as people moved away to find work.

Tip: Corabia has a harbor with a ferry to the Bulgarian city Zagražden.

Take the main road, which is lined with tall old trees, out of Corabia and proceed for about 30 kilometers through the villages and towns. Most of the traffic on this road consists of horse-drawn wagons and herds of livestock and fowl. The next villages are **Garcov** and **Islaz**.

About 4 kilometers after Islaz you cross the **Olt River** and then the **Saiu** before riding into **Turnu Măgurele**.

Turnu Măgurele
Telephone area code: 040
- Ferry to Nikopol
- Catedrala Sfantul Haralambie
- Muzeul Turnu Măgurele
- Ruins of a Roman bridge across the Danube. The bridge was built by the Emperor Constantine the Great in the year 330 AD.

Turnu Măgurele lies near the mouth of the Olt River and the Danube across from the Bulgarian city of Nikopol. The name means "mountain tower" and refers to a defensive tower from the 6th century. It was part of a fortification built by the Byzantine ruler Justinian.

Tip: The first larger city since Calafat. There are good stores where you can buy supplies, a nicely tended park and a number of attractive buildings, including the church, which can be viewed.

Turnu Măgurele to Giurgiu — 113 km

The harbor and the ferry to Nikopol are about 4 kilometers south of the city center.

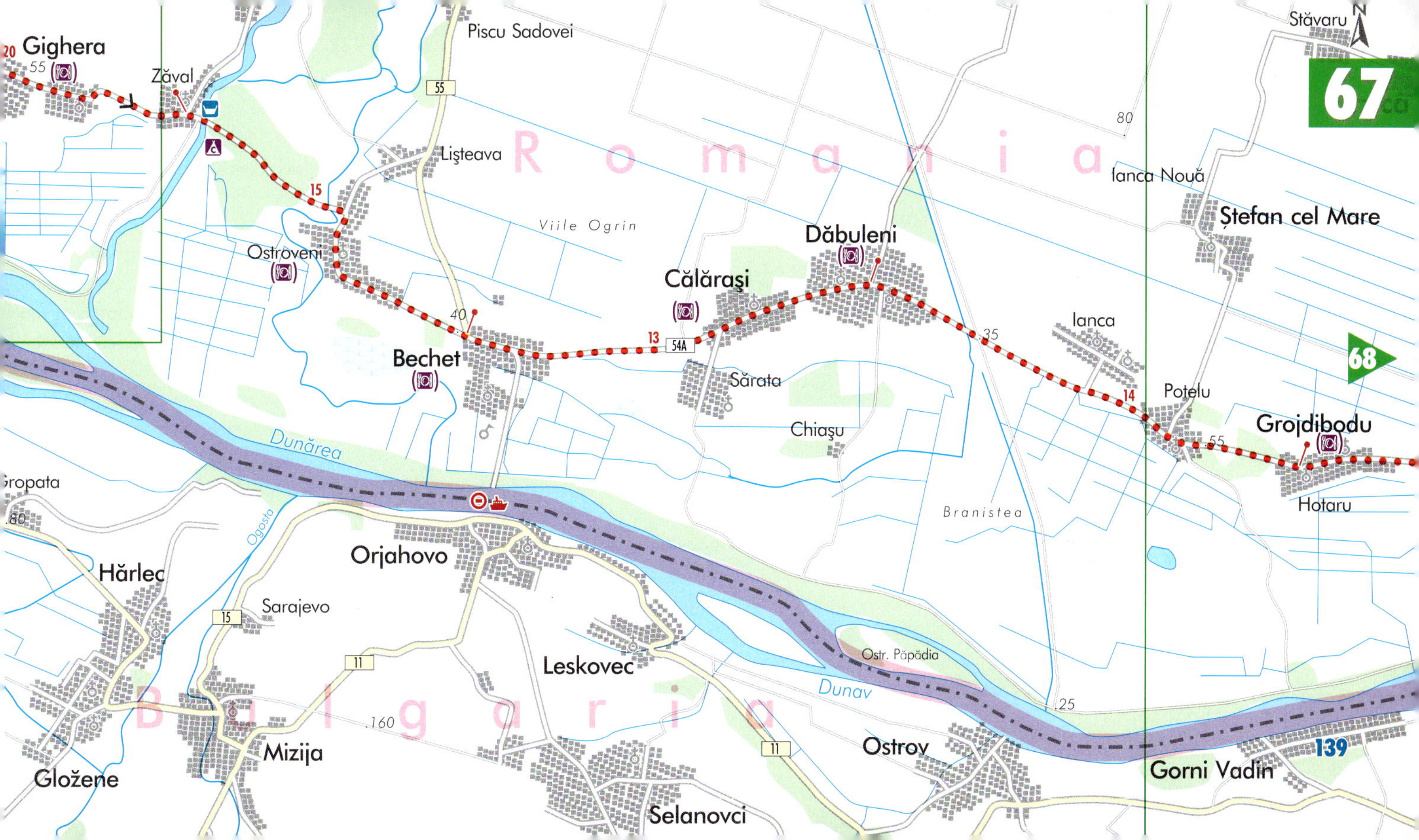

67
68
139
Gighera
Zăval
Piscu Sadovei
Stăvaru
Lişteava
Romania
Viile Ogrin
Ostroveni
Bechet
Călăraşi
Dăbuleni
Ianca Nouă
Ştefan cel Mare
Ianca
Sărata
Chiaşu
Potelu
Grojdibodu
Hotaru
Branistea
Dunărea
Gropata
Ogosta
Orjahovo
Hărlec
Sarajevo
Leskovec
Ostr. Păpădia
Dunav
Bulgaria
Mizija
Gloženе
Selanovci
Ostrov
Gorni Vadin
55
54A
15
11

Take the main street through Turnu Măgurele ~ pass the church with the "twisted" towers on the right and then turn left on **Route 65A** towards **Pitești** at the next junction go straight towards Giurgiu via the towns of **Ciuperceni, Traian, Seaca, Navodari, Vânatori**.

In Vânatori the road turns towards the north and you ride around Lakul Suhaia ~ and finally ride into the village of **Lisa**.

Lisa

In Lisa, cross the **Calmatui River** several times ~ in the village turn right at the intersection ~ after 2 kilometers, as you enter Piatra, turn right towards **Viișoara** ~ and proceed towards the south again through **Viișoara, Suhaia, Fântânele**.

About one kilometer before the next town cross railroad tracks ~ just before the edge of **Zimnicea** cross the railroad tracks again

Turnu Magurele

~ and then turn left at the main 4-way intersection in Zimnicea.

Zimnicea
🚢 **Ferry to Svištov** in Bulgaria

The remains of fortifications dating to the 4th century to first century BC have been found near Zimnicea. Archaeologists believe the complex was built to protect the area from Lysimachos, a general who served under Alexander the Great and was sent to Dacia as governor.

The earliest known records about the city date to the year 1385, in reports by Christian pilgrims returning to Europe from Jerusalem. Zimnicea became an important station on the trading route between central Europe and the Balkans.

During the Romanian war of independence (1877-78) it was the headquarters for Russian troops that helped the Bulgarians in their war against the Turks.

In 1977 the city was almost completely destroyed by an earthquake. Decades later there are still many buildings that have been only partly restored or where repairs were never completed. Some parts of Zimnicea look like a ghost town.

After the fall of the Ceaușescu regime in 1989, the city's industrial base started to collapse and the population started to shrink. The city government now hopes to revive the flagging economy with tax incentives.

Proceed straight ~ and then through a long S-curve as you leave the town ~ at the edge of town cross the railroad tracks again and continue towards **Zimnicele** and **Bujoru**.

About 3 kilometers after Bujoru the road starts to climb ~ the climb is followed by a 4% descent into **Pietroșani**.

Pietroșani

After Pietroșani continue through the villages of **Pietrișu, Gaujani, Cetatuia, Vedea**.

After Vedea the road's designation changes to Route **5C** ~ a short distance later you ride into Malu.

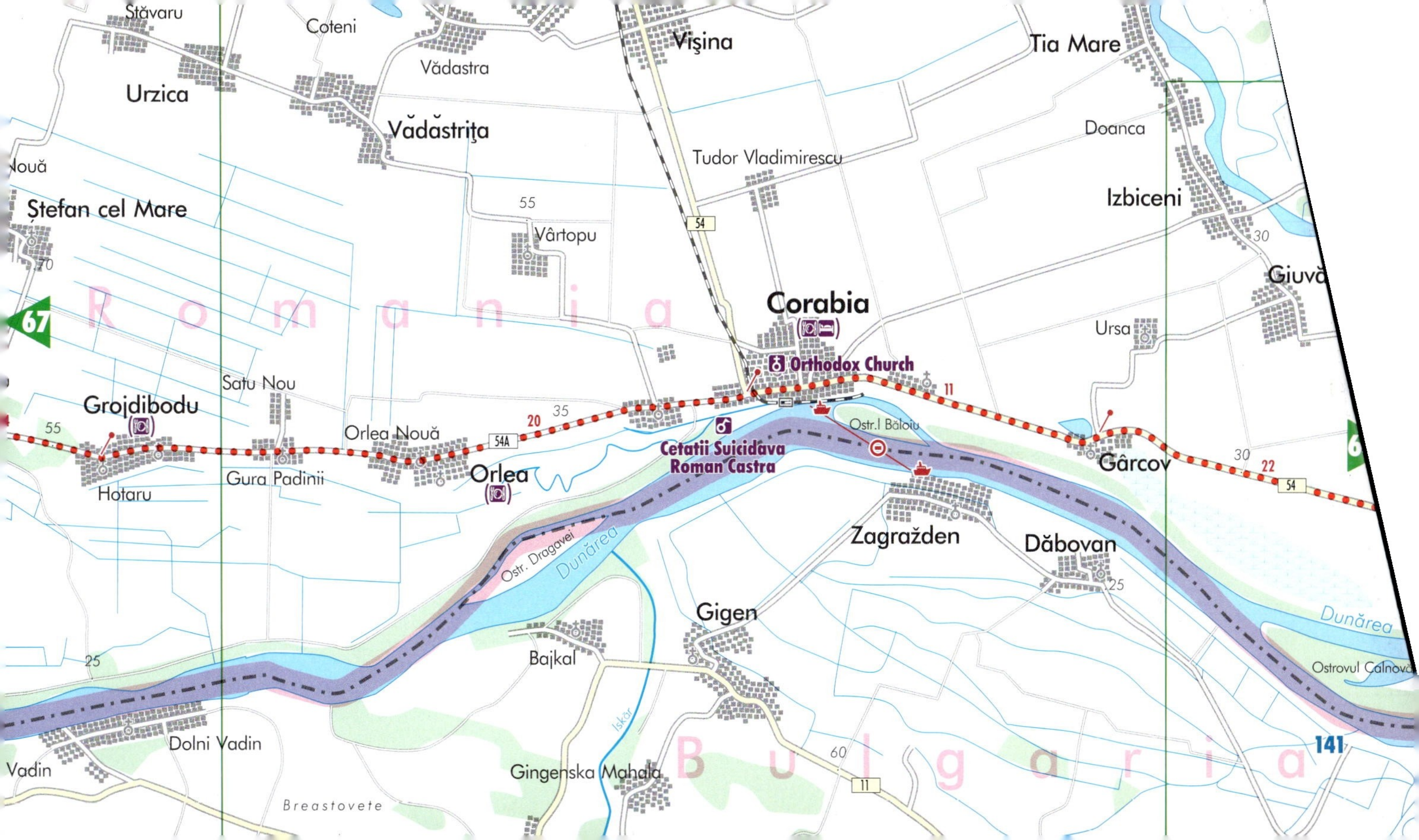
Stăvaru
Coteni
Vădastra
Vişina
Tia Mare
Urzica
Vădastriţa
Doanca
Tudor Vladimirescu
Nouă
Izbiceni
Ştefan cel Mare
55
54
Vârtopu
30
70
Giuvă
Corabia
67
R o m a n i a
Ursa
Orthodox Church
Satu Nou
11
Grojdibodu
35
20
Ostr.l Băloiu
55
Orlea Nouă
54A
Cetatii Suicidava
Roman Castra
30
Gârcov
22
54
Orlea
Gura Padinii
Hotaru
Zagraždan
Dăbovan
Ostr. Dragavei
Dunărea
25
Gigen
Dunărea
Bajkal
25
Ostrovul Calnovăț
Dolni Vadin
Vadin
Iskăr
60
Gingenska Mahala
B u l g a r i a
11
Breastovete

68 to **Slobozia**
a rest area on
of the road.

...d leads you into

..y to **Ruse** in Bulgaria
...etatii lui Mircea cel Batran (ruin)
Double-level bridge to Ruse in Bulgaria

The only bridge across the Danube with a border crossing between Romania and Bulgaria stands between the cities of Giurgiu and Ruse. The 4,000 meters long bridge is one of the longest spans in Europe, and is named the "bridge of friendship." For many years this was a bit of a misnomer, because no one was allowed to use the bridge.

From the 16th century to 1829 Giurgiu was a harbor town under Turkish control. In the 20th century it emerged as an important loading station for petroleum, making it a target for bombing raids that caused heavy damage and casualties during World War Two. In 1941 Axis forces build the longest pontoon bridge in military history to cross the Danube into Bulgaria.

More recently, Romania and Bulgaria agreed to build a third bridge between the two countries. The span near Silistra is to be funded in part by the European Union.

Public park in Turnu Magurele

Giurgiu to Călărași — 149 km

Follow **Bulevardul 1907** towards the center ~ the Bulevard goes through a curve to the right and becomes **Mircen cel Batran** ~ which you take to the large plaza with the clock tower ~ go straight across the plaza to **București** street ~ which takes you out of the city ~ follow Route **E70 (or E85)** towards București (Bucharest) out of the city ~ after a short distance pass through **Remuş**.

Remuş
Follow the main road straight through the village ~ to the next village, **Daia**.

Daia
After Daia there is a railroad crossing ~ after the road curves to the left it becomes a motorway ~ at the fork just after the curve go to the right onto the smaller country road ~ and proceed uphill on the curving road towards **Plopşoru**.

Plopşoru
In the village the road starts to descend again ~ and continues downhill through curves to the next larger town, **Baneasa**.

Tip: The landscape changes significantly as you head east from Giurgiu. The countryside is hillier and you ride mainly through vineyards.

The next villages you pass through are named **Pietrele**, **Prundu**, **Greaca**.

Between **Greaca** and **Căscioarele** the road is straight as an arrow as it crosses several gentle hills and many vineyards ~ past a small

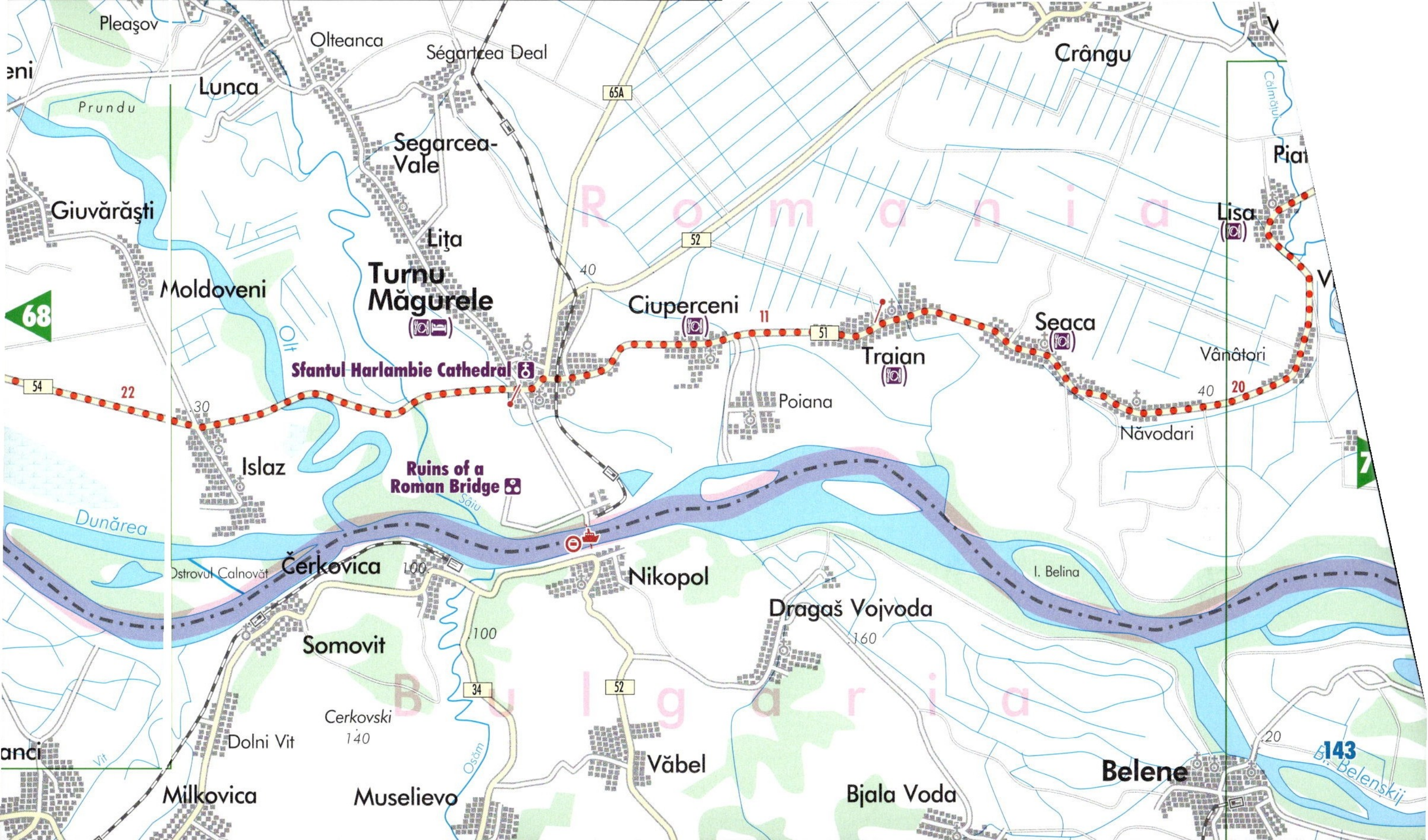
Pleaşov
Olteanca
Ségartcea Deal
Crângu
Lunca
Prundu
65A
Segarcea-Vale
Giuvărăşti
Liţa
Turnu Măgurele
Moldoveni
Olt
52
40
Romania
Lisa
Ciuperceni
11
51
Seaca
Traian
Vânâtori
68
Sfantul Harlambie Cathedral
54
22
30
Poiana
40
20
Năvodari
Islaz
Ruins of a Roman Bridge
Sâiu
Dunărea
Ostrovul Calnovăt
Čerkovica
100
Nikopol
I. Belina
Dragaš Vojvoda
160
Somovit
100
34
52
Bulgaria
Cerkovski
140
Dolni Vit
Vit
Osăm
Văbel
20
Belene
Br. Belenskij
Milkovica
Muselievo
Bjala Voda

69

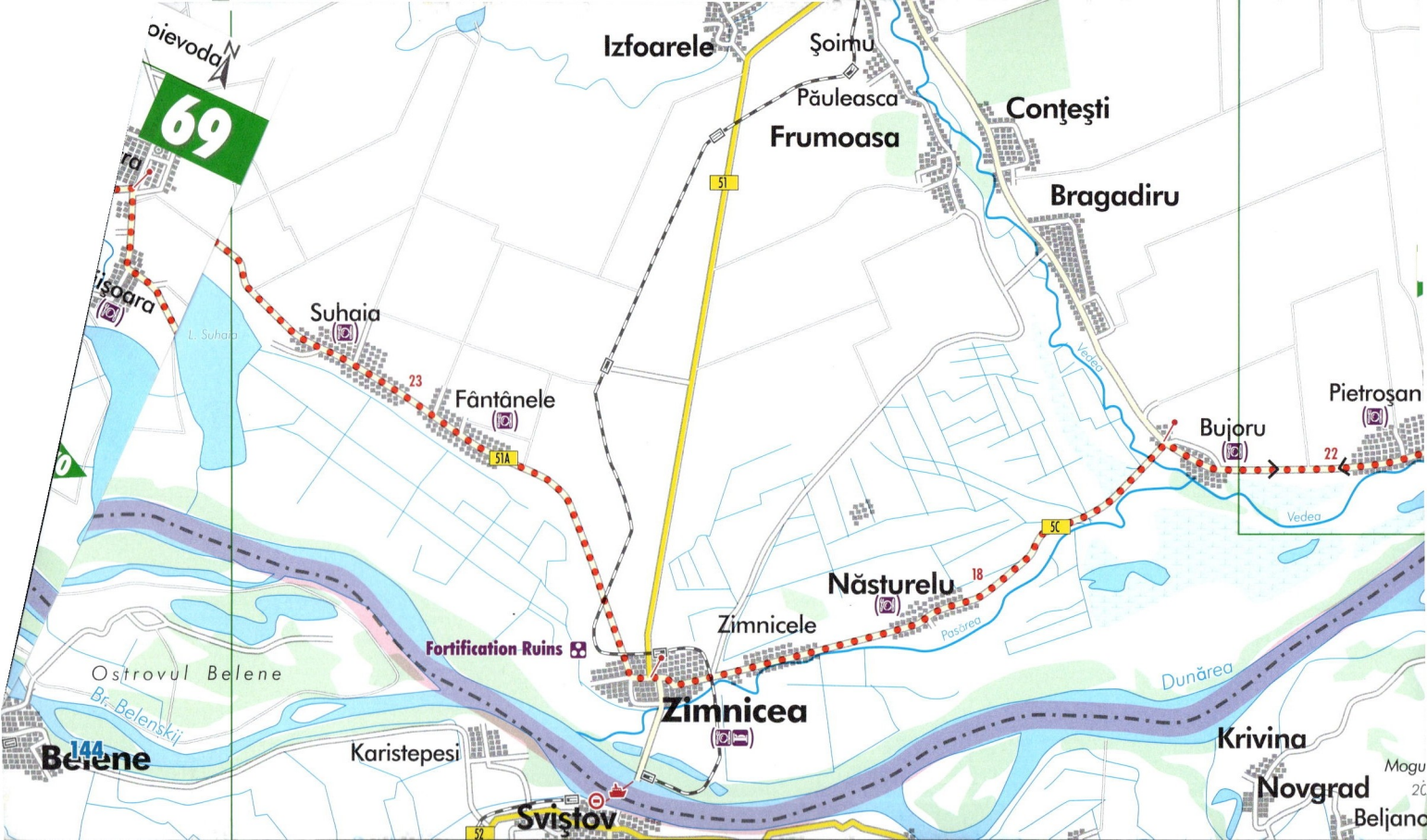

- Izfoarele
- Şoimu
- Păuleasca
- Frumoasa
- Conţeşti
- Bragadiru
- Suhaia
- L. Suhaia
- Fântânele
- Pietroşan
- Bujoru
- Vedea
- Năsturelu
- Zimnicele
- Pasărea
- Fortification Ruins
- Ostrovul Belene
- Br. Belenski
- Dunărea
- Belene
- Karistepesi
- Zimnicea
- Krivina
- Novgrad
- Beljana
- Sviştov

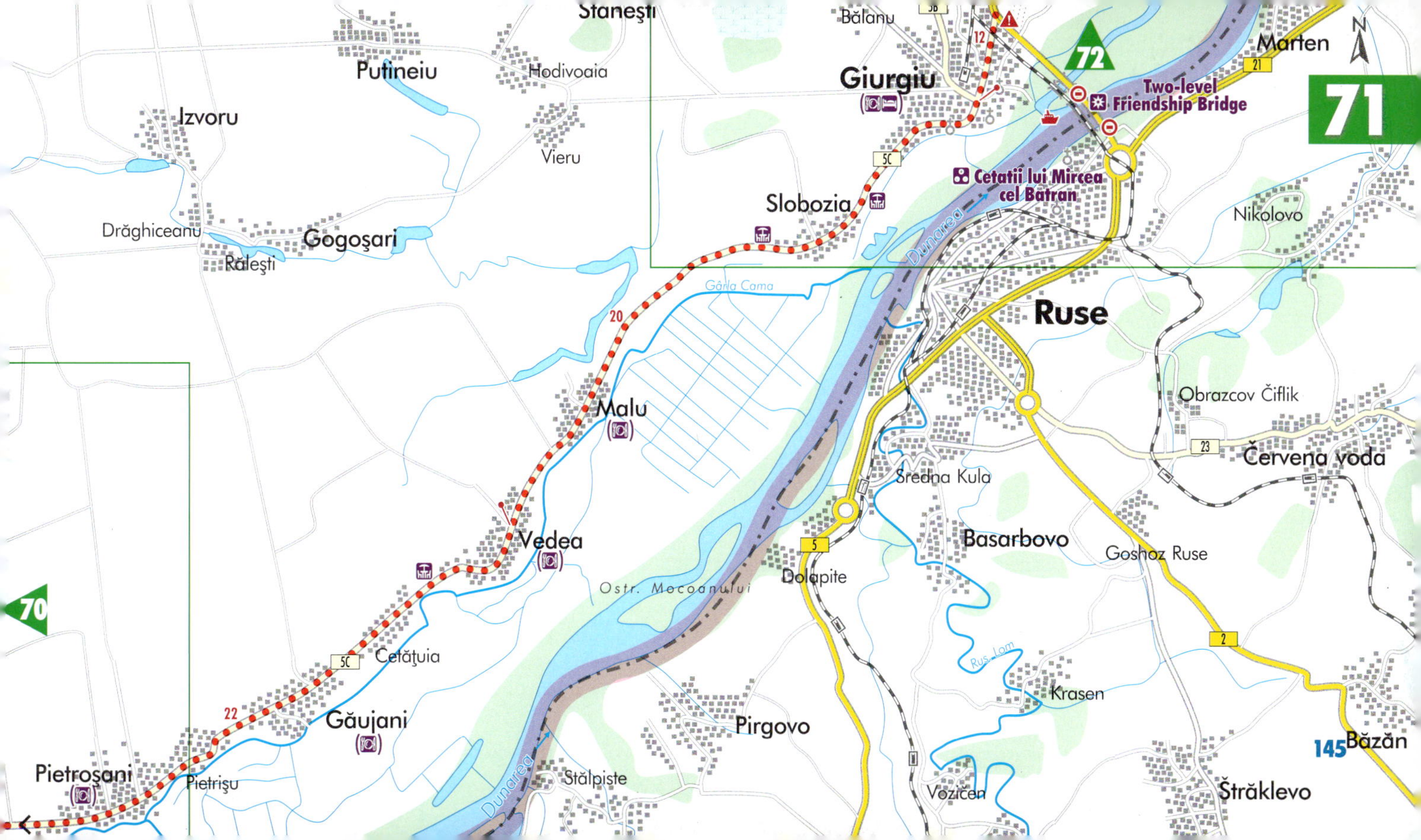

Stanesti
Bălanu
Marten
72
71
Putineiu
Hodivoaia
Giurgiu
Two-level Friendship Bridge
Izvoru
Vieru
5C
Cetatii lui Mircea cel Batran
Slobozia
Nikolovo
Drăghiceanu
Gogoşari
Răleşti
Dunarea
Gârla Cama
20
Ruse
Malu
Obrazcov Čiflik
23
Červena voda
Sredna Kula
Vedea
Basarbovo
5
Goshoz Ruse
Ostr. Mocoanului
Dolapite
70
2
5C
Cetățuia
Rus. Lom
22
Krasen
Găujani
Pirgovo
Băzăn
Pietroşani
Pietrişu
Stălpiste
Dunarea
Vozičen
Štrăklevo

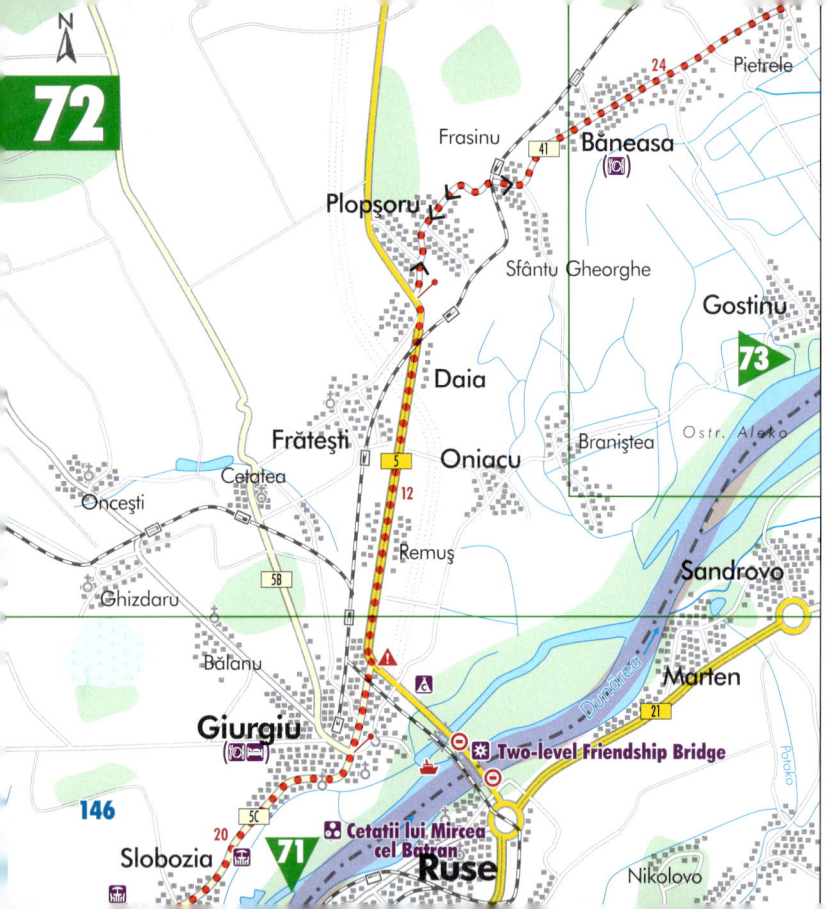

pond on the right side ⤳ the road becomes somewhat hillier near **Căscioarele**.

Căscioarele

After the town the road goes downhill again ⤳ and over a small bridge ⤳ then back uphill and through several curves ⤳ to the next town, **Chirnogi**.

Chirnogi

Simply follow the main road through the town and proceed to **Oltenița**.

Oltenița

🛥 **Ferry to Tutrakan** in Bulgaria

In Oltenița you ride across a large bridge over the Arges River ⤳ on the left side there is an open air pool ⤳ proceed straight ahead to the next larger intersection ⤳ go straight ⤳ at the next smaller intersection keep going straight ⤳ turn left at the intersection with the stop sign ⤳ to the right there is a railroad crossing ⤳ follow the road ⤳ which brings you to the main road ⤳ where you can see signs pointing towards Călărași to the right. The next village is **Ulmeni**.

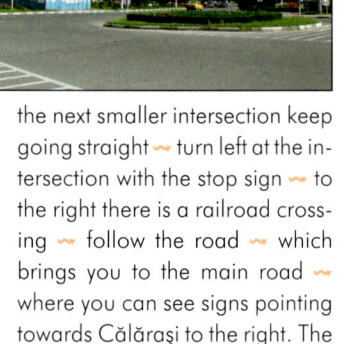

Ulmeni

Keep following the road towards **Cetatea Veche**. Villages and hamlets follow in quick succession: **Spanțov**, **Stancea**,

Chiselet and Mânăstirea.
Mânăstirea
🏛 Museum Al. Sahia

The next towns are named **Dorobanțu**, **Varasti**, **Ciocănești**, **Bogata**, **Rasa**, **Cunești**, **Grădiștea**.

Follow Route 31 to until you reach the big confusing-looking intersection with Route 3 ~ turn right toward Călărași (there are signs) ~ the traffic is somewhat heavier now ~ ride straight towards Călărași. It is an industrial city, with many tall chimneys and large factory complexes visible.

Just before entering the city you pass a

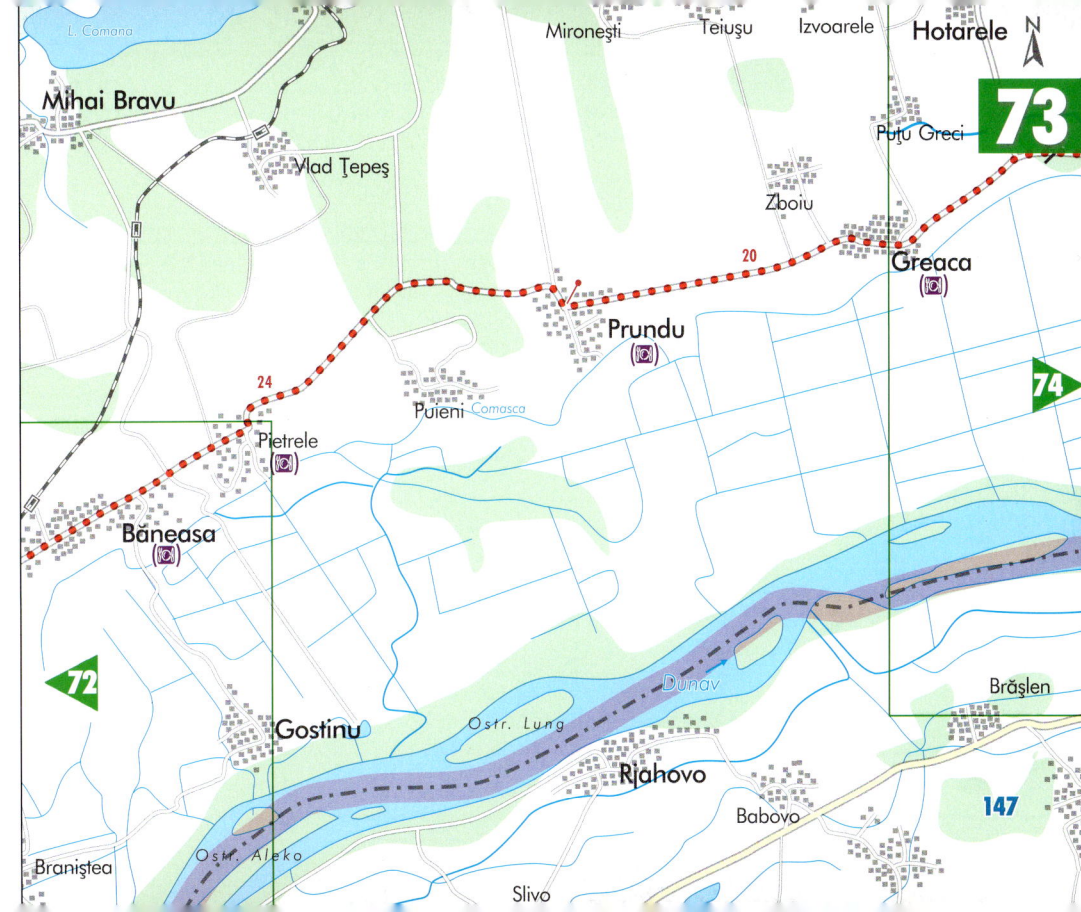

On the ferry in Călărași

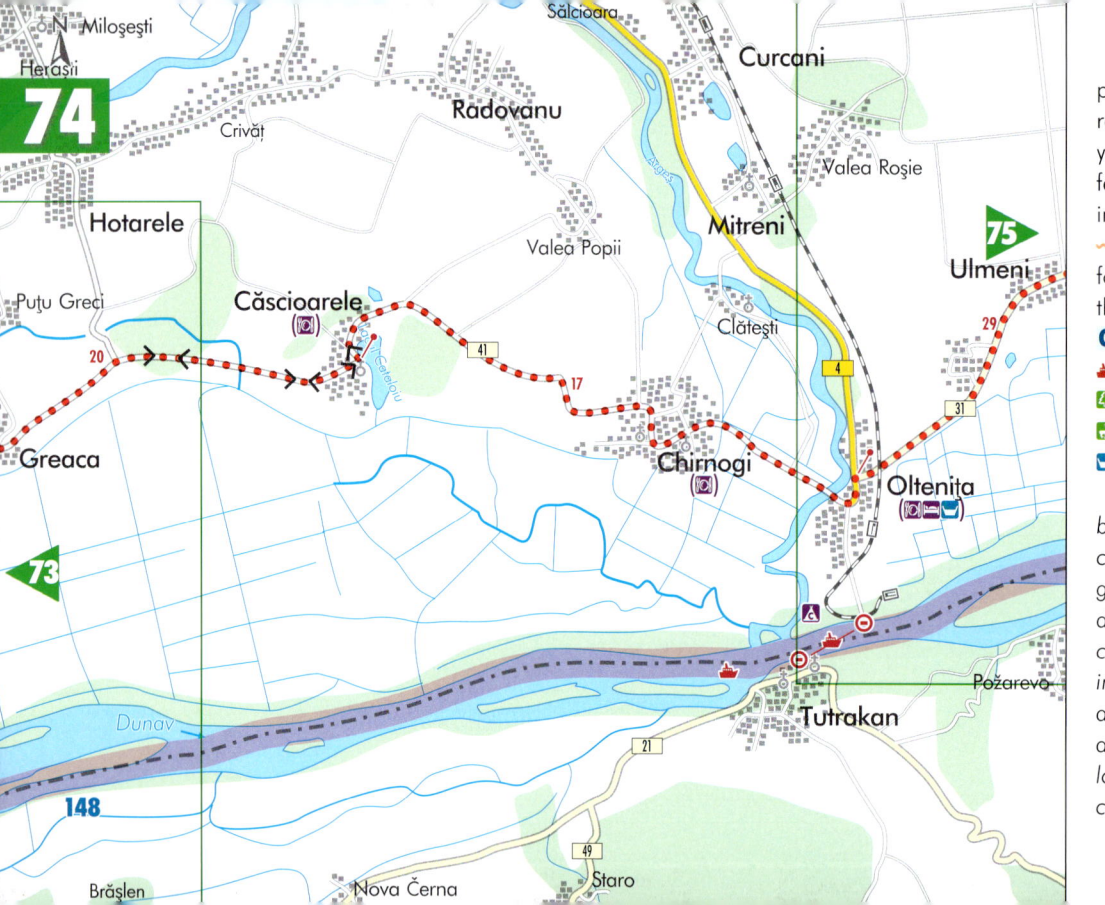

petrol station on the left side ～ the national road Route 3 bypasses Călăraşi and brings you down to the Danube where there is a ferry station for a ferry to Ostrov or Silistra in Bulgaria. Keep going to the next junction ～ where you stay to the left. There is a sign for Constanţa. Keep going until you reach the ferry landing in Călăraşi.

Călăraşi

- Ferry to Ostrov or Silistra in Bulgaria
- Botanical garden
- Zoo
- Beaches on the Bratul Borcea (an arm of the Danube)

Even from a distance Călăraşi can easily be recognized as an industrial city. Like the capital Bucharest, during the Ceauşescu regime much of Călăraşi's old center was torn down and replaced by a planned modern city. The result, with expansive neglected industrial areas and big concrete-slab apartment blocks, is not attractive. Only a handful of buildings worth taking a look at remain. They include several old churches, the city hall, the prefecture and the architecturally-interesting modern palace of culture.

Călăraşi to Constanţa — 134 km

After getting off the ferry follow Route 3 towards Constanţa. The road runs directly next to the border between Romania and Bulgaria. The city of Silistra is divided, with the right side of the road in Bulgaria and the left side in Romania.

Tip: This section of the route offers many climbs and descents that help make the ride more varied and interesting. It also passes the ruins of many old fortification, which help make the ride to Constanţa especially interesting.

Ostrov

Tip: The road through Ostrov has a cobblestone surface.

After Ostrov the road lies close to the Danube and you ride through beautiful flood-plains.

Just before Galiţa you pass Dervent Monastery and a lake on the right.

Dervent Monastery

Dervent Monastery. The monastery church has three altars. They are dedicated to "The God-fearing Paraschiva", "The healing spring" and "St. George". The interior features beautiful wall and ceiling decorations. The entrance portal, which also functions as bell-tower, is an architectural masterpiece. People traveling alone can spend the night here.

The name "Dervent" means roughly "beyond the creek". The monastery was built near the former fortress Dervent. A monk named Elefterie Mihai collected money from the surrounding towns and villages between 1929 and 1936 to fund construction of the monastery. In 1959 the monks living there were evicted by the communist regime and the property was taken over by the management of the local farming cooperative. The monastery served as village church. In 1990 the monks returned and restored the property to its original use. Today about 17 monks live and work there.

The monastery is often visited by sick people looking for cures, especially on September 14, the "day of the holy cross".

Silistra, Bulgaria, seen from the ferry from Călărași to Ostrov

Tip: There are often many begging children at the monastery. Keep a close eye on your possessions.

Galița

Tip: The route now veers away from the Danube and heads across southern Romania towards Constanța and the Black Sea coast. You will not see the Danube again until you reach the river's delta north of Constanța.

Stay on Route 3 after Galița. The road has less traffic now and goes over gently-rolling landscape ~ just after the town there is a one-kilometer stretch on cobblestones ~ cross a bridge ~ and continue on the cobblestone surface ~ through **Băneasa** where you must use special care on the uneven stones as you ride through town.

Băneasa

There is one last stretch of cobblestones.

Ion Corvin

Just before you ride out of the village there is a sign pointing to a monastery complex 4 kilometers to the left ~ the following kilometers feature many curves and some steep climbs and descents that bring you first to **Crangu** and then on to **Adamclisi**.

Adamclisi

Postal area code: 907010; Telephone area code: 0241

Monumentul Tropaeum Traiani — 30 meter victory monument. Erected in the year 109 by Roman Emperor Trajan, it shows scenes from the Roman victory over the Dacians.

Ruins of Adamclisi fortress (Cetatea) with the remains of 22 towers, 4 gates, cobblestone paved streets, sewers and 4 early Christian churches.

Tropaeum Traiani Museum, ✆ 618763, Open: Tues-Sun 9-18 o'clock. Museum for artifacts recovered from digs at the

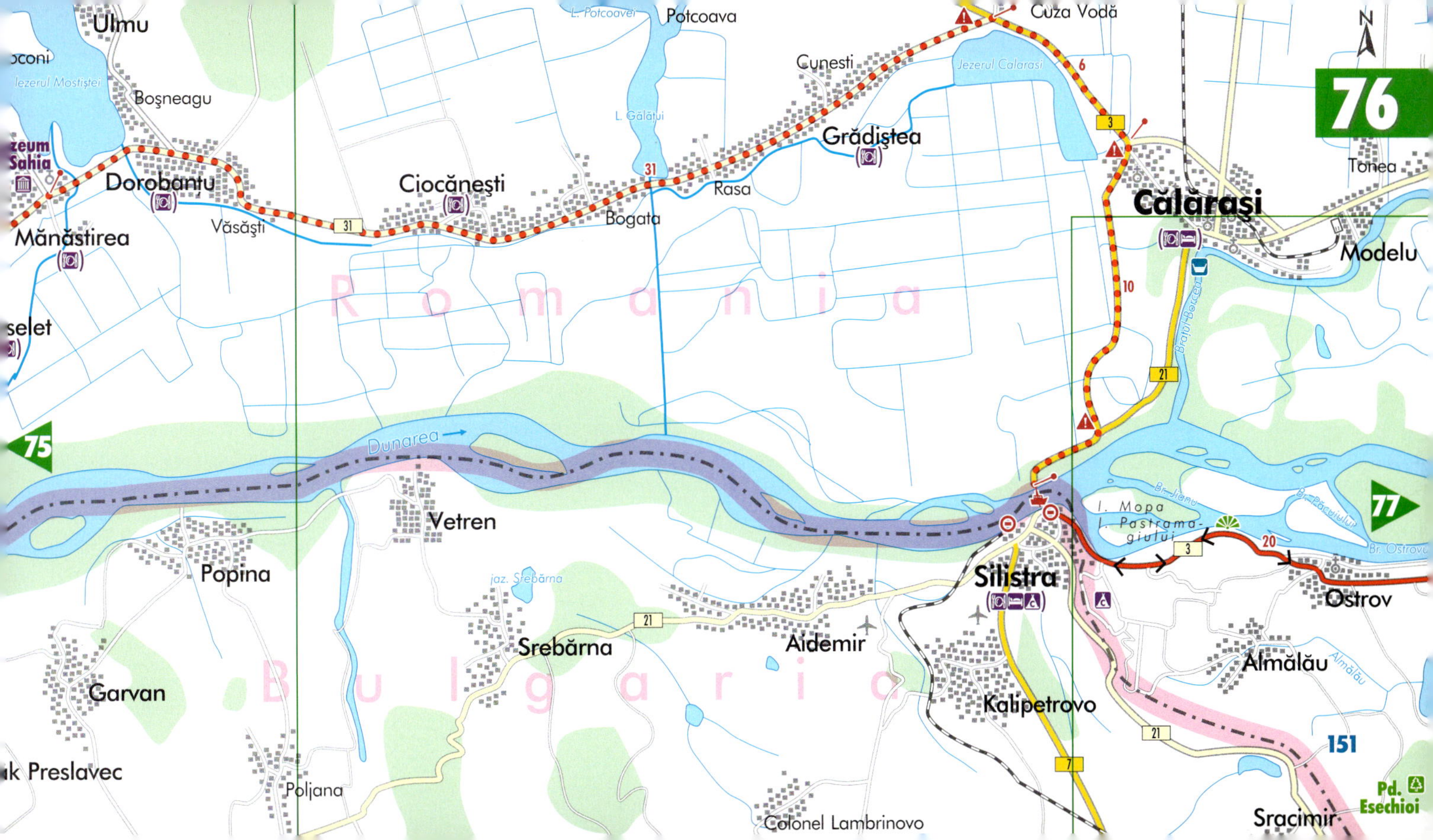

76
Ulmu
Boşneagu
Dorobanţu
Mănăstirea
Văsăşti
Ciocăneşti
Bogata
Rasa
Grădiştea
Cunesti
Potcoava
L. Potcoavei
L. Gălăţui
Cuza Vodă
Jezerul Calarasi
Iezerul Mostiştei
Călăraşi
Tonea
Modelu
Braţul Borcea
Romania
Dunarea
75
77
Vetren
Popina
Srebărna
jaz. Srebărna
Aidemir
Silistra
Kalipetrovo
Ostrov
Almălău
I. Mopa
I. Pastrama-giului
Br. Jianu
Br. Păcuiului
Br. Ostrovu
Garvan
Preslavec
Poljana
Colonel Lambrinovo
Sracimir
Pd. Esechioi
Bulgaria
151
31
3
21
7
20
6
10

site, including original elements from the monument.

The name Adamclisi or Adamklissi comes from the Turkish name Adam Kilise, which means church of the people. The Turks mistakenly believed the ancient monument to be an early church.

The earliest settlement at the site was probably a Roman legionnaires encampment named "Civitas Tropaensium". About 200 AD the settlement attained Roman city status. After the Romans withdrew from Dacia, the city was run by Goths. Emperor Constantine ordered the construction of new fortifications and the city enjoyed a second period of prosperity. But it was destroyed in 587 AD by the Avars and subsequently lay forgotten for centuries. In the 14th century, after the Ottoman Turks conquered the area, Turks and Avars started settling in the region.

The museum and the archaeological sites are to the left from the town. Outside Adamclisi the road becomes hillier and there are many curves ~ the next town is **Deleni**.

Deleni
Continue through the hilly countryside to **Pietreni**.

Pietreni
There is another steep climb before you ride into Viişoara.

Viişoara
After Viişoara there is a gentle descent down to **Cobadin**.

Cobadin
The road curves to the left and delivers you into Cobadin ~ continue along Route 3, the main street ~ the next few kilometers are a steady up and down across hilly country to **Ciocirlia** ~ before riding into the town there is a railroad crossing.

Ciocirlia
After the railroad crossing go uphill ~ and then downhill into **Ciocirlia de Sus**.

Dervent monastery

Ciocirlia de Sus
There is more traffic now and you ride mostly down a tree-lined road ~ downhill again before you get to Basarabi ~ about one kilometer before the city the road surface becomes cobblestones ~ just before the edge of the city there is a bridge across the Danube-Black Sea canal.

Basarabi
Go straight until you reach the traffic circle ~ turn right on **Route 3** towards Constanţa. The road has 4 lanes here and traffic is much heavier but leads you straight into Constanţa on the Black Sea.

Basarabi has no visible border between the next town, Valu lui Traian.

Valu lui Traian
Much of the road is lined with trees on both sides and is pleasantly shaded. The right lane is mostly occupied with parked cars that allow

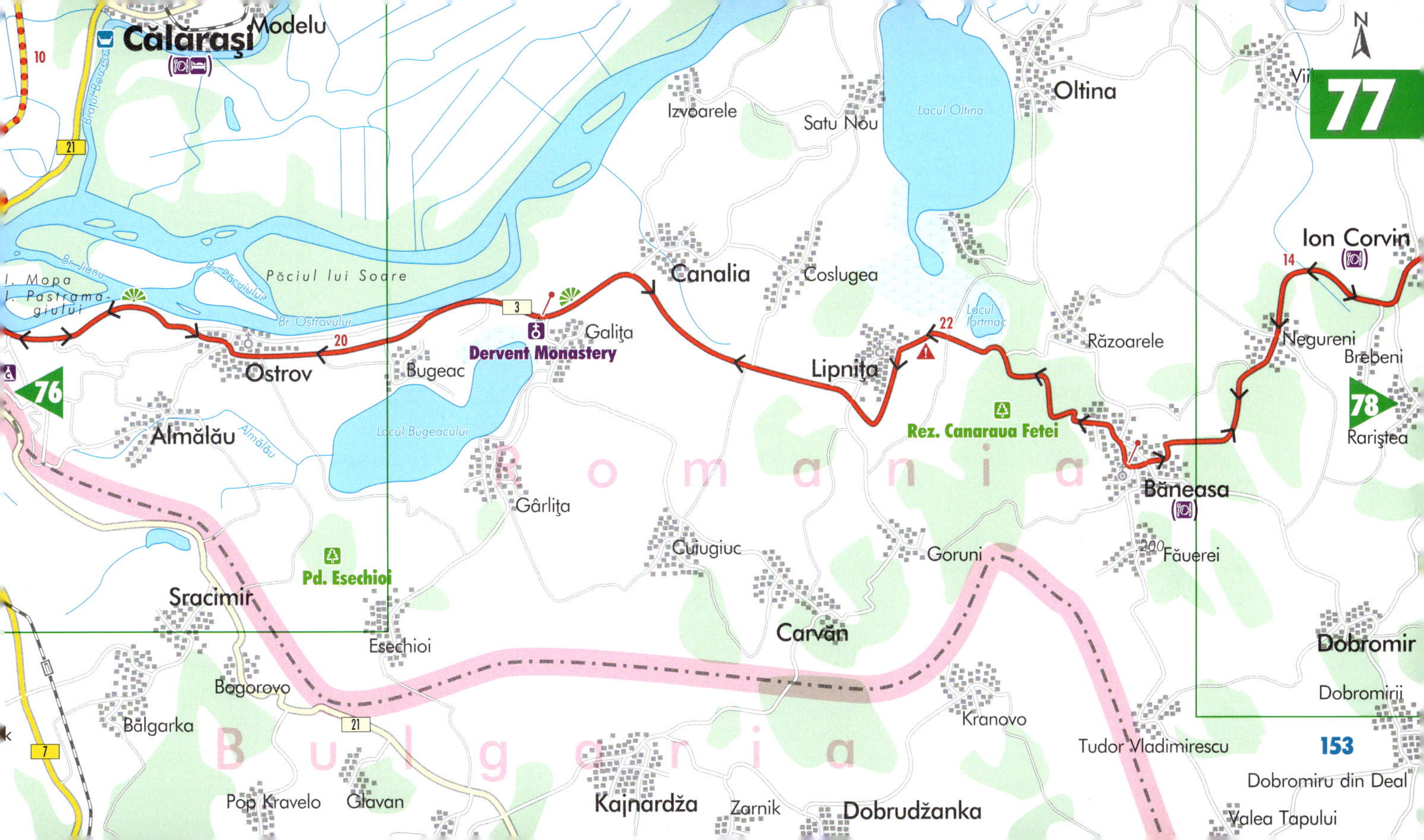

Călăraşi
Modelu
10
Braţul Borcea
21
Oltina
Izvoarele
Satu Nou
Lacul Oltina
Viile
77
Ion Corvin
14
I. Mopa
I. Pastramagiului
Br. Jianu
Br. Păcuiului
Păciul lui Soare
Br. Ostrovului
Canalia
Coslugea
3
Galiţa
Dervent Monastery
20
Ostrov
Bugeac
Lacul Iortmac
22
Lipniţa
Răzoarele
Negureni
Brebeni
76
78
Rariştea
Almălău
Lacul Bugeacului
Rez. Canaraua Fetei
Romania
Gârliţa
Băneasa
200
Făuerei
Cuiugiuc
Goruni
Pd. Esechioi
Sracimir
Carvăn
Esechioi
Dobromir
Dobromirii
Bogorovo
Bălgarka
21
7
Kranovo
Bulgaria
Tudor Vladimirescu
Dobromiru din Deal
Pop Kravelo
Glavan
Kajnardža
Zarnik
Dobrudžanka
Valea Tapului

the bicyclist to deal with heavy traffic without too much trouble.

About 10 kilometers before you reach Constanţa the road starts to rise ~ at kilometer 9 there is another short climb ~ as well as at kilometer 8 ~ one the right side you pass an old coast guard patrol boat that has been placed next to the road. In Constanţa use caution with the electric busses that take their power from overhead wires and do not have much space for maneuvering.

After this long ride into the city you come to a large intersection ~ turn left on **B-dul Ferdinand** towards **Port Tomis** ~ proceed to the next large intersection with signals ~ and turn right on **B-dul Tomis** towards Mamaia. This street brings you to **Piaţa Ovidiu**, just a few hundred meters from the harbor promenade and the fabulous Cazino.

Constanţa
Postal area code: 900605; Telephone area code: 0241

- Info Litoral Tourist Information center, Str Traian 36, ✆ 555000
- Contur Travel, Piaţa Ovidiu 14, ✆ 619777

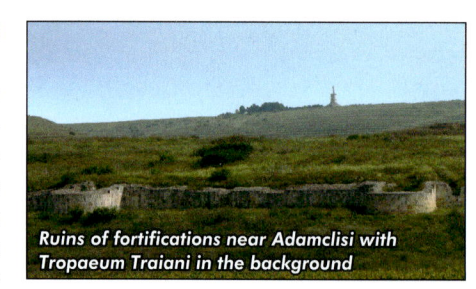

Ruins of fortifications near Adamclisi with Tropaeum Traiani in the background

- Danubius, B-dul Ferdinand 36, ✆ 615836
- Roman Mosaic (3rd century), Open: June-Sept, Tues-Sun 9-20 o'clock, Oct-May, Tues-Sun 10-18 o'clock. The 700 square-meter floor-mosaic was discovered in 1959. It is part of a large complex that is thought to have been the commercial center of the Roman city of Tomis. Vaulted storage rooms and spaces are beneath the mosaic floor.
- Museum of History and Archaeology, Piaţa Ovidiu 12, ✆ 618763, Open: June-Sept, Tues-Sun 9-20 o'clock, Oct-May, Tues-Sun 10-18 o'clock. Exhibits include mammoth tusks, 2nd century bones, Roman statues and coins
- Statue of Ovid (1887), Piaţa Ovidiu. In memory of the Roman poet Ovid who was banished to Tomis by the Emperor Augustus in the year 8 AD. It is believed that Ovid's grave lies under the status.

- **Ion Jalea Museum**, Str Arhiepiscopiei 13, ✆ 618602, Open: Thurs-Sun 10-18 o'clock. Works by the sculptor Ion Jalea.
- **Mahmudiye Mosque** (1910), Str Arhiepiscopiei. The main mosque in Romania. The minaret is open to the public and offers excellent views of the city.
- **Orthodox cathedral** (1885), Decembrie 1989. Handsome domed church with impressive interior architecture.
- **Cazino** (1907-10), B-dul Elisabeta 2, ✆ 617416. Commissioned by King Carol I, who wanted to transform Constanţa into a glamorous seaside resort, the casino was designed by the architect Daniel Renard and built after World War One. The neo-classical building has a good restaurant as well as gambling.
- **Planetarium**, Bd-ul Mamaia 267, Open: Mon-Sun 9-20 o'clock
- **Genoese light house** (13th century) on the beach boulevard
- **Aquarium**, near the casino, with fish and other sea-creatures from the Black Sea.
- **Dolphinarium**, B-dul Mamaia, Open: Mon-Sun 9-19 o'clock.

The city was first established by Greek settlers in the 6th century BC. They named the town Tomis, which comes from an ancient word for "cut" and refers to the myth of Medea,

78

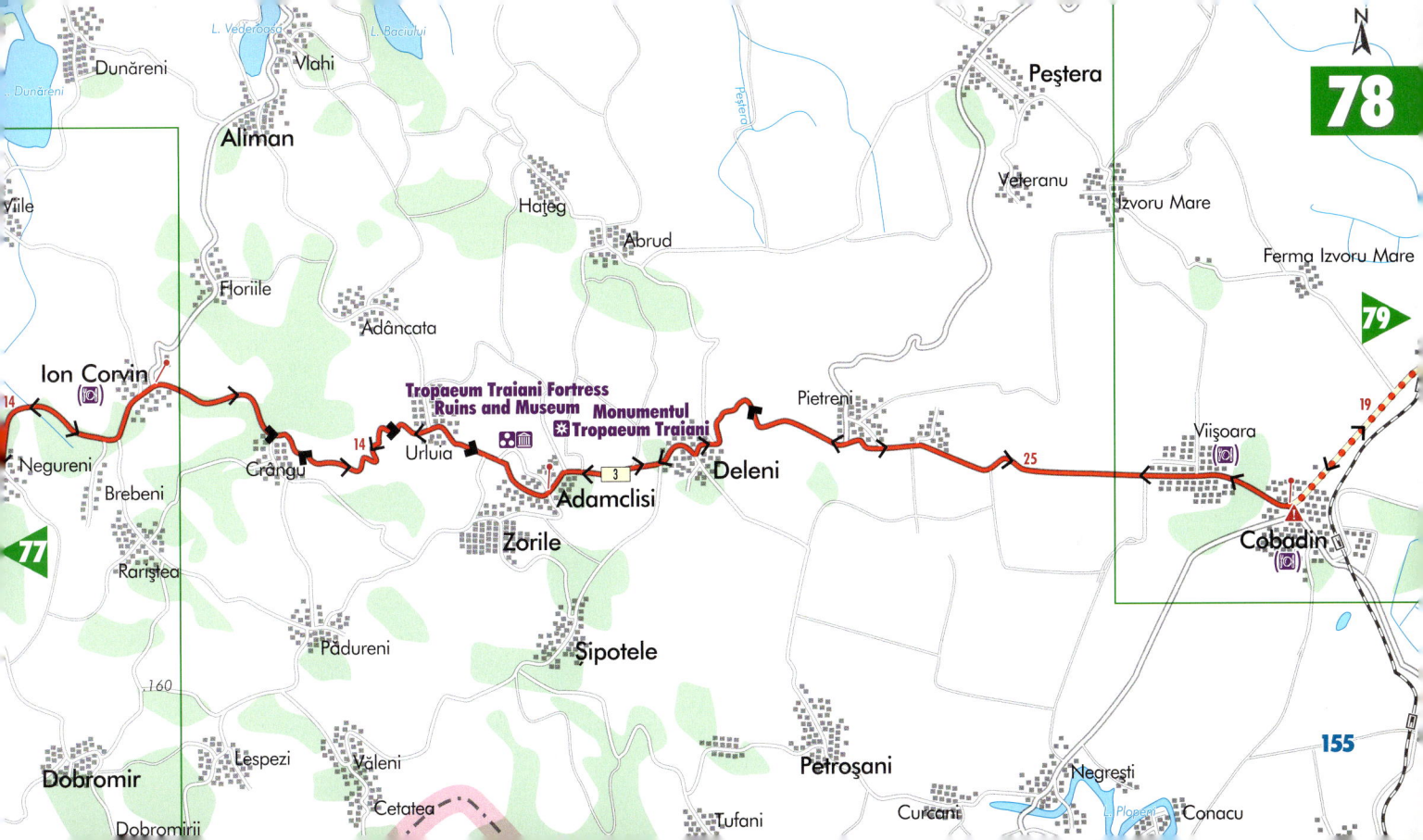

Peștera

L. Vederoasa
L. Baciului

Dunăreni
Vlahi
Veteranu
Izvoru Mare
Aliman
Ferma Izvoru Mare
Viile
Florile
Hațeg
Abrud
Adâncata
Dunăreni

Ion Corvin
Tropaeum Traiani Fortress Ruins and Museum
Monumentul Tropaeum Traiani
Pietreni
Viișoara
Negureni
Crângu
Urluia
Deleni
Brebeni
Adamclisi
Cobadin
Rariștea
Zorile
Pădureni
Șipotele
Dobromir
Lespezi
Văleni
Petroșani
Negrești
Conacu
Dobromirii
Cetatea
Tufani
Curcani

77
79

155

Yacht harbor in Constanţa

Jason and the Argonauts. When Medea fled with Jason and the Argonauts, she took her brother Apsyrtus. When their father pursued them, Medea killed Apsyrtus and cut his body into pieces and threw them into the sea to delay her father, who she knew would stop to collect the remains of his son.

The Romans captured the region from the Odrysians in 29 BC, and in 8 AD Caesar Augustus banished the Roman poet Ovid to the city. He died here, but not before completing some of his most important works, including "Tristia" and "Epistulae ex ponto".

In the 4th century the Emperor Constantine the Great renamed the city after his sister, Constantia. After the split of the Roman Empire, Constanţa fell to the Byzantine Empire before being besieged and destroyed several times by Avars and Slavs. The Ottoman Turks took control of the city in the early 15th century and held it until 1877, when the Kingdom of Romania was established after the Romanian war of independence.

Since the end of the 19th century, the city has steadily gained in significance and in the 20th century it became a popular seaside resort.

Today it is the third largest city in Romania and the country's main seaport, mixing elements of the Orient and Europe into a multi-cultural atmosphere that we urge you to enjoy for a few days.

Constanţa – Archaeological Museum and Ovid Statue

Constanţa to Tulcea — 154 km

Despite the heavy traffic, leaving Constanţa is easy. Take **Marcus Aurelius** street from the eastern end of **Piaţa Ovidiu** and follow it through a curve to the left and proceed until it ends at a T-intersection turn left and go to the next intersection where you turn right on **Mircea cel Batran** which you can follow straight out of the city. The city of Mamaia borders directly on Constanţa.

Tip: Riding along the beaches in the city one must almost give more attention to the many pedestrians than to the motorized traffic. People are constantly coming and going to and from the beach, crossing the road or walking along it. There are numerous

79

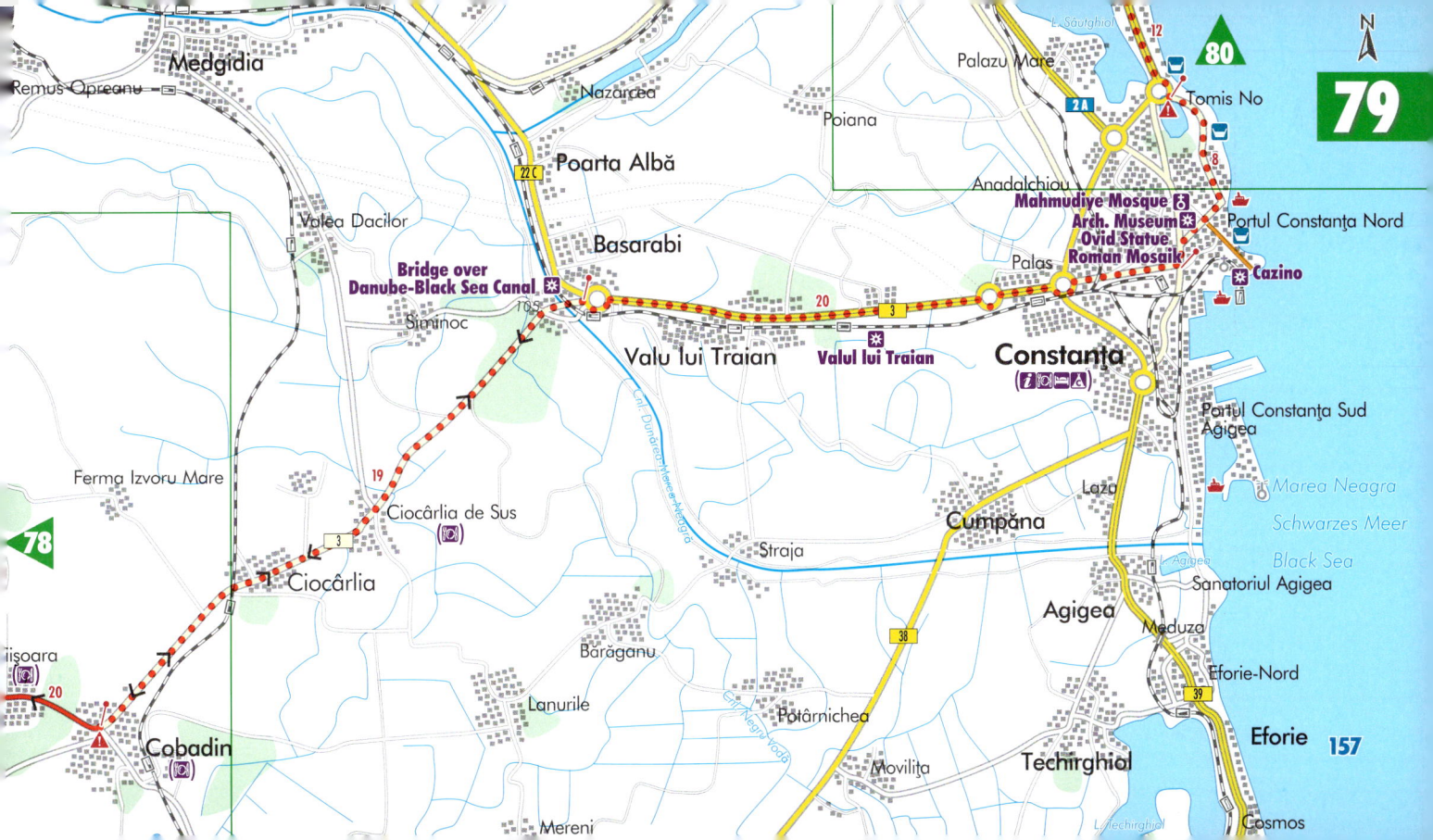

80
78
157

Medgidia
Remus Opreanu
Nazarcea
Palazu Mare
L. Siutghiol
Tomis No
Poiana
Poarta Albă
Anadalchiou
Mahmudiye Mosque
Arch. Museum
Ovid Statue
Roman Mosaik
Portul Constanța Nord
Valea Dacilor
Basarabi
Palas
Cazino
Bridge over Danube-Black Sea Canal
Siminoc
Valu lui Traian
Valul lui Traian
Constanța
Portul Constanța Sud Agigea
Ferma Izvoru Mare
Ciocârlia de Sus
Laza
Marea Neagră
Schwarzes Meer
Black Sea
Ciocârlia
Straja
Cumpăna
Sanatoriul Agigea
Agigea
Meduza
Băraganu
Lanurile
Eforie-Nord
Cobadin
Potârnichea
Movilița
Techirghiol
Eforie
Mereni
Cosmos

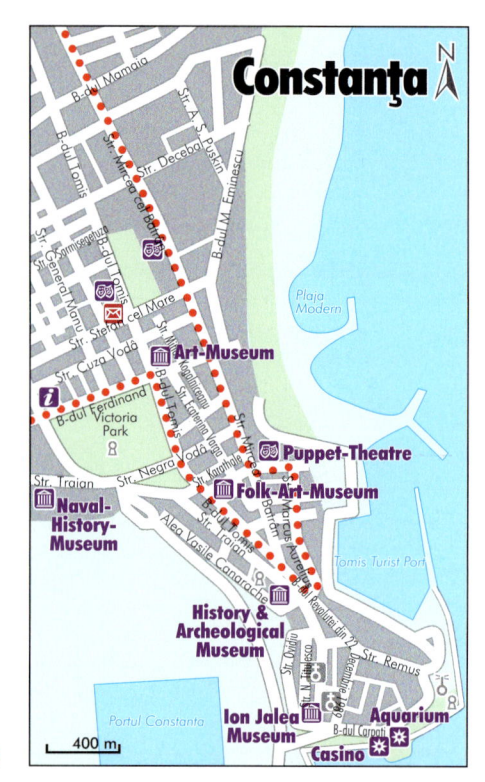

hotels, guest-houses and campgrounds on the right, as well as an outdoor swimming complex. Beach chairs and tourists crowd the beach and create a lively holiday atmosphere that contrasts starkly with the hundreds of kilometers of simple rural countryside that lie behind you.

If you have gotten this far and do not wish to miss the Danube delta, the ride now continues northward towards Tulcea.

After Mamaia stay on the main road north towards Năvodari ~ straight across a bridge ~ and past Năvodari off to your left ~ turn right after the bridge ~ immediately after turning right there is a posted bicycle path on the right side ~ proceed past a petro-chemicals complex and an industrial harbor ~ here you must endure some unpleasant odors.

The road narrows from four lanes to two lanes and goes over another bridge ~ where the bicycle path ends ~ keep going on this smaller road where there is less traffic ~ on the left side you can see lake Lacul Corbu as you continue to the next town, Corbu.

Constanța – Cazino and the Black Sea

Corbu

After Corbu you ride along a pretty tree-lined road that has a rough asphalt surface ~ and proceed northwards towards the Danube delta ~ the road starts to climb before you ride into the next town.

Sacele

Camp ground

Ride downhill and through curves as you enter the town ~ and follow the road through Sacele ~ and depart the town through a left-hand curve as the road starts to climb again ~ then back downhill ~ followed by another

Constanța – Mahmudiye Mosque

climb that ends in a curve to the right 〰 and then straight ahead 〰 to the right you can see the Black Sea on the horizon.

About halfway to Istria there is a turn-off to the right that leads to a campground and an archaeological site named "Cetatea Histria."

Cetatea Histria
- **Archaeological dig** at the site of a 5th century BC Greek harbor town
- **Museum** directly adjacent to the open-air site has exhibits with coins and sculptures and other items found at the dig. There is also a café.

Today nothing remains of this ancient city but a field of ruins on the edge of Lake Sinoe. It is impressive nevertheless. With a little imagination one can almost envision a busy town with a market, temples and public baths. The walls with 10 towers and two gates are still fairly well preserved. Long ago it was a significant harbor town until silting and shifting sands made the harbor inaccessible and the town was abandoned.

159

Constanţa harbor

Continue along Route **226** to the town of **Istria**.

Istria
Proceed through the town and on towards **Sinoie**.

Sinoie
The main road through the village curves around to the left and heads towards **Mihai Viteazu** and the main road Route **22** or **E87**.

Mihai Viteazu
Over a small railroad crossing ⚠ **Caution!** The crossing is very uneven ~ after a few hundred meters you come to the B 22 main road ~ turn right at the intersection towards Tulcea and Baia ~ the road starts to go uphill ~ the climb ends when the road curves to the right. There are fine views at the top towards the west, with forests, lakes and lines of hills in the distance as you coast easily down into **Baia**.

Baia
Cross a small bridge and ride into the town ~ past a hotel and a shop and straight through the town.

At the north end of the town there are huge grain elevators left over from a former kolkhoz farm that is no longer in operation and has been abandoned to the elements.

Kolkhoz and Sovkhoz farms
Kolkhoz farms were large cooperatives mainly in the Soviet Union but also in other socialist countries, including Romania. The first were formed in 1917 by peasants who voluntarily combined their properties. After 1929, they were increasingly established by government decree as a means of eliminating private property.

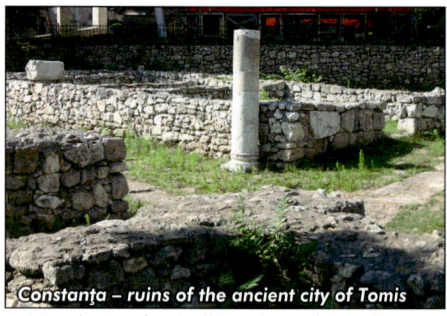

Constanţa – ruins of the ancient city of Tomis

Members of a kolkhoz farm formally were owners of production equipment but not of the land, which remained property of the state. Management of these cooperatives was dictated to a large extent by the state, which also demanded delivery of a portion of the crop determined according to soil and climate conditions. Any surplus that the kolkhoz produced could be sold at unregulated prices on local markets, where individual farmers could also sell any goods they produced on their private plots.

Sovkhoz farms were state-run operations at which workers were salaried employees. These

Bike path near Navodari

were initially formed in 1919 to demonstrate to farmers the advantages of centrally-run large-scale farm operations. Sovkhoz farms were also often set up in less productive areas where the risk of crop failure was higher. Today many of these farms continue as highly-specialized farms for seed and breeding livestock.

On the left side of the road a short distance after the grain elevators there are ruins of another agricultural complex which has seen better days ~ proceed down the tree-lined road to a 4-way intersection with a petrol station and small inn ~ turn right towards **Jurilovca**.

The next town you ride through is named Ceamurlia de Jos ~ on a lightly-traveled well-paved road ~ after about one kilometer go through an underpass for the railroad ~ and continue to **Ceamurlia de Jos**.

Ceamurlia de Jos

Proceed straight towards **Lunca**.

Lunca

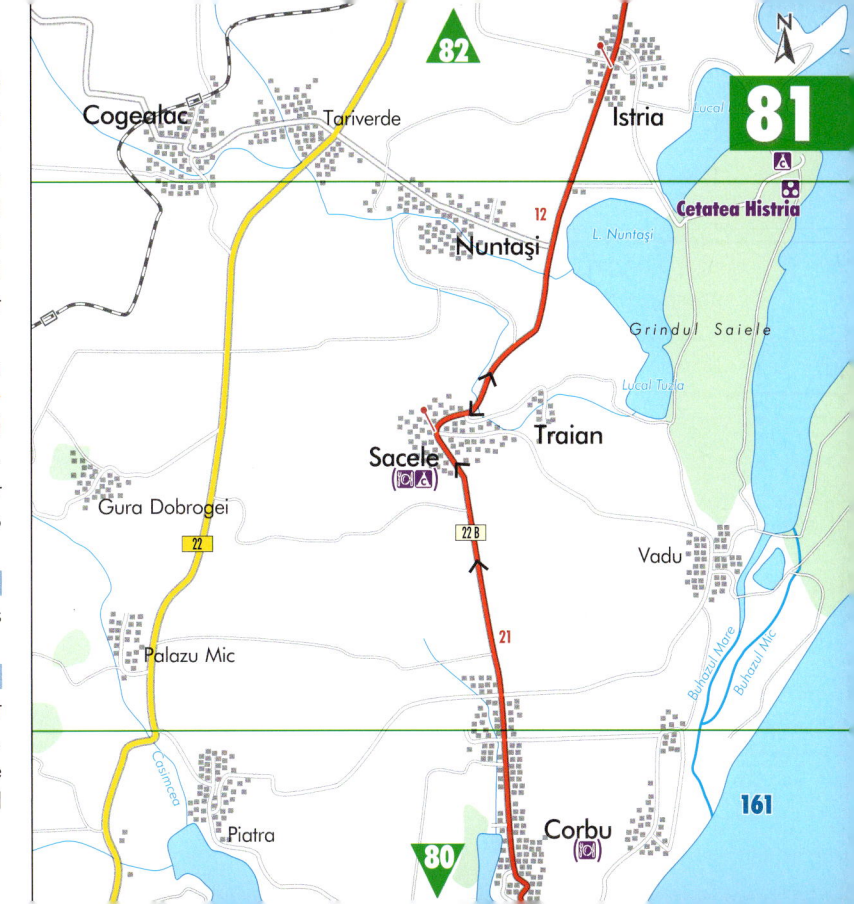

After Lunca proceed straight towards the next town, Vişina. Just before you get there ride past another large agricultural complex which is still partially in operation.

Vişina

The route now brings you close to the Black Sea again and an area with a harbor ~ to the right you can see **Lacul Goloviţa**, which has access to the sea. Proceed another 3 kilometers to **Jurilovca**.

Jurilovca

As you enter the town you ride past a petrol station ~ and proceed to a T-intersection where you can only turn left or right. Turning right brings you down to the harbor, while left goes towards the town of Sălcioara.

Tip: To the right, past a large church, the road street goes down to the harbor of Jurilovca. Here you can board a ferry or a boat to the island of Grindul Cosa, which has a nature preserve and habitat for many various birds. There are information boards about what lives on the island. There is also a campground at Portiţei on the island.

From the harbor take **Str 6 marchi** straight out of the town towards Sălcioara ~ the road

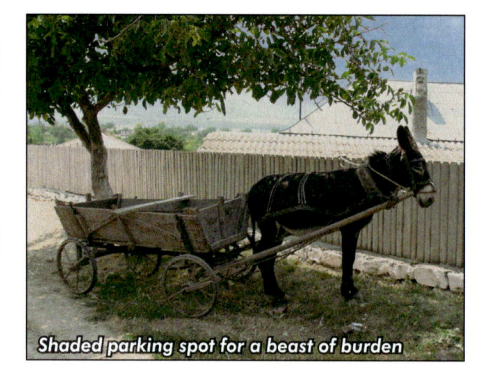

Shaded parking spot for a beast of burden

surface becomes worse here with many potholes and cracks.

The road descends into the town and must be ridden with caution. But also try to catch a glimpse of the Black Sea and the Danube delta stretching away to the horizon to the north and east.

Sălcioara

Tip: This next piece of road is in very poor condition! Wherever possible, you may wish to ride along the unpaved edge of the road.

Ride out of the town along an avenue lined with very old trees ~ the road surface improves about halfway to Enisala. The road also becomes wider and the countryside seems to change with every passing kilometer ~ to the left lie forested hills while on the right is a vast former fish farm and, beyond the old pools, stony karst hills.

A short distance later the ruins of the ancient fortress of Cetatea Heracleea become visible on one of the karst hills to the right.

Ride past a small pond ~ and continue uphill ~ then back downhill just before the town ~ **Lacul Razim** is off to your right ~ and continue downhill into the town of Enisala.

Enisala

✠ **Ruins of Cetatea Heracleea**, probably a Roman fortress

Tip: Here you have the option of a detour to the town of Babadag to visit the mosque or various museums.

Excursion to Babadag   9 km

In Enisala turn left towards Babadag.

The countryside around Babadag changes dramatically as you enter forested hills.

In the town turn left at the next intersection ~ the mosque is to the left, to the right a small plaza with a stone sculpture.

Babadag

- **Oriental Museum**, Casa Panaghia, Open: Weds-Sun 9-16 o'clock. Exhibits documenting the Turkish history of Babadag.
- **Exhibits of oriental art**
- **Ethnographic Museum**
- **Mosque Ali Gazi Pasha** (1522), Str Mihai Viteazul, Open: 8-21 o'clock. The oldest Moslem structure in Romania.
- **Lacul Babadag**

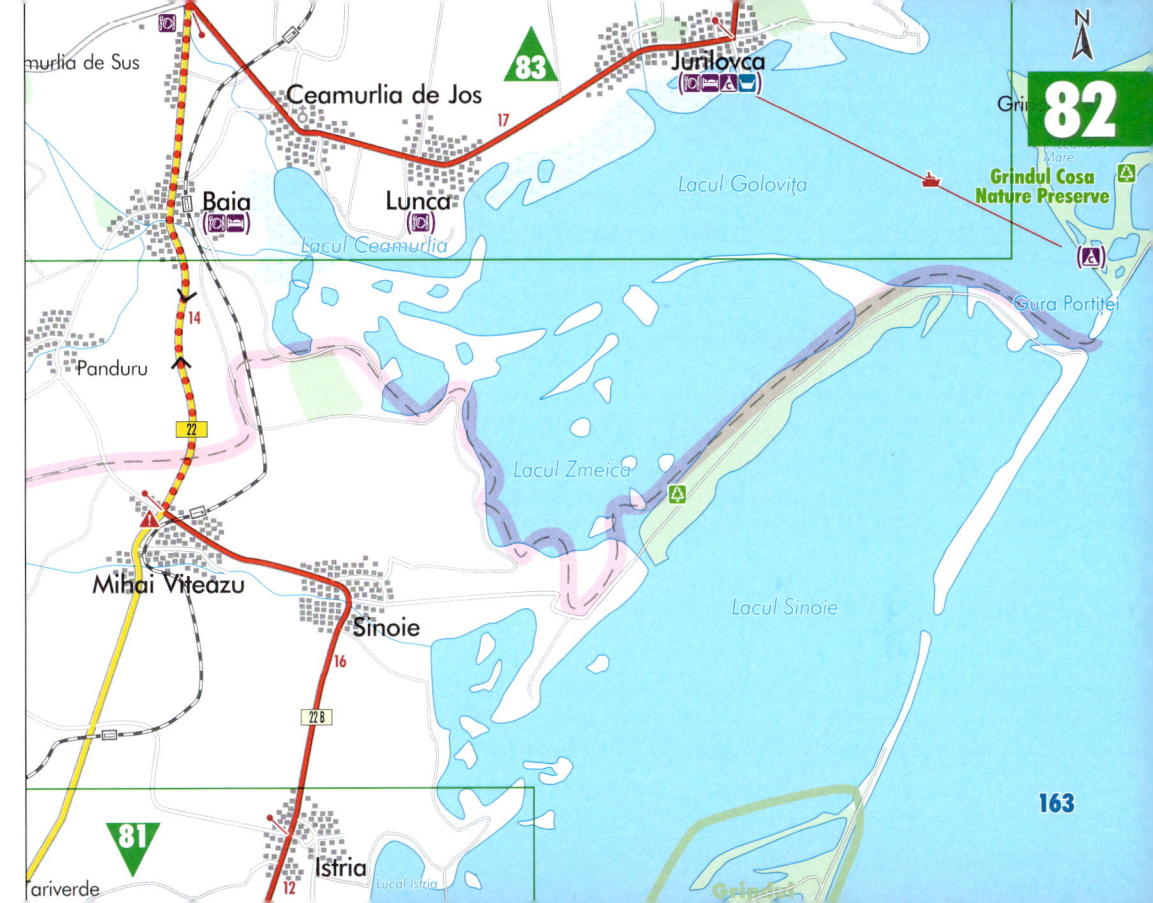

The name Babadag means "father of the mountains" in Turkish. The town lies on Lacul Babadag, which is separated from Lacul Razim only by a thin swampy strip. Remains of an Ice Age settlement and various Roman and Byzantine ruins can be *found along the lakefront.*

Return to the main route by the same roads.

On the main route, turn right at the next junction towards Sarichioi and make a short climb ⁓ at the edge of town go through a right-curve and back downhill. There is a ruin to the right, small ponds and farmsteads on the left and a road lined with poplars ⁓ keep going downhill.

Tip: Here you enter the Danube delta nature preserve.

Pass a small fishery on the left side ⁓ the road winds through swamps and reeds with water reaching almost to the road on both sides ⁓ over a small bridge ⁓ and straight across the flat landscape to the village of **Sarichioi**.

Sarichioi

After gaining a few meters elevation there is a gentle descent into Sarichioi.

Sabangia

The road becomes somewhat hillier between Sabangia and Agighiol until you come to a straight section of road that leads into Agighiol.

Agighiol

- Archaeologists uncovered the 4th century tomb of a Dacian lord. Burial objects included gold and silver jewelry and ceramic items.

Agighiol is to the south-east of Tulcea and is a popular resort. It lies amid protected nature preserves and an important paleological site.

Ride across a small bridge in the town and proceed north towards Tulcea.

Tip: If you wish to see some more of the Danube delta you can take a detour through the villages of Murighiol and Nufaru on the way to Tulcea. To do so turn right after the bridge in Agighiol. This detour adds about 50 kilometers to your total distance, but is very scenic and passes several ancient ruins.

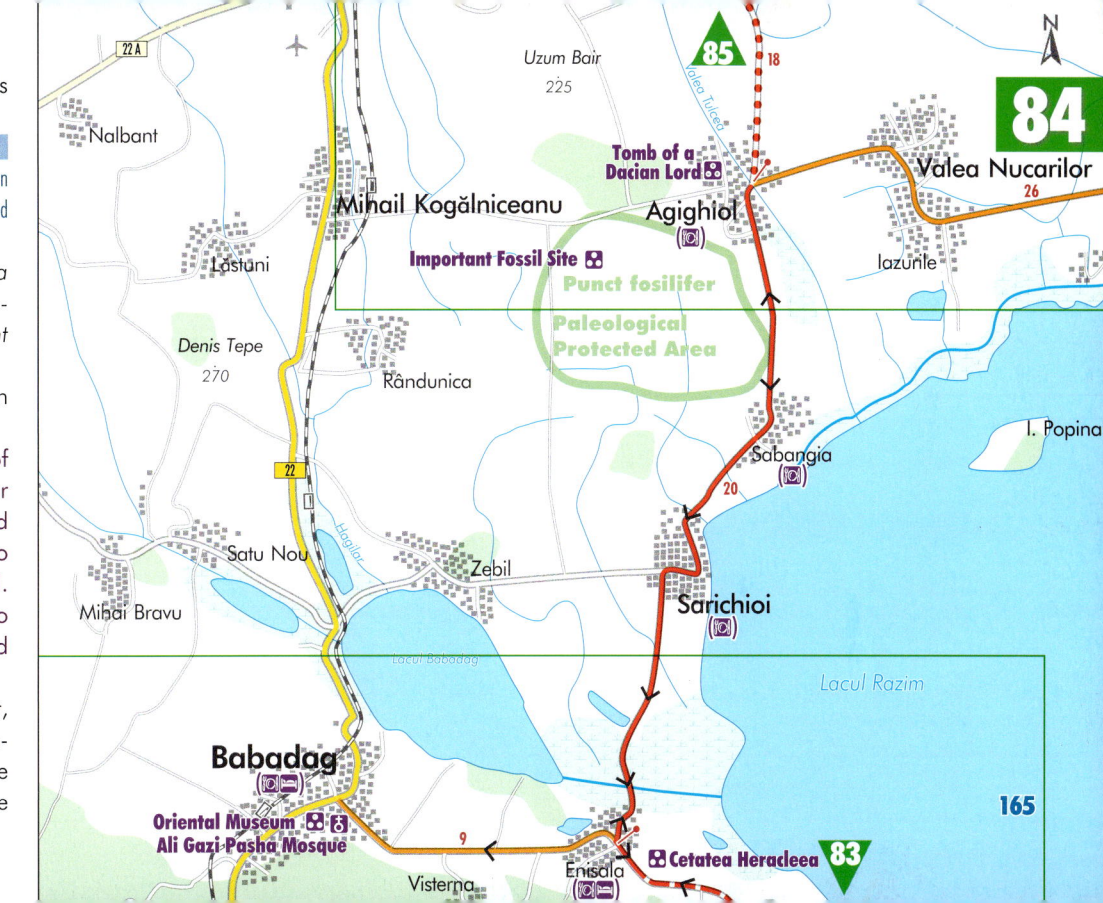

The shorter main route takes you, in part, through forested hills and a tree-lined country avenue after about 10 kilometers the road starts to descend steadily just before entering Tulcea you pass a picnic area and a small woods on the right side.

The road into Tulcea rises steeply at first ~ then back downhill ~ over railroad tracks and a bridge ~ after the bridge the street is paved with cobblestones and goes uphill again ~ until you come to a main road ~ turn right on this main road, which is **Str Mahmudiei**, and ride downhill into the city ~ continue to the next T-intersection ~ and turn right on **Str Pacii** ~ go straight to the traffic circle ~ the third exit from the circle brings you straight to the harbor promenade and **Str Isaccei** and the train station.

Tree-lined road near Salcioara

Tulcea
Postal area code: 820000; Telephone area code: 0240

- **Tourist Information**, Atbad, Str Babadag 11,
- **Danubius Travel Agency**, Hotel Europolis, Str Pacii 20, ☎ 512443
- **Ibis Tours**, Str Babadag 6, Ap 14, ☎ 512787
- **Information and Ecological Education Center**, Hotel Delta, Str Isaccei 2, ☎ 514720
- **Tourist information center for the Danube delta biosphere preserve offices**, Str Portilui 34a, ☎ 518924
- **Danube delta research institute**, Str Babadag 165, ☎ 524550
- **Ferry connections to Sulina** daily from Navrom train station or with one of the many private ferry services. One way about 3 hours, 90 minutes by hydrofoil boat
- **Excursion cruises into the delta**: from private boat companies directly on the harbor. Caution: do not immediately accept the first price you are offered. Most of the captains are willing to negotiate.
- **Parcul Monumentului Independentei**, next to the history museum. Ruins of the old citadel.
- **Archaeology and history museum**, Str Gloriei&Str Chindiei, ☎ 513626, Open: May-Aug, Tues-Sun 9-18 o'clock, Sept-April, Tues-Sun 8-16 o'clock

Cetatea Heracleea near Enisala

- **Folklore museum**, Str 9 Mai, ☎ 516204, Open: May-Aug, Tues-Sun 9-18 o'clock, Sept-April, Tues-Sun 8-16 o'clock. Turkish and Romanian ceremonial costumes, fishing nets, carpets, etc.
- **Natural history museum with aquarium**, Str Progresului 32, ☎ 515866, Open: May-Aug, Tues-Sun 9-18 o'clock, Sept-April, Tues-Sun 8-16 o'clock.
- **St. Nicholas church**, Str Progresului 37. A memorial to the victims of the 1989 revolution stands in front of the church.
- **Greek Orthodox bishops church**, Str G Doja
- **Azizie Mosque** (1863), Str Independenei
- **International Folk festival of the Danube nations**, every August

Tudor Vladimirescu
Ilganii de Sus
Partizani
Maliuc
Baba Rada
85
Gorgova
Vulturu
Bratul Sulina
Ferry Connections to Sulina
Cetatea Aegyssus
Tulcea
Picnic Area
22
Ilganii de Jos
Lacul Gorgova
86
Cnl. Gura Lictov
Nufăru
Malcoci
Victoria
Băltenii de Sus
Băltenii de Jos
Danube Delta National Park
Lacul Isacov
Br. Sf. Gheorghe
Lacul Uzlina
34
18
Beştepe
Mahmudia
Uzlina
Uzum Bair
225
Valea Tulcea
Lucal Murighiol
Lucal Sărătura
Pelican
Tomb of a Dacian Lord
Valea Nucarilor
26
Murighiol
Dunavăţu de Sus
167
Agighiol
Coline
Sarinasuf
Plopul
Important Fossil Site
84
Iazurile
Dunavăţu de Jos
L. Tătarului
Gârla Şontea
Lacul Obreitinul Mare

- **Fishing**, Infos from the local anglers and hunters association, Str Isaccea 10, ✆ 511404. A fishing permit is available in every community.

Tulcea was established by Greeks in the 8th century BC, who named it Castrum Aegyssus. Today it is known as the "gateway to the Danube delta". After being conquered by the Romans, Tulcea served as the main base for the Roman Black Sea fleet. After the Fall of Rome, it changed hands repeatedly until the Ottoman Turks took control in 1416 and named the city "Hora-Tepe", or Tolçu.

Today Tulcea remains an important harbor, and is the base for Romania's river navy.

The many factories and wharfs do not give Tulcea great charm, but along with a growing tourism industry they do represent an important part of the local economy. The city is the gateway for all visitors who wish to go to the delta, whether for pleasure or for research. It is also the starting or ending point for many cruise ships, with the harbor filled with boats and ships that serve as floating hotels and offer visitors cheap accommodations. Many of these boats also offer excursions of varying lengths into the Danube delta.

In the Danube delta

The adventurous bicycle tourist who has made it this far must not fail to make the last leg of this great trip: the 70-kilometer boat ride through the delta to the town of Sulina.

The Danube delta

The entire Danube delta has been designated a UNESCO world heritage site and as a biosphere preserve shared by Romania and Ukraine. It is a unique natural treasure and especially worthy of protection. The Danube splits into three arms at Tulcea: the Chilia-Arm which forms the border with Ukraine and is the longest of the three arms, some 100 kilometers long; the 70-kilometer Sulina Arm, which is the shortest connection to the Black Sea and is, with its canal, the arm that can be navigated by large ships; and the St. George's Arm, which winds its way through many loops

In the Danube delta

towards the Black Sea. These three main arms are also connected by countless constantly shifting and changing smaller arms and canals and many lakes. The delta covers a surface of approximately 4,500 square kilometers. Its width grows by about 40 meters per year as alluvium carried by the river collects in the delta. About 20 percent of the area is solid ground. The rest is water, wetlands, reed and marshy islands that form a rich and diverse habitat for more than 300 species of birds, including many protected species like pelican, cormorants and ibis. These make the

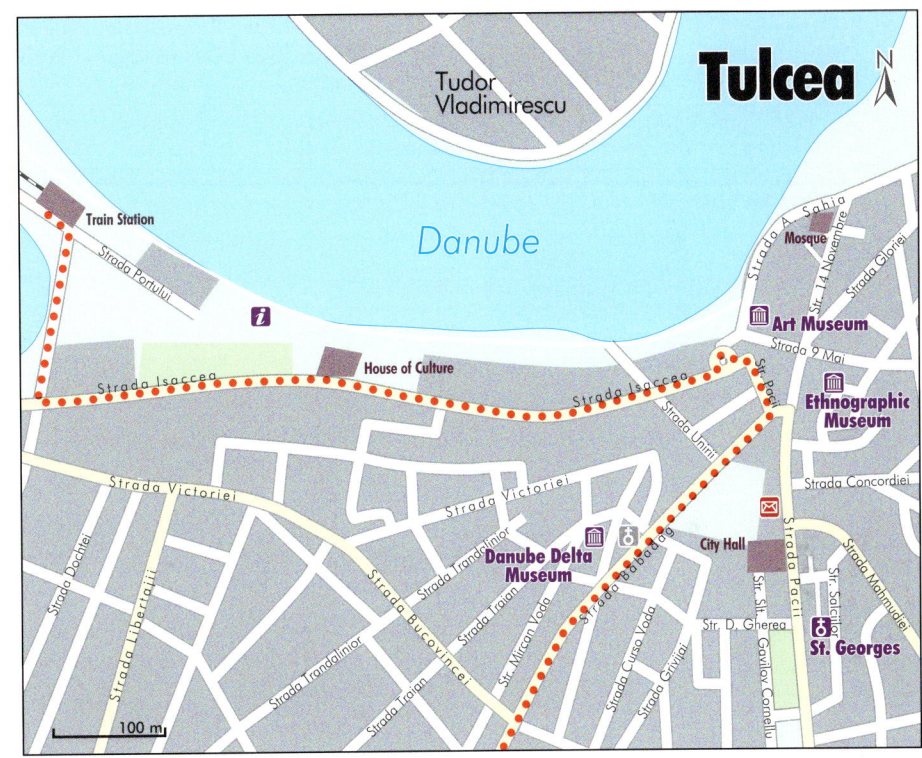

Tulcea waterfront

delta one of the largest and most interesting bird sanctuaries in the world.

The delta is also home to hundreds of different kinds of plants and trees, ranging from poplars and willows to wild apple and pear, oak, elm and many other trees. Wildlife includes many snakes, marten and fox as well as deer and wild pigs.

About 15,000 people live in this unique environment. Most of them fish for their living, exploiting the more than 100 species of fish that can be found in the waters. Only a small portion of the area is cultivated, and there is little livestock. Among the delta's inhabitants is a community of Lippovans, or Old Believers, who came from Russia more than 200 years ago and sought refuge in the delta.

Because there are virtually no roads through the delta, inhabitants and visitors must depend on boats and ships to travel through the area. These vessels range from simple motorboats and kayaks to houseboats and floating hotels. Fast catamarans and hydrofoil boats provide public transportation between the larger communities and towns. One warning should be taken seriously: The countless unmarked channels and lakes make it very easy for visitors to get lost in the delta. If you wish to explore some of the more remote parts of the delta, go with an experienced guide and do not forget to bring a good insect repellent because the air is filled with bugs and mosquitoes between May and September.

Sulina

DDBR Office, House No. 1

* **Lighthouse** (1870). At river kilometer No. 0. With a fine few of the Black Sea coast some 2 kilometers away.
* **Cemetery in the dunes near the cemetery**. Gravestones and reliefs testify to Sulina's multicultural past. Peoples from 25 different nations have lived and died here.

We are especially pleased that you chose this guide for your bicycle tour down the Danube. We hope you were satisfied with the book and that it helped you complete a tour that will long remain a fond memory. The bikeline team also hopes other volumes in our **bikeline**, **cycline** and **skateline** series may be useful to you in the future.

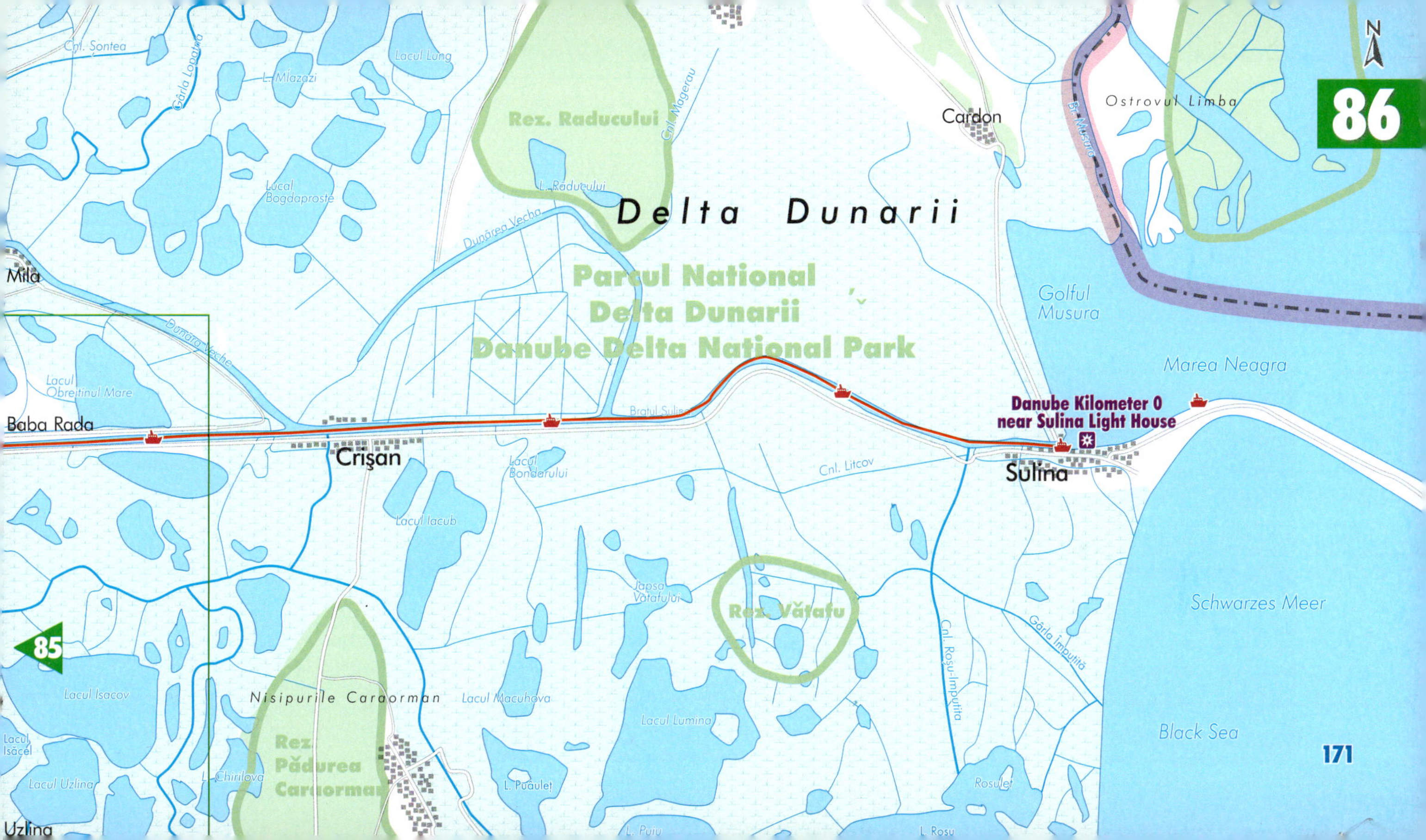

86
85
Delta Dunarii
Parcul National Delta Dunarii
Danube Delta National Park
Rez. Raducului
L. Raducului
Rez. Vătafu
Rez. Pădurea Caraorman
Nisipurile Caraorman
Danube Kilometer 0 near Sulina Light House
Cnl. Sontea
Gârla Lopatna
Lacul Lung
L. Mlazazi
Lucal Bogdaproste
Cnl. Magerau
Dunărea Vecha
Dunăra Veche
Cardon
Ostrovul Limba
Br. Musura
Golful Musura
Marea Neagra
Schwarzes Meer
Black Sea
Mila
Baba Rada
Lacul Obreitinul Mare
Bratul Sulina
Crişan
Sulina
Lacul Bondarului
Cnl. Litcov
Lacul Iacub
Japsa Vatafului
Cnl. Roşu-Împuţita
Gârla Împuţită
Lacul Isacov
Lacul Isăcel
Lacul Uzlina
L. Chirilova
Lacul Macuhova
Lacul Lumina
L. Puaulet
Rosulet
L. Puiu
L. Rosu
Uzlina

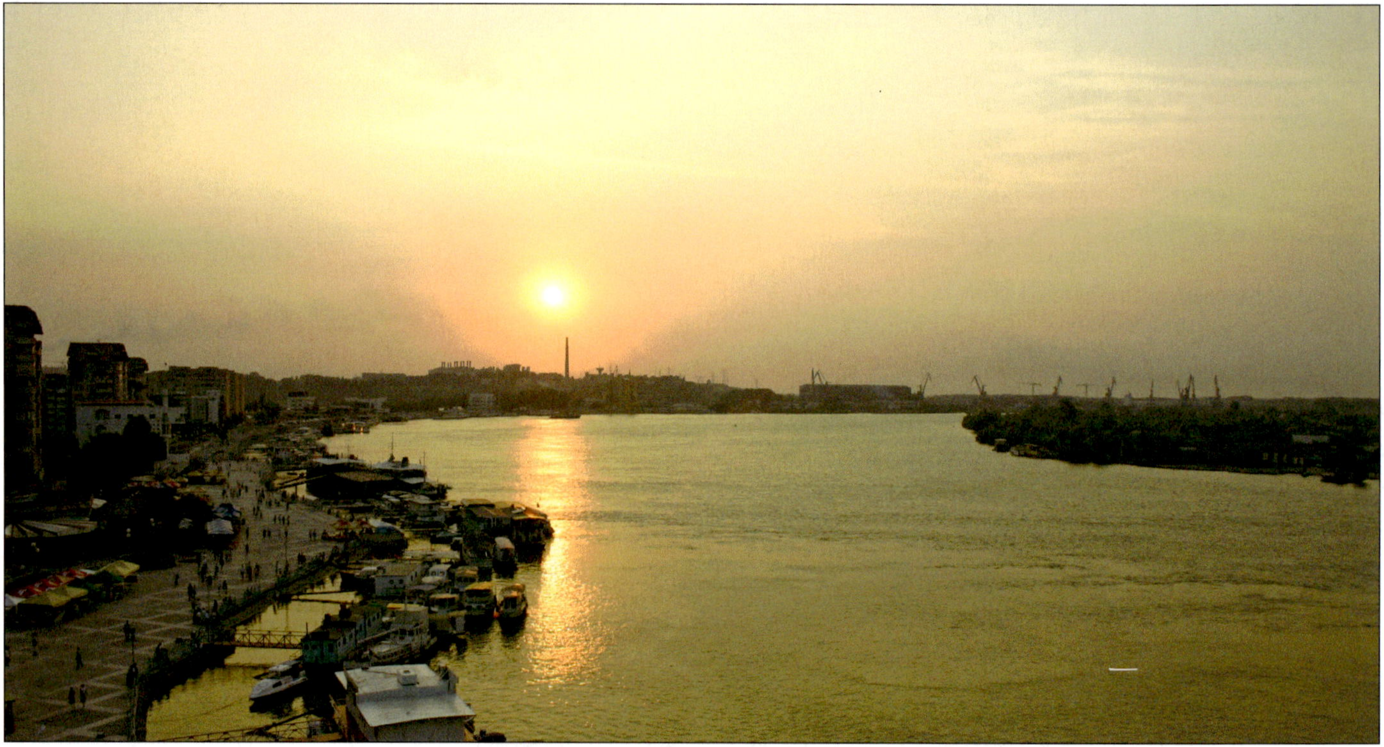

Accommodations

The following lists overnight accommodations in a number of categories:

H	Hotel
Hg	Hotel garni
M	Motel
Gh	Inn
P	Pension, Guest house
Pz	Private room
BB	Bed and Breakfast
Fw	Vacation apartment (selected)
Bh	Farm
Hh	Hay hotel
🏠	Youth hostel, hostel
▲	Campground
△	Tent site

We have not attempted to list all available accommodations and these listing should not be construed as any kind of recommendation.

The Roman number (I–VII) after the telephone number indicates price range. These fall into the categories shown below:

I	under € 15 Euros
II	€ 15 - 23 Euros
III	€ 23 - 30 Euros
IV	€ 30 - 35 Euros
V	€ 35 - 50 Euros
VI	€ 50 - 70 Euros
VII	over 70 Euros

These categories are based on the price per person in a double room equipped with shower or bath, with breakfast, unless otherwise indicated. Rooms with bath or shower in the hall are indicated with the symbol ⚿.

Because we wish to expand this list and keep it up-to-date, we welcome any comments, additions or corrections you may have. There is no charge for a listing.

Budapest

Postal code: 1011; Telephone area code: 01

ℹ️ Tourist information, Vörösmarty tér/Süto utca 2, ✆ 4388080

ℹ️ Tourist information, Liszt-Ferenc tér 11, ✆ 3224098

H Hilton, Hess András tér 1-3, ✆ 8896922, VI
H Thermal Hotel Aquincum, Árpád fejedelem útja 94, VI
H Kempinski Corvinus, Erzsébét tér 7-8, ✆ 4293777, VI
H Hyatt Regency, Roosevelt tér 2, ✆ 2661234, VI
H Budapest Mariott, Apáczai Cserer János utca 4, ✆ 2667000, VI
H Thermal Hotel Margitsziget, Margitsziget, ✆ 8894752, IV-VI
H Art'otel, Bem rakpart 16-19, ✆ 4879487, VI
H Dunapart, Királyokb útja 261, ✆ 3879361, III-VI
H Victoria, Bem rakpart 11, ✆ 2018644, V-VI
H Alba Hotel Budapest, Apor Péter utca 3, ✆ 8894235, V-VI
H Orion, Döbrentei utca 13, ✆ 3568583 or 3568933, V-VI
H Gellert, Szent Gellért tér 1, ✆ 3852200, VI
H Mercure Buda, Krisztina körút 41-43, ✆ 4888100, V-VI
H Rege, Pálos utca 2, ✆ 3915100, V-VI
H Budapest, Szilágyi erzsébét fasor 47, ✆ 4889800, V
H Panda, Pasaréti út 133, ✆ 3941932, V
H Hunor, Pünkösdfürdo utca 40, ✆ 2430949, V-VI
H Flamenco, Tas vezér utca 7, ✆ 8895650, IV-V
H Wien, Budaörsi út 88-90, ✆ 3102999, V
H Rubin Apartman, Dayka Gábor utca 3, ✆ 3193231, V-VI
H Sas Club, Törökbálinti út 51-53, ✆ 2464643, IV-V
H Olympia, Eötvös út 40, ✆ 3956451, IV-VI
H Normafa, Eötvös út 52-54, ✆ 3956505, V-VI
H Agro Panorama, Normafa út 54, ✆ 4583900, III-VI
H Novotel Budapest Centrum, Rákóczi út 43-45, ✆ 4775300, VI
H Inter-Continental, Apáczai Csere János utca 12-14, ✆ 3276333, VI
H Korona, Kecskeméti utca 14, ✆ 4868800, V-VI
H Erzsébet, Károlyi Mihály utca 11-15, ✆ 8893746, VI

H Aastoria, Kossuth Lajos utca 19-21, ✆ 8896060, V-VI

H Taverna, Vaci utca 20, ✆ 4853100, VI

H Béke Radisson, Teréz körút 43, ✆ 8893939, VI

H Liget, Dózsa Györgyút 106, ✆ 2695300, V-VI

H Benczúr, Benczúr utca 35, ✆ 4795650, III-VI

H Grand Hotel Hungária, Rákóczi út 90, ✆ 8894455, VI

H Emke, Akácfa utca 1-3, ✆ 4783050, IV-VI

H Nemzeti, József körút 4, ✆ 4772000, V-VI

H Aero, Ferde utca 1-2, ✆ 3479700, IV-V

H Ibis Budapest, Ráday utca 6, ✆ 4564100, IV-VI

H Expo, Expo tér 2, ✆ 2637500, V-VI

H Grand Hotel Margitsziget, Margistsziget, ✆ 8894752, V-VI

H Volga, Dózsa György út 65, ✆ 3290400, IV-V

H Helia, Kárpát utca 62-64, ✆ 8895822, VI

H Family, Ipoly utca 8b, ✆ 3201284, V-VI

H Stadion, Ifúság útja 1-3, ✆ 8895351, V

H Citadella, Citadella sétány, ✆ 4665794, IV

H Vénusz Motel, Dósa utca 2-4, ✆ 3687252, III

H Minol, Batthyány utca 45, ✆ 2430777, III

H Touring, Pünkösdfürdo utca 38, ✆ 2503184, IV

H Griff, Bartók Béla út 152, ✆ 2040044, V

H Ventura, Fehérvári út 179, ✆ 2081232, III-VI

H Sunlight, Eötvös utca 41, ✆ 3956583, III-V

H Ábel Panzio, Ábel Jenö utca 9, ✆ 3810553, III

H City Panzió Mátyás, Március 15. tér 8, ✆ 3384711, III-VI

H City Panzió Pilvaz, Pilvaz köz 1-3, ✆ 2667560, III-VI

H City Panzió Ring, Szent István krt. 22, ✆ 3405450, III-VI

H Délibáb, Délibáb utca 35, ✆ 4798600, III-VI

H Medosz, Jókai tér 9, ✆ 3743000, II-III

H Metropol, Rákóczi út 58, ✆ 3421175, IV

H Baross Panzio, Baross tér 15, ✆ 4613010, III

H Platánus, Könyves Kálmán körút 44, ✆ 3336505, V

H Diáksport, Dózsa György út 152, ✆ 3408585, II

H Flandria, Sszegedi út 27, ✆ 35032181, III

H Terminus, Csavargyár utca 1-3, ✆ 3501728, II

H Ében Nagy Lajos király útja 15-17, ✆ 2523333, IV

H Zugló, Nagy Lajos király útja 15-17, ✆ 2512455, III

H Marco Polo, Nyár utca 6, ✆ 4132555, II-IV

P Korona, Sasadi út 127, ✆ 3191255, III

ℹ Sirály Youth Hostel, Margitsziget, ✆ 3293952, II

▲ Római Fürdö Kemping, Szentendrei út 189, ✆ 3887167

▲ Zugligeti Niche Kemping, Zugligeti út 101, ✆ 2008346

Szigetszentmiklós
Postal code: 2310; Telephone area code: 024

H Gastland MO, MO autóút 19, ✆ 446484, III

P Tóth, Petofi S. út 41, ✆ 441190

M MO Autohof, Csepeli út 20, ✆ 9005

M MO Túra, Gyári út 49, ✆ 403509

Szigetszentmárton
Postal code: 2318; Telephone area code: 024

H Szent Márton, Dunapart-alsó 84, ✆ 456866

Ráckeve
Postal code: 2300; Telephone area code: 024

ℹ Tourist information Ráckeve, Kossuth L. u. 51, ✆ 429747

H Schlosshotel Savojai, Kossuth lajos útca 95, ✆ 485253

H Apaj Schlosshotel, Kiskunlacháza, Hajós Major, ✆ 430275

H Kék-Duna Wellness, Dömsödi út 1, ✆ 523230, V-VI

H Savoyai Schlosshotel, Kossuth L. u. 95, ✆ 485253, III

Gh Kata, Keszeg sor 99, ✆ 422131

Gh Kis Szárcsa, Keszeg sor 2, ✆ 485531

Gh Ráckevei, Kossuth L. 38, ✆ 385720

P Bálványos, Dömsödi út 34, ✆ 422585

P Flóra, Délegyháza, Magyar Naturista Egyesület telep, ✆ 412262

P Kis Duna, Dunaharaszti, Fo utca 130, ✆ 460109

P Laguna, Kossuth L. u. 108, ✆ 422939

P Leányvári, 51-es fo út 44, ✆ 535478

P Zöld Sziget, Taksony, Sziget sétány, ✆ 477477

Szigetbecse
Postal code: 2321; Telephone area code: 024

Gh Vízparti, Királyréti dunasor 185, ✆ 2751666

Dunaújvaros
Postal code: 2400; Telephone area code: 003625

H Dunaferr, Epotik Utja 2, ✆ 381073

H Álom Szállás, Erdösor 1/a, ✆ 413646

H Klub Hotel, Építok utca 2, ✆ 500477

H Föiskola Kerpely Aural Kollégium, Dózsa György utca 33

H Sportszállo, Eszperantó utca 4, ✆ 411255

Dunaföldvár
Postal code: 7020; Telephone area code: 075

ℹ Tourist information Dunaföldvár, Rákoczi u. 2, ✆ 341176

H Jurik Motel, Vaci M.str. 2, ✆ 9977605, III

H Zafír Fogado, Vilmospusztala, ✆ 700035

H Panoráma Üdülöházak, Templom utca 78, ✆ 342748

H Turi Panzió Dunapart Vendégház, Beszédes sar 2-3. ✆ 541096, II

H Hidfö Panzió, Sóház utca 15, ✆ 343216, I-II

P Sipos Pazio, Ilona str. 5, ✆ 343702

P Prajda Panzio, Kossuth L. str. 22, ✆ 342182, ✆ 9372424

P Varro Panzio, Petöfi str. 20, ✆ 342055 or 341810

P Liget Szallo, Kossuth L. str. 24, ✆ 342137 or 3008284

P Túri Panzió, Beszedes str. 2-3, ✆ 9939747 or 541096

P Zafir fogado, Vilmos puszta 1./a., ✆ 700035

🏨 Hásök ter 166, ✆ 341529

⛺ Kek Duna, Hösök platz 26, ✆ 541107

Paks
Postal code: 7030; Telephone area code: 075

ℹ️ Tourist information Paks, Szent István tér 2, ✆ 421575

H Duna Hotel, Dózsa György str 75, ✆ 31089

H Paks, Cseresznyéspuszta 57, ✆ 421521

Kalocsa
Postal code: 6300; Telephone area code: 078

ℹ️ Tourist information Kalocsa Tours Kft., Szent István Kft., Szent István király út 5, ✆ 481819

H Kalocsa, Szentháromság tér 4, ✆ 461244, III

H Két Gólya Fogadó, Móra Ferenc utca 12, ✆ 462259

H Pirosarany, Szent István király út 37, ✆ 462220, II

H Danubius Beta, Szentháromság tér 4, ✆ 561180

Pz Kalocsa-Korona-Tours-Büro, Szent István király út 5, I-II

Fadd
Postal code: 7133; Telephone area code: 074

H Aranypart Hotel és étterem, Dunasor 7, ✆ 437037

P Napfény, Tavasz street 12, ✆ 446130

M Motel Club Dombori, Dunasor 22, ✆ 447337

M Margaréta, Volent-öböl 65, ✆ 447463, III

Szekszárd
Postal code: 7100; Telephone area code: 0036

ℹ️ Tourist information, Garay tér 18, ✆ 511263

ℹ️ Tourist information, Széchenyi utca 38, ✆ 418365

H Gemenc, Mészáros Lázár utca 1, ✆ 311722, III

H Alicsa Hotel, Kálvária utca 1, ✆ 312228, III

H Zodiaco, Szent Lászlo u. 19, ✆ 511150, III

P Alfa Megacentrum, Tartsay Villmos street 8, ✆ 511060, II

P Fritz Panzió, Aranydomb-dülő, ✆ 409596, III

P Gyógygödör Vendéghaz, Csatári street 70, ✆ 319018, II

Pz Touristinformation, Széchenyi utca, ✆ 418365, II-III

Baja
Postal code: 6500; Telephone area code: 079

ℹ️ Tourist information Baja, Szentháromság tér 5, ✆ 420793

H Duna, Szentháromság tér 6, ✆ 324844, II

H Sugovica, Fi-sziget, ✆ 321575, II-III

H Country House, Márc sétány 15, ✆ 326585

H Kaiser Panzió, Hattyu utca 2, és Kálmán utca 12, ✆ 520450

P Bácska Ipartestület Panzió, Petófi-Sziget 10, ✆ 324907, I

P Kolibri, Batthyány utca 18, ✆ 321628

P Vizafogó Panzió és Etterem, Fi-Sziget, ✆ 422134 or 326585

M Napfény Motel, Monostori utca 47, ✆ 321052

⛺ Sugovica Kemping, Petofi-sziget, ✆ 321755

Dunafalva
Postal code: 7713; Telephone area code: 069

P Marika, Park útca 1, ✆ 332075

Mohács
Postal code: 7700; Telephone area code: 069

ℹ️ Tourist information, Széchenyi utca 1, ✆ 505515

ℹ️ Mecsek Tourist, Szentháromság utca 2, ✆ 511020

H Csele-Mohacs, Szent Mihály tér 6-7, VI

H Szabadság, utca 9, ✆ 510383

P Duna panzió, Felső Dunasor 14, ✆ 302450

P Korona, Jókai utca 2, ✆ 311480, II

P Duna, Felső Dunasor 14, ✆ 302450, II

P Autós étterem és Panzió, Szent János street 1, ✆ 322228

P Pegazus Lovasfarm, Eszéki ut 3, ✆ 301244

M Révkapu, János utcá 1, ✆ 303474, I-II

Croatia

Bilje
Postal code: 31327; Telephone area code: 031

ℹ️ Tourist Info, Kralja Zvonimira 1b, ✆ 751400

P Mazur, Kneza Branimira 2, ✆ 750294

P Sabo, Kneza Branimira 23, ✆ 750163

Pz Galic, Ritska 1, ✆ 750393

Pz Crvendac, Biljske satnije 5, ✆ 750264

Pz Baranjska Oaza, P. Sandora 63, ✆ 751007

Pz Lackovic, Vinogradska 5a, ✆ 750850

Pz Lutra, Tina Ujevica 2, ✆ 750960

Fw Vrata Baranja, Vinogradska 17, ✆ 751450

Osijek
Postal code: 31000; Telephone area code: 031

ℹ️ Tourist Association Osijek, Županijska 2, ✆ 203755

H Osijek, Samacka 4, ✆ 230333

H Waldinger, Zupanijska 8, ✆ 250450

H Silver, Martina Divalta 84, ✆ 582535

H Vila Ariston, Andrije Kacica Miosica 6, ✆ 251351

H Central, Trg Ante Starcevica 6, ✆ 283399

H Mursa, Bartola Kasica 2a, ✆ 224909

H Ritam, Kozjacka 76, ✆ 310310

H Royal, Kapucinska 34, ✆ 210103, VI-VII

Pz Domin, Sv. Ane 84, ✆ 506290

Vukovar
Postal code: 32000; Telephone area code: 032
- Tourist Info, J. J. Strossmayera 15, ✆ 442889
- H Lav (Lion), J. J. Strossmayera 17, ✆ 445100
- H Dunav, Trg Republike 1, ✆ 441285

Ilok
Postal code: 32236; Telephone area code: 032
- Tourist Info, Trg Nikole Ilokog, ✆ 590020
- H Dunav, Julija Benesica 62, ✆ 569500
- P Masarini, Radieva 4, ✆ 981646855

Serbia

Backa Palanka
Postal code: 21400; Telephone area code: 021
- Tourism information, Veselina Masleše 8, ✆ 741644
- H Fontana, Jugoslovenske Armije 11-15, ✆ 740055 or 742022
- H Grand Club, Industrijski put bb, ✆ 7550000
- M Poloj, Celarevska suma 2, ✆ 745370
- P Idila Plus, Jugoslovenske Armije 59, ✆ 751830

Bezdan
Postal code: 25000; Telephone area code: 025
- Fw Kod Srecka Bezdan, Sebesfok bb, ✆ 810200

Bački Monostor
Postal code: 25000; Telephone area code: 025
- Pz Maricic, Bedanska 43, ✆ 807015

Sombor
Postal code: 25000; Telephone area code: 025
- Tourist information Sombor, Trg Cara Lazara 1, ✆ 468141
- H Internacion, Trg Republike 1, ✆ 463322
- M Beli Dvor, Apatinski put bb, ✆ 27268
- M Kronic, Conopljanski put 30, ✆ 29900
- M Kallos, Staparski put bb, ✆ 440220
- P Tamara, Apatinski put bb, ✆ 434110
- P Piccolina, Avrama Mrazovića 2, ✆ 22820
- P Renesansa, Zlatne grede 4, ✆ 420706

Vrbas
Postal code: 21460; Telephone area code: 026
- H Backa, Save Kovacevica bb, ✆ 707376

Veternik
Postal code: 21000; Telephone area code: 021
- M Stari Krovovi, Novosadski put 115, ✆ 402882 or 394793
- Pz Kamenjar, ✆ 468409

Beocin
Postal code: 21000; Telephone area code: 021
- P Karas, Naselje Dunav bb, ✆ 874633
- P Kod Steve, Naselje Dunav 62, ✆ 870000

Begec
Postal code: 21000; Telephone area code: 021
- Pz Salas „Cveja", Nikola Tesla 2, ✆ 898045

Futog
Postal code: 21000; Telephone area code: 021
- P Dunavac, Dunavska, ✆ 895406

Novi Sad
Postal code: 21000; Telephone area code: 021
- Tourist information Novi Sad, Mihajla Pupina Bulevar 9, ✆ 431811
- H Vojvodina, Trg Slobode 2, ✆ 622122
- H Putnik, Illje Ognjanovica 26, ✆ 615555, II-IV
- H Park, Novosadskog sajma 35, ✆ 4888888, VI-VI
- H Aleksandar, Bulevar Cara Lazara 79, ✆ 4804444I
- H Sajam, Hajduk Veljkova 11, ✆ 420266
- H Novi Sad, Bulevar Jasa Tomica, ✆ 442511, II-IV
- H Fitness Gymnas, Teodora Pavlovica 28, ✆ 469285, II-III
- H Zenit, Zmaj Jovina 8, ✆ 6621444, III-VII
- H Brankovo kolo, Episkopa Visariona 3, ✆ 528236 or 422784 or 622160, I
- H Varadin, Petrovaradinska tvrdjava 8, ✆ 431122 or 431184
- H Danube Cottages Resort, Fisherman's Island at Kameniccka ada bb, ✆ 466977 or 466978
- H Vila Una, Avijátcarska 9, ✆ 518101, II-III
- H Rimski, Jovana Cvijica 26, ✆ 443237 or 333587
- H Mediteraneo, Illije Ognjanovica 10, ✆ 427135
- M Jet Set, Temerinski put 41, ✆ 414511, II-III
- M Bor, Temerinski put 57a, ✆ 412424, II-V
- M Bela Lada, Kisacka 21, ✆ 616594, I
- P Bonaca, Kisacka 2, ✆ 446600
- P Voyager, Strazilovska 16, ✆ 453711
- P Duga Cirila i Metodija 11a, ✆ 364191
- P Fontana, Nikole Spasica 27, ✆ 6621779
- Hostel Brankovo kolo, Episkopa Visariona 3, ✆ 528263

Sremska Kamenica
Postal code: 21000; Telephone area code: 021
- P Olimp, Milosa Obilica 8, ✆ 463295
- P Kordun, Mose Pijade 10 a, ✆ 462860
- P Evandjelina, Branislava Bukurova 2, ✆ 464111
- P Villa Mali raj, Kosteljnikova 5, ✆ 064/1119004
- M Konak, Trg Kralja Petra 1, ✆ 463819
- M Ilidza, Ledinacki put 1, ✆ 461158

Sremski Karlovci
Postal code: 2100; Telephone area code: 021
- Tourist information, Branka Radicevica 7, ✆ 882127
- H Dunav, Dunavska 5, ✆ 883735 or 883139
- H Boem, Trg Branka Radicevica 5, ✆ 881038, II

Beška
Telephone area code: 022
- H Božić, Obala Dunava bb, ✆ 551176 or 552468
- P Sidro, ✆ 021/889099
- P Centar, Kralja Petra 1-2, ✆ 571043

Inđija
Telephone area code: 022
M Lovac, Novosadski put bb, ✆ 567450

Novi Banovci
Telephone area code: 022
M Oaza, Kresina 32, ✆ 342382

Zemun
Postal code: 11000; Telephone area code: 011
H Zlatnik, Slavonska 26, ✆ 3167511, VII
H Skala, Bezanijska 3, ✆ 196605
Hg Lav (Lion), Cara Dusana 240, ✆ 3163289
△ Camping Dunav, Batajnicki drum bb, ✆ 199072 or 3167630

Belgrade
Postal code: 11000; Telephone area code: 011
🛈 Tourist information, Airport Belgrade, ✆ 601555
🛈 Tourist information, main train station, ✆ 3612732
🛈 Tourist information, Knez Mihailova 18, ✆ 2629992
H Aleksandar Palas, Kralja Petra 13-15, ✆ 3305300, VII
H Beograd Inter-Continental, Vladimira Popovica 10, ✆ 3113333
H Hyatt Regency, Milentija Popovica 5, ✆ 3011234, VI-VII
H Best Western, Bulevar JNA 56a, ✆ 3090401 or 3972560
H Sumadija, Sumadijski trg 8, ✆ 3554255
H Majestic, Obilicev venac 28, ✆ 3285777
H Moskva, Balkanska 1, ✆ 2686255, V-VII
H Palas, Toplicin venac 23, ✆ 185585 or 2637222
H Metropol, Bulevar revolucije 69, ✆ 3230911
H Jugoslavija, Bulevar Nikole Tesle 3, ✆ 2600222
H Astoria, Milovana Milanovica 1a, ✆ 2645422
H Kasina, Terazije 25, ✆ 3235574, III
H Nacional, Bezanijska kosa bb, ✆ 2601122
H Union, Kosovska 11, ✆ 3248022
H Park, Njegoseva 4, ✆ 3234723
H Prag, Narodnog fronta 27, ✆ 3610422
H Rex, Sarajevska 37, ✆ 3611862
H Royal, Kralja Petra I 56, ✆ 2626426
H Le Petit Piaf, Skadarska 34, ✆ 3035252, VII
H Balkan, Prizrenska 2, ✆ 2687466
H Excelsior, Kneza Milosa 5, ✆ 3231381
H N, Bileceka 57, ✆ 3972183
H Posta, Slobodana Penezica Krcuna 3, ✆ 3614260
H Radmilovac, Smederevski put bb, ✆ 3416131
H Slavija, Svetog Save 1, ✆ 2450842
H Slavija lux, Svetog Save 2, ✆ 2450842
H Srbija, Ustanicka 127c, ✆ 2890404
H Tas, Beogradska 71, ✆ 3243507
H Trim, Kneza Viseslava 72, ✆ 3540669
H Lav, Cara Dusana 240, ✆ 3163289
H Dom, Kralja Milutina 54, ✆ 685696
H Bristol, Karadordeva 50, ✆ 631895
H Central, Glavna 10, ✆ 191712
H Putnik, Palmira Toljatija 9, ✆ 697221
H Turist, Sarajevska 37, ✆ 3611862
H Centar, Savski Trg 7, ✆ 644055
H on ship, Jahting klub Kej, ✆ 3165432
Hg Splendid, Dvorska 5, ✆ 3235444
Hg Beograd, Balkanska 52, ✆ 2645199
M Mihajlovac, Pozeska 31, ✆ 3555458
Fw Kosutnjak, Kneza Viseslava 17, ✆ 3555127
🏛 Dorcol, Gospodar Jovanova 42, ✆ 064/2588754
🏛 Tis, Koste Abrasevica 17, ✆ 3800650
🏛 Jelica, Krunska 8, ✆ 3248550
🏛 Belgrade Eye, Krunska 6b, ✆ 3346423

Pancevo
Telephone area code: 013
H Tamis, Dimitrija Tucovica bb, ✆ 342622
M Miss, Novoseljanski put 56, ✆ 371920

Banatski Brestovac
Telephone area code: 013
△ Camping, Jabukev cvet, ✆ 063/213742

Skorenovac
Telephone area code: 13
Pz Dani, Bratstva i jedinstva bb, ✆ 764066

Smederevo
Postal code: 11300; Telephone area code: 026
H Smederevo, Izletnicka bb, ✆ 222511
M Car, Djure Danicica 66, ✆ 642042 or 229760
M Zlatnik, Kovinski put bb, ✆ 651411

Stara Palanka
Telephone area code: 013
P Dunav, ✆ 841026

Vračev Gaj
Telephone area code: 013
△ Camping, Milos gaj, ✆ 755595

Bela Crkva
Postal code: 26340; Telephone area code: 013
🛈 Tourist Organisation of Bela Crkava, J Popovica bb, ✆ 26340 or 851091
H Turist, Kozaracka bb, ✆ 851094
H Vacation Complex Jezero, Begradska bb, ✆ 851152
H Veltours, 1. oktobra 77, ✆ 851152

Pozarevac
Postal code: 12000; Telephone area code: 012
H Dunav, Lenjinova 3, ✆ 539200

Kostolac
Postal code: 12208; Telephone area code: 012
H Kostolac, Trudbenicka bb, ✆ 241622
M Dunavski dragulj, Kanal bb, ✆ 241428

Veliko Gradište/Srebrno Jezero
Postal code: 12220; Telephone area code: 012
H Srebrno Jezero, Srbija i Crna Gora, ✆ 62992

P VilaLago am Silbersee, ☎ 62759 or 063/7718400

P Dunavski cvet, Freizeitzentrum Beli Bagrem, ☎ 063/7718003

P Stevic, Freizeitzentrum Beli Bagrem,

P Madera, Freizeitzentrum Beli Bagrem, ☎ 61252

P Srbija, Freizeitzentrum Beli Bagrem, ☎ 61152

▲ Camping, Srebrno jezero, ☎ 62619 or 063/351298

Vinci
Telephone area code: 012
P Villa Dunavski raj, ☎ 79616

Golubac
Postal code: 12223; Telephone area code: 012
H Golubacki Grad Hotel, Golubacki trg., ☎ 78207 or 78182

Brnjica
Telephone area code: 012
Fw Toma, ☎ 73041 or 063/323096

Dobra
Telephone area code: 012
Pz Stanojevic, ☎ 69502
Pz Cvetkovic, ☎ 69087

Donji Milanovac
Postal code: 19220; Telephone area code: 030
H Lepinski Vir, Donji Milanovac, ☎ 86210 or 86211
Pz Open gallery, ☎ 86869 or 063/86869

Tekija
Postal code: 19320; Telephone area code: 019
M Tekija, Avrama Petronijevica 12, ☎ 85116

Kladovo
Postal code: 19320; Telephone area code: 019
H Plaza, Kladovo-Kostol, ☎ 87999
H Djerdap, Dunavska bb, ☎ 81010
Fw OSK Djerdap, ☎ 81394

Negotin
Telephone area code: 019
H Krajina, Srbe Jovanovica bb, ☎ 546852

Romania

Oroşva
Postal code: 22000 ; Telephone area code: 0252
M Continental, E 752, ☎ 329235

Eşelniţa
P Pensiunea „Steana Dunarii", 0040/722-207918

Drobeta-Turnu Severin
Postal code: 22000; Telephone area code: 0252
H Continental Parc, B-dul Republicii, ☎ 312851, V
H Traian, Bulevardul Tudor Vladimirescu 74, ☎ 312851
M Continental GuraVaii, Calea Timisoarei, ☎ 326778

Turnu Măgurele
Telephone area code: 047
H Turris, Str Independentei 1, ☎ 416560, VI

Giurgiu
Telephone area code: 0246
H Steaua Dunarii, Str Mihai Veteazul 1, ☎ 217270, I-II
M Prietenia, Blvd Prieteniei 1, ☎ 231340

Călăraşi
Postal code: 8500; Telephone area code: 0242
H Perla, Bd 1 Mai Nr. 12, ☎ 115980
H Clrai, Str. G-I Vasile Milea Nr. 2, ☎ 2315858

Constanţa
Postal code: 900605; Telephone area code: 0241
ℹ Tourist information, Piata Ovidiu 14, ☎ 619777
H Tineretului. B-dul Tomis 24, ☎ 613590, II
H Maria, D-Dul 1 Decembrie 1918, ☎ 616852, V
H Guci, Str Rascoala din 1907, ☎ 695500, VI
H Intim.Strada Nicolae Titulescu 9, ☎ 617814, II-III
H Capri, Strada Mircea cel Batran 109, ☎ 553090, VI
H Sport, Strada Cuza Voda 2, ☎ 617558, II
H Astoria, Strada Mircea cel Batran 103, ☎ 614696, II
H Unrii, Strada Unirii 32-34, ☎ 617855, II

Murighiol
Telephone area code: 0240
H Pelican, Judetul Tulcea, ☎ 516386, III
BB Riviera, ☎ 545910, II

Victoria
Telephone area code: 0240
H Victoria,Piata Libertatii, ☎ 241916, VI
P Palermo, Str 1 Decembrie 1918, ☎ 242973, I-II

Tulcea
Postal code: 820000; Telephone area code: 0240
ℹ Information and Ecological Education Centre, Str Portului 34 A, ☎ 519214
H Delta, Str. Isaccei 2, ☎ 514720, V
H Europolis, Str. Pacii 20, ☎ 512443, II-III
H Egreta, Strada Pacii 1, ☎ 517103, II
H Cormoran, Sate Uzlina, ☎ 656227, V

Sulina
Telephone area code: 0240
ℹ Tourist information Sulina, DDBR office, House No. 1 at the docks
H Sulina, B-dul Alexandru cel Bun 1, ☎ 234571104
P Delia, sat Crisan 50, ☎ 547018

Index of Places

Page numbers printed in *green* refer to the list of accomodations

A
Adamclisi	150
Agighiol	165
Apostag	34

B
Babadag	163
Backa Palanka	*176*
Bački Monostor	*176*
Baia	160
Baja	48, *175*
Balta Verde	129
Banatska Palanka	116
Băneasa	150
Banoštor	76
Basarabi	152
Batajnica	86
Batina	60
Batoți	128
Bátya	47
Bechet	134
Begec	*176*
Bela Crkva	116, *177*
Belegiš	84
Belgrade	87, *177*
Beocin	*176*
Beočin	76
Berzasca	119
Beška	84, *176*
Bezdan	*176*
Bijelo Brdo	68
Bilje	64, *175*
Bölcske	34
Boljetin	109
Borovo	68
Brestovik	93
Brnjica	*178*
Budapest	21, *173*
Burila Mare	129

C
Calafat	131
Călărași	148, *178*
Căscioarele	146
Ceamurlia de Jos	161
Cetate	130
Cetatea Histria	159
Chirnogi	146
Ciocirlia	152
Ciocirlia de Sus	152
Ćirikovac	98
Cobadin	152
Constanța	154, *178*
Corabia	138
Corbu	158
Coronini	119
Čortanovci	84
Cozla	119
Crivina	128

D
Daia	142
Dalj	68
Deleni	152
Dervent Monastery	150
Dobra	108, *178*
Donji Milanovac	110, *178*
Draž	60
Drencova	119
Drmno	99
Drobeta-Turnu Severin	125, *178*
Drobeta Turnu-Severin	125
Dubova	122
Dunaegyháza	34
Dunafalva	54, *175*
Dunaföldvar	34
Dunaföldvár	*174*
Dunakömlöd	34
Dunapataj	37
Dunaszentbenedek	38
Dunaùjvaros	*174*
Dunavecse	33

E
Enisala	162
Eșelnița	124, *178*

F
Fadd	44, *175*
Fajsz	48
Foktő	38
Futog	*176*

G
Gajić	60
Galița	150
Gârla Mare	130
Géderlak	36, 38
Gerjen	44
Gighera	134
Giurgiu	142, *178*
Gogoșu	129
Golo Brdo	112
Golubac	102, *178*
Golubinje	111
Grabovac	64
Grocka	93
Gruia	130

H
Hajós	41
Hajósi pincek	41
Harta	37
Hinova	128
Hladna Voda	109

I
Ilok	71, *176*
Inđija	*177*
Ion Corvin	150
Istria	160
Izvoarele	130

J
Jurilovca	162

K
Kalocsa	38, *175*
Kaluđerovo	116
Kladovo	*178*
Klenovnik	98
Kličevac	99
Kneževi Vinogradi	64
Kölked	58
Koruška	76
Kostolac	98, *177*
Kozica	108
Krčedin	84

L
Lakihegy	28
Lisa	140
Liubcova	119
Lug	64
Lunca	161

M
Măcești	118
Madocsa	34
Maglavit	130
Makád	32
Mala Krsna	96
Malu	142
Mânăstirea	147

Index of Places

Mihai Viteazu	160	P		Sălcioara	162	Szekszàrd	*175*	Uszód	38
Miske	41	Paks	35, *175*	Sarichioi	164	Szekszárd	45	V	
Mohács	55, *175*	Palánkpuszta	45	Sarvaš	68	Szeremle	51	Valu lui Traian	152
Moldova Veche	118	Pancevo	*177*	Simian	128	Sziget-Szentmiklós	28	Vardarac	64
Moreni	130	Petfitelep	34	Sinoie	160	Szigetbecse	32, *174*	Veliko Gradište	100, *177*
Mosna	111	Pietreni	152	Sip	125	Szigetcsép	29	Veternik	*176*
Murighiol	*178*	Pietroşani	140	Skobali	96	Szigethalom	29	Victoria	*178*
N		Piscu Vechi	132	Skorenovac	*177*	Szigetszentmàrton	*174*	Viişoara	152
Negotin	*178*	Plopşoru	142	Slobozia	142	Szigetszentmiklós	*174*	Vinci	102, *178*
Neštin	76	Poiana Mare	132	Smederevo	94, *177*	Sziget Szentmárton	30	Vişina	162
Novi Banovci	84, *177*	Pojejena	118	Solt	36	T		Vračev Gaj	116, *177*
Novi Sad	76, *176*	Pozarevac	*177*	Sombor	*176*	Tass	33	Vrancea	128
O		Požarevac	96	Sotin	70	Tekija	114, *178*	Vranovo	96
Ogradena	124	Požežena	102	Srebrno Jezero	*177*	Ţigănaşi	129	Vrata	130
Olteniţa	146	R		Sremska Kamenica	*176*	Tismana	128	Vrbas	*176*
Opatovac	70	Ráckeve	30, *174*	Sremski Karlovci	81, *176*	Tolna	44	Vukovar	68, *176*
Oroşva	*178*	Radimna	118	Stara Palanka	*177*	Topolje	60	Z	
Orşova	124	Radinac	96	Stari Banovci	84	Tulcea	166, *178*	Zatonje	100
Osijek	66, *175*	Ram	100, 116	Sulina	170, *178*	Turnu Măgurele	138, *178*	Zaval	134
Osipaonica	96	Remuş	142	Surduk	84	U		Zemun	86, *177*
Ostrov	149	S		Susek	76	Udvar	58	Zimnicea	140
Ostroveni	134	Sabangia	164	Suza	64	Újmohacs	54	Zmajevac	62
Ostrovo	100	Sacele	158	Sviniţa	122	Ulmeni	146		
Ostrovu Corbului	128	Salcia	130	Szalkszentmárton	33	Usije	102		